Reanimating grief

Reanimating grief

Waking the dead in literature, theatre and performance

William McEvoy

MANCHESTER UNIVERSITY PRESS

Copyright © William McEvoy 2024

The right of William McEvoy to be identified as the author of this work has been asserted in accordance with the Copyright, Designs and Patents Act 1988.

Published by Manchester University Press
Oxford Road, Manchester, M13 9PL

www.manchesteruniversitypress.co.uk

British Library Cataloguing-in-Publication Data
A catalogue record for this book is available from the British Library

ISBN 978 1 5261 7669 1 hardback
ISBN 978 1 5261 9469 5 paperback

First published 2024
Paperback published 2026

The publisher has no responsibility for the persistence or accuracy of URLs for any external or third-party internet websites referred to in this book, and does not guarantee that any content on such websites is, or will remain, accurate or appropriate.

EU authorised representative for GPSR:
Easy Access System Europe – Mustamäe tee 50,
10621 Tallinn, Estonia
gpsr.requests@easproject.com

Typeset by Newgen Publishing UK

To my parents

Contents

Acknowledgements	*page* viii
Preface	x
Introduction	1
1 Genealogies of grief: classic reanimations	17
2 Animate objects of mourning	40
3 Grief, fiction, passion	61
4 Dead forms, living characters	88
5 Burying the living and the dead	112
6 Musical afterlives	133
7 Mothersongs	148
Conclusion: impossible reanimations	177
Bibliography	182
Index	191

Acknowledgements

Many people have contributed to my thinking in this book and have supported my work over the past few years.

I am grateful to staff at a number of research libraries for their support, including colleagues at the Bibliothèque historique de la ville de Paris, the Bibliothèque nationale de France, the British Library, the Bodleian Library, Oxford, Trinity College, Dublin, and the libraries of NUI Galway and the University of Sussex.

I have presented ideas from this book at several conferences in the UK and France and am grateful to conference participants for their insightful comments. I would like to thank editors and reviewers at *C21 Literature: Journal of 21st-century Writings*, *Studies in Theatre and Performance*, and the British Library 'Discovering Literature' series, for comments on earlier versions of materials that appear here in revised form. The book's cover image, by Shyam, is a stack of granite, and is reproduced under the Unsplash licence.

Special thanks to my colleagues at the University of Sussex for their critical friendship while the writing of this book has been in progress. These include in particular colleagues in Drama, Theatre and Performance, and my former department of English. Matthew Dimmock has been a huge source of encouragement over many years.

I warmly thank colleagues at Manchester University Press for all their support and meticulous attention to detail throughout the publication process. It has been a pleasure working with them. I also extend my thanks to the anonymous peer reviewers who gave me such insightful comments on my original proposal.

Acknowledgements

A number of current and former colleagues and friends have provided me with feedback on work-in-progress. Warm thanks to Louise Sheffield for her brilliant observations. Vincent Quinn offered an excellent set of critical comments for which I am very grateful. Other friends who have contributed to the development of my ideas include Anne Robatel, Caroline Johnson, Vicky Lebeau, Deborah Philips, Garry Whannel, Eleftheria Ioannidou and David Barnett. Numerous friends have supported me in countless ways not diminished by their anonymity here: I express my warmest gratitude to them.

Dimitris Papanikolaou has supported this project from the start. His critical acumen and unstinting encouragement have been invaluable.

My siblings Anne, Christopher, Michelle, Mary and Catherine have lived through the bereavements at the heart of this book and I thank them for their love and understanding as it took shape. Their partners have been a source of endless support to all of us. To my nieces and nephews Olivia, Maggie, Niamh, Erin, Joseph, Katie, Daniel and George: I look forward to you reading this book one day.

Finally, I thank my parents, Patrick and Margaret, who always supported me having my head in books, even when I should have been dancing. This book is dedicated to them.

Preface

The death of each of my parents was followed by a period of intensive research.

When my father died in 2001, we had to embark on a search for documents that took us to registry offices in London and Dublin, archives of births and baptisms. We were looking for traces, for legal reasons, but also to reconstruct the past and piece together our shared histories. The grief detectives found very little evidence. We started mapping out our parents' movements from the late 1960s, hoping that old filing cabinets in back offices might contain some of the necessary numbers and letters. The investigation had to be conducted in secret and culminated in a document registering a child without a name.

When my mother died in 2015, it felt like the sequel to that earlier death. The research process was different. I remember conversations we had, those before the diagnosis, those after, the latter shaped by imminent grief. I also remember the absence of those confessional, intimate exchanges over the preceding decades.

Researching grief for this book led me to think about the relationship between critical and creative writing, the drive to anatomise grief and mourning and the concurrent desire to perform the affect through elegy or memorial. The research process took me on itineraries across genres, revisiting past texts and selves through encounters with works of literature and theatre, performance, music and songs. Each of the books, plays and performances in *Reanimating grief* is linked to my past as a reader, critic, spectator or teacher. Re-engaging with them in the wake of grief meant multiple reanimations: the memory of viewing them for the first time, previous periods and spaces of reading – these works are hinges between the before and after of grief, embodying its complex temporality.

The case studies in this book are not intended as a comprehensive survey of episodes or types of reanimation in literature and theatre. Instead, they offer an autobiography of grief as it emerges through the retrospective examination of previously encountered works of art which resonate in the context of loss: works that revive the dead, that explore death's uncanny double-takes; works that are themselves suffused with grief and mourning, or explore aesthetic questions through metaphors of death and revival. Furthermore, the book reflects on the incompleteness of memory and the fragmentary quality of grief's recollections. Reanimations in the book are often abbreviated, defined by the very absence they intermittently make present.

Reanimating grief, therefore, proposes to integrate the critical, the reflective and the creative, operating through reconstruction and elegy, creating a composite text that veers between theorising grief and memorialising the dead. It brings together grief and performance throughout, linking the phenomenological memory of songs from childhood, or the delivery of an impromptu eulogy in a private performance of loss, with other literary texts, theatre and performances remembered and revisited in the wake of bereavement. In these cases, grief prompts a re-engagement with these works, in the form of listening 'on repeat', delving deeply into embodied memories of reading, viewing, singing. This is a book about the multiple reanimations that grief and mourning produce, of the dead, of our memories of living with the dead, of the enchanting works of fiction, theatre or performance we encountered while they were alive and which are now haunted by the shape of their absence.

Introduction

Well I'll be damned
Here comes your ghost again
                          Joan Baez, 'Diamonds and Rust' (Baez, 1975)

The dead are deceased, but as deceased, they do not cease accompanying us, and we do not cease living with them.
                                                  (Nancy, 2008: 38–9)

… we persevere in *vivacentrism*, the fiercest and perhaps the founding bigotry of all: the illusion that the living may eradicate the dead through burial, cremation, and forgetfulness.
                                                         (Ellmann, 2004: 84)

Reanimations

This book investigates the concept of reanimation in literature, theatre and performance as a way of exploring the phenomenon of grief. It reflects on my own personal experience of grief while examining a range of cultural works that represent or evoke bereavement and loss. At its heart is the way the concept of reanimation blurs the distinction between the living and the dead. The book sees reanimations as sites of enchantment in which literature, theatre and performance engage in magic and impossible acts: making inanimate things animate, giving the negativity of grief a poetic eloquence, reversing time or bringing the (apparently) dead back to life. Along the way, the book deals with the ontological, epistemological and aesthetic questions that reanimations ask: how they help us conceptualise death, find a language for grief and mourning, and contribute to a poetics and aesthetics of loss.

As a term, 'reanimations' refers to a reversal whereby something taken to be dead or inanimate, a lost, grievable or mournable object, is revived or reappears. This book explores a wide variety of reanimations, figurations of loss across different cultural and aesthetic works. It looks at the return of the dead in the form of ghosts, revenants and phantoms, as well as reversals of perceived or fabricated deaths, and the reappearance of the dead in the more fragmented, multi-sensory forms of verbal, visual or auditory memory. Reanimations, I suggest, act as a conceptual space linking different manifestations of grief together, enabling us to find articulations of our loss in literary texts and theatre performances, in their echoes of one another, and in the critical and creative connections we make between them. Reanimations allow us to express and sing our grief while acknowledging some of its impossible demands (the return of the dead) and its painful knowledge about fragmentation, silence, and even the guilt of undertaking creative work and critical reconstruction in the wake of bereavement.

The return of the dead as ghosts, vampires, zombies and the undead has prompted critical concepts such as ghosting, hauntology, apparitionality and others. As Alice Rayner notes, '[g]hosts have made the transition between poststructuralist critical theory to postmodern culture' (Rayner, 2006a: xxxiv). This book is not, however, focused on ghosts in/as theory, on ghost stories as a specific narrative genre, nor on the role of ghosts and revenants in gothic literature or horror. Instead, my focus is on reanimations of the dead more generally for what they tell us about loss and how they help us conceptualise death and the complex emotions it produces in the living.

In what follows, I bring together critical reflections with memories of reading or viewing texts and performances, often returning to art works I first encountered pre-grief and thinking about how bereavement reframes them. Cultural works echo and augment our grief – in the wake of loss, we read them anew for their encounters with the dead, or for the elements that transmit both the presence and absence of the deceased. This book explores, as well as engages in, expressions of grief, adding a personal voice to more critical investigations of works of fiction, theatre and performance. Underpinning this is the desire to understand more about death and the affective structures of grief and mourning, as well as the recognition that the pain of loss remains unique to each individual. For me, grief meant wanting to research, to find out more about the dead, but also about how we conceptualise death, and why art brings the dead back to life in a way that risks reiterating our grief and confirming our loss. What also became noticeable as I grieved and then began thinking critically about the subject were the politics of grief: the way this most singular but universal of affects is socially mediated and regulated.

Researching for and writing this text in the wake of loss, between two griefs, and in their wake, taught me about the power of the unsaid, about guilt and regret, and about my unconscious investments in the different kinds of cultural works this book explores. The process has led me to ask questions about who I am and how I remember, about how my upbringing, caught between national and social formations, inflects the texts, performances and songs I explore with class associations, identity markers, and memories of people, places and objects. Looking at the chapters, each one is shaped by recurring knots in my self-understanding, contradictions around being British and Irish, between heteronormativity and queerness, between literature and performance, high and popular culture, grief as a lived affect and reanimation as literary or theatrical metaphor.

The genesis of this book is closely linked to the Irish folk song 'Finnegan's Wake', which I discuss in detail in Chapter 7. I used to listen to this song as I was growing up in London to Irish immigrant parents. It is associated in my mind with my childhood but also with my sense of national and cultural displacement. The song contains a striking scene of reanimation in which the apparently dead protagonist, Tim Finnegan, comes back to life at his own funeral wake, and the title would famously go on to be the name of James Joyce's last monumental work *Finnegans Wake* (1939). The song 'Finnegan's Wake' embodies many of the key themes of the book as a whole: the links between the living and the dead, between literature and song, high and popular art, and between different versions of grief and forms of mourning. It is a song which brings the dead back to life in an impossible reanimation, injecting laughter into the scene of mourning, reviving the living as well as the provisionally deceased.

My book is attracted to the concept of reanimation for a number of reasons. First, reanimation operates as what Mieke Bal calls a 'travelling concept', offering 'miniature theories, and in that guise, help[ing] in the analysis of objects, situations, states and other theories' (Bal, 2009: 19). It ranges from literal acts of reanimation of the dead, the puzzling reanimations of ghosts and phantoms, to the poetic reanimations of the dead via elegy. In addition, it looks at the shift between animacy and inanimacy in performance, as well as exploring how literature and song represent memory and/or become objects of memory, especially in the context of bereavement.

Second, reanimations tie into elements of literature, theatre and performance that revolve around the non-rational, the counterfactual or magical. Recent critical work on the idea of enchantment explores links between fiction, fantasy and imaginary worlds (Saler, 2012) but also new forms of engagement with art more open to its enigmatic, irrational qualities (Felski, 2008, 2011). The artistic return of the dead, in whatever reanimated form, is bound up with an impossible reversal. Discussing the period after her husband's death, Joan Didion writes, 'I was thinking as small children think, as if my thoughts or wishes had the power to reverse the narrative, change the outcome' (Didion, 2012: 35), while a little later she writes, '"Bringing him back" had been through those months my hidden focus, a magic trick' (Didion, 2012: 44). Reanimations in art embody the desire to revive the dead, testifying to the reconstructive power of literature and theatre through encounters with ghosts, plot reversals that bring dead characters back to life, objects, symbols, gestures and memories that recall the dead, as well as signalling the complex emotions around remembering and forgetting.

As well as exploring enactments of death, grief and reanimation, my book examines what literature, theatre and performance can offer us in the light of death's finality and grief's force. In *The Archaeology of Loss*, Sarah Tarlow talks about grief for her father in these terms:

> When my father died, that was grief, a grief that only takes from you, peels you away, leaves nothing in the middle. Grief that lies in wait in empty armchairs and unsolved crossword clues. It still, ten years on, ambushes me when I am weeding the garden or in the middle of a run, and I am suddenly, embarrassingly, sobbing by a hedge and I cannot get my breath. Grief is your life as it was before, but less. A diminishing. (Tarlow, 2023: 222–3)

The disjunction between grief as 'a diminishing' (Tarlow, 2023: 223) and grief as a reparative process leads a critic like Eugenie Brinkema to be sceptical about art forms 'commuting the negativity of mourning into a productive new state' (Brinkema, 2014: 56). This book highlights the tensions between different ways of grieving: as melancholia, loss and negation, or as a source of creativity and poetic elegy, even as a celebration of choreography, physicality and sexual desire. One of the challenges the next chapters document is how to balance these contradictions, to articulate the pain of death and its ruptures with the playfulness of art, theatre and literature, full of fantastical images of ghosts, funerals and burials, plays-within-plays and farcical metatheatre.

Reanimations demonstrate grief's multiple modalities, as simultaneous acts of reconstruction and evasion. Allowing grief's contradictions to be visualised or verbalised, reanimations permit us to say the unsayable, or to create a space for it. In works such as Shakespeare's *Hamlet* and Enda Walsh's *The Walworth Farce*, the book explores the relationship between the poetic expression and evasion of grief, where creating plays-within-plays or theorising (self-) performance become reflections on grief's communicability.

Reanimation: etymology; early uses of the word

Reanimation as a concept is richly evocative, with cognates including returning, reimagining, recreating, reawakening, revising, revisiting, reigniting, rekindling and re-enlivening.

The OED gives three definitions of *reanimation*: 1a. 'the fact or process of returning to life', first used in 1633; 1b. 'the fact or action of restoring to life. Also figurative', first used in 1653, and 2. 'Renewal of vigour or liveliness', first use cited is 1711. The examples given in relation to meanings 1a and 1b mostly link reanimation to bodies, ghosts or resurrections from the dead, while definition 2 gives examples using the term in a wider figurative sense. One of the earliest recorded uses in English dates back to 1626, from *Contemplations vpon the Historicall Part of the Old Testament* by I. H. Dean of Worcester, author Joseph Hall, where the word is used in the context of the impossibility of reviving the corpse of a dead person: 'The body that is once cold in death, hath no more aptitude to a reanimation, than that which is moldred into dust' (Hall, 1626: 134).

The word 'animation' has an earlier origin in English, appearing in the forms 'anymacyon' in the 1500s and in the 1500s–1600s as 'animacion'. It comes to English through Latin and French, and has a cluster of connected meanings around 'vital principle' and 'fact of possessing life', its connotations moving between 'vivacity' and 'liveliness' to include 'impulsive', 'bringing into action' and 'being animate or alive'. These in turn link back to the Latin word 'anima', which Lewis and Short's Latin dictionary defines as 'air', 'breeze', 'wind', 'breath', 'vital principle', 'life', 'living being', 'rational soul' and 'consciousness'.

While the various meanings and uses of the words 'animus'/ 'anima' dominate etymologies of the word 'reanimation', it is also worth focusing on the importance of the prefix 're' in the term, since part of my argument in this book relates to the meaning of 're' in words such as repetition, rehearsal and re-hearing. As accounts of the prefix 're' tell us, it comes from Latin with the indication of 'again', a repetition or second iteration, and at the same time often has the sense of looking or going backwards, as in words such as 'revert', 'retrace' or 'remake'. As the OED notes, 're-' 'sometimes denot[es] that the action itself is performed a second time, and sometimes that its result is to reverse a previous action or process, or to restore a previous state of things'.

The temporal duality caught between moving forward and looking back is a key torsion within grief too and one which this book explores from the outset. 'Re' brings an odd temporality, a shift forwards that is also a pull backwards; an attempt to reposition the past in the present or future, but also drawn inexorably backwards to become associated with nostalgia and memory. Take the word 'repetition', for example, an internally divided phenomenon, caught in the lexical drama of temporal oscillation. This instability is more pronounced in the case of literary language designed to be read recurrently, or for poetic utterance to be read or spoken, even more so in the context of songs and theatre, both predicated on their iterability and future embodiment in performance. Indeed, the compulsion to repeat a song is one of the most singular markers of its success and yet that repetition is fraught with memory and nostalgia, oriented towards the future but reanimating our former encounters with it, an issue I explore in further detail in Chapters 6 and 7.

The word 'reanimation' therefore comes to connote a complex revival that occurs for the first time but can also feel like a repetition. It is a term that points towards the future but looks back to the past, that promises new perspectives, which may fail or simply mimic or repeat. As the following chapters show, reanimations are often attempts to explore the singularity and finality of death through a temporal contradiction. Reanimations reverse the usual life trajectory from animacy to inanimacy, from living to dead. They are counter-intuitive, magical and enchanting, critiquing rationality, defying sense.

Reanimations: key claims

The book examines the concept of reanimation from a number of perspectives. The first sees reanimations in literature, theatre and performance as a space in which to process and conceptualise death. While we might be able to understand death scientifically, cognitively and philosophically, confronting the reality of death, emotionally and psychologically, is a complex and unpredictable process. Neuroscientist Dorothy P. Holinger suggests in *The Anatomy of Grief* that:

> When news of a death reaches the survivor, abstract thinking – so very important to the decision-making orchestrated by the frontal cortex – is overridden by our senses, which drive the brain's 'bottom-up processing.' These systems process what we are perceiving through sight, sound, smell, taste, and touch. (Holinger, 2020: 55–6)

Some of this processing relates to acknowledging what happens to the human body after death, the shift from animacy to inanimacy, and our unconscious anxieties about whether the dead are really dead, or will stay dead, manifested in the form of the haunting doubles, living versions of the dead, and objects coming to life that characterise Freud's uncanny.

In addition to conceptualising the changed ontological status of the dead, reanimations allow us to communicate with the dead and/or to express our sometimes contradictory emotions about them. As Didion asks, '[i]f the dead were truly to come back, what would they come back knowing? Could we face them? We who allowed them to die?' (Didion, 2012: 152). Reanimations provisionally revive the dead to permit us to say what has been left unsaid, to atone or confess, to explore emotions about the dead that we could not think or express while they were alive. For Jean Laplanche, '[m]ourning is hardly ever without the question: what would he be saying now? What would he have said? hardly ever without regret or remorse for not having been able to speak with the other enough, for not having heard what he had to say' (Laplanche, 1998: 254). We can say to or through ghosts or spectres things we could never say to the living. We reanimate the dead to cope with unfinished business; to express love or regret, guilt or anger; to act out the desire to make poetry from our loss, art from absence or to impress the dead with our performances of grief. We may even be reanimating them to atone for the fact that our knowledge of them while living was incomplete. As Philip Kennicott suggests:

> After death delivers its initial shock, one wanders the world exploring loss, how it operates, how it reveals things that were concealed, how loss completes our often limited sense of the person who died and begins the process of fixing that person in our memory. (Kennicott, 2020: 36)

Reanimations often play a role in helping us come to terms with our own mortality and future death. Even though they are bound up with grief for the deceased, they are as much about the living as they are about the dead. As Kennicott says, 'with our parents' deaths we rediscover [death] as unavoidable and universal. Ideally, they help us learn to die, sometimes explicitly, giving us insight, consoling *us* for *their* death, so that ours will be easier when it comes' (Kennicott, 2020: 10; italics in original). Reanimations engage us in a seriality that ends with our own death. They are about accepting that a part of us has died with those we grieve, about our desire to revive them and about our intensified apprehension of our own finitude. As Didion says, we are 'so wired that when we mourn our losses, we also mourn, for better or for worse, ourselves. As we were. As we are no longer. As we will one day not be at all' (Didion, 2012: 198).

In aesthetic terms, reanimations explore the relationship between death, grief and art by being aligned with fiction and fabulation, with magic, enchantment and transformation. By reviving the dead, an impossible act, they communicate the power of fiction to embody alternative versions of the real, to undo absence, to articulate the intensity and hallucinatory quality of loss. As such, reanimations can be acts of transformation, often with a corrective or utopian dimension: they recreate the dead, perhaps even reinvent them. As Kennicott notes, '[w]hen grief looses its hold, you return to the world you once knew, only to find it transformed by the thing that is missing' (Kennicott, 2020: 36). They permit us to think through and beyond the fantastical and to find in death and loss a new understanding of the fantastical altogether. For Laplanche: 'Demons already are quite clearly human creations. But neither do the dead – any more than demons – exist. In one sense, they too are a creation' (Laplanche, 1998: 246). In reanimations, we conceptualise and poeticise death, we articulate the contradictions of grief, we celebrate art's enchantment and magical powers, and we transform the void of bereavement into 'something rich and strange'.

Reanimating grief looks at literary texts which record reanimations of the dead bound up with the grieving process in a variety of ways. Works such as *Odyssey*, *Aeneid* and 'The Dead' all feature ghosts or powerful portrait-memories of the dead. These encounters act as precursors for future works of fiction, theatre or performance. At the same time, grief can be reanimating in the way it generates intertextual pathways and networks between and across genres and media. The ontology of ghosts and the epistemology of memory are intertwined with the wider notion of textual and aesthetic reanimation within and across different cultural forms. They also depend on performance and iterativity.

Theatre as an art form embodies this interdependence of forms of memory, the text haunting the live performance, bodies onstage reanimating texts, characters, readings, or sometimes earlier performances of a role. Indeed, theatre becomes the very space in which to theorise the valency of the metaphorical concept of reanimation further. In the words of Alice Rayner:

> In theatrical space, performance does not inter the past so much as raise the dead, in a ghostly repetition that is the same insofar as it is mortal. That is, it raises the dead from within the paradoxical space of sameness and repetition, sameness and difference. It must be haunted if it is to be effective. It must take the ghosts from the tombs of written memorialization and return to an audience the affective sorrow of experience rather than the sealed tomb of memorialization.
> (Rayner, 2006a: 61)

For Rayner, theatre juxtaposes the living and the dead in a form of reanimation which is physical and spatial as well as textual. From the page to the world of live performance, theatre's reanimations shift us away from memorialisation towards a re-encounter with the tangible body, object or voice of grief. Theatre's rehearsals and repetitions augment this haunting sense of engagement with ghosts of the dead. In Chapter 2, which theorises the event known as the *coup de théâtre*, I examine the way in which performance 'raises the dead' (Rayner, 2006a: 61) by experimenting with animacy and inanimacy, while theatre's playfulness with death, its eloquent acts of grieving at fabricated deaths and constructed scenes of mourning, are explored in sections on Sophocles' *Electra* and *Hamlet* in Chapters 1 and 3.

Reanimations have a specific resonance for art forms that are predicated on rehearsal and repetition. Peggy Phelan makes a claim for the role of theatre and performance in relation to bereavement: 'it may well be that theatre and performance respond to a psychic need to rehearse for loss, and especially for death. Billed as rehearsal, performance and theatre have a special relation to art as memorial' (Phelan, 1997: 3). Building on this insight, I suggest that grief leads us to bring these qualities of performance to a wider range of literary, poetic or textual forms, prompting us to return to them, re-reading, re-viewing and reconceptualising them as a form of memorial, an act of memory. Grief leads us to remember and rehearse those works of fiction, theatre or song which once enchanted us, now bringing the affective force of bereavement to the scenes of death, revenance or mourning which we may have encountered pre-grief.

Music and songs likewise operate within this economy of reanimation as they engage with the logics of rehearsal and repetition. In Chapters 6 and 7, I examine the power of the musical fragment to convey the involuntary and apparitional quality of grief. These chapters examine aural epiphanies, snatches of songs, half-remembered melodies or lines, sometimes mishearings, viewing them as time-travelling reanimations of grief, loss and mourning, but also of desire, love and passion. These fragments – aural glimpses, the few notes we hear or remember – often signal a tension between the part and the whole, opposing the desire for completion against the transient irruptions of grief. The sonic fragment is a metonym for the dissolutions that grieving enacts on our memory of the dead, communicating to us the multiple fragmentations of grief's emotional force.

In summary, this book looks at reanimations across literature, theatre and performance as a memorial for the dead, as a series of theoretical acts about fiction and literary enchantment, and as a way of dealing with our own mortality and future death.

Grief and mourning: defining terms

For the purposes of this book, grief is viewed as the immediate reaction to the death of someone close to us. In contrast, mourning is taken to be the process by which grief is psychologically processed and contextualised. Grief irrupts, whereas mourning reframes and narrates. As David Kessler points out, grief is a private act while mourning is public:

> Too often outsiders who may have the best of intentions will suggest to a bereaved person that it's time to move on, embrace life, and let go of grief. But grief should be a no-judgment zone ... Grief is what's going on inside of us, while mourning is what we do on the outside. (Kessler, 2019: Chapter 2, para. 8)

The contrast between grief as private and mourning as more external is echoed by other critics. Harry Robert Wilson quotes Brinkema's distinction between grief, the 'private passion (feelings, sentiments, experiences)', and mourning, 'the public manifestation of that interior state to the outside world (rituals, customs, shared beliefs)' (Brinkema, 2014: 72 in Wilson, 2019: 107). Wilson continues: 'From this position, grief can be considered as the felt affect and mourning as the naming of the emotion and subsequent cultural practice of working through that emotion' (Wilson, 2019: 107).

Some critics go so far as to theorise mourning as the theatre of grief – its ritual enactment and performance. By this analysis, grief might be said to precede mourning. In her discussion of grief in *Hamlet*, Laurie Maguire suggests that mourning is the public, shared performance of grief, a kind of grief in costumes:

> Mourning, like memory, is performative … In that it demands action, mourning differs from grief: it is the performance of grief. Grief is internal – 'I haue that Within, which passeth show;/These, but the Trappings, and the Suites of woe' declares Hamlet … distinguishing the costumed ritual of mourning from the internal grief it denotes.
> (Maguire, 2002: 68)

Grief by this reading feels like an ontological change, a new way of being, whereas mourning involves adopting public forms of emotion, engaging in visible rituals. For Didion, grief is a state, whereas mourning is a more active process: '[u]ntil now, I had been able only to grieve, not mourn. Grief was passive. Grief happened. Mourning, the act of dealing with grief, required attention' (Didion, 2012: 143).

For Brinkema, the inner turmoil of grief contrasts with the performative quality of mourning:

> In this usage, grief involves emotional, cognitive, and physical responses to loss centred around affective reactions such as anger, rage, anxiety, fear, nausea, hysteria, numbness, and denial. Mourning, by contrast, is often figured as formalized or ritualized responses to death: funerals, eulogizing, memorial services, and burial habits.
> (Brinkema, 2014: 72)

Brinkema argues that we need to distinguish grief and mourning more explicitly. She defines 'grief' as the 'peculiar painfulness' (Freud's phrase) of profound loss that cannot be figured or recuperated. Drawing on Roland Barthes's idea in *Camera Lucida* about the non-translatability of the photographic image, Brinkema says:

> I want to suggest that one way to theorize grief as irresolvable – undialectical, unproductive, a bad investment, and peculiarly

painful – precisely involves letting the dead become life-cluttering photographs. Far from ameliorating the affective pang, the becoming-photograph of the dead materializes the untransformative and untransformable dimension of loss's pain. (Brinkema, 2014: 75)

Brinkema takes the idea of grief's untransformability from Barthes's claim that the photograph, in capturing the ephemeral via the action of light, is undialectical, registering an unrepeatable loss like the singularity of death. In Barthes's words, '[i]f dialectic is that thought which masters the corruptible and converts the negation of death into the power to work, then the photograph is undialectical: it is a denatured theatre where death cannot "be contemplated," reflected and interiorized' (Barthes, 2000: 92, quoted in Brinkema, 2014: 82).

Grief's inexpressibility takes different forms in the scenes of reanimation in this book. Whether it is through ephemerality and evanescence (the *coup de théâtre*), scepticism about the presence of ghosts (*Hamlet*), realism's limits (Chekhov), representation under erasure (Beckett) or farcical re-enactments (Walsh), these works leave space for grief to escape expression, for its resistance to figuration or reconstruction.

'Expressive' and 'critical' writing

In *Camera Lucida*, his essay on photography which is also a meditation on death and grief, Barthes talks about 'the uneasiness of being a subject torn between two languages, one expressive, the other critical' (Barthes, 2000: 8). Exploring death and loss precipitates this exact quandary as we reflect critically on grief, its definitions, and its role in literature and theatre, and at the same time feel the impulse to write expressively or elegiacally about our own grief. My book builds on Barthes's observation about the relationship between critical and expressive modes of writing to suggest that their combination provides valuable insights into the affective power and subjective investments we make in literature, theatre and performance. In an essay on Freud and Barthes, Kathleen Woodward makes a similar observation:

> I have wished for a discourse about mourning more expressive than that provided by psychoanalysis, a discourse that would combine the

affective dimension of the experience of mourning with theoretical descriptions of mourning as a process. (Woodward, 1990: 94)

As a result, my book incorporates short sections of creative writing, autobiographical reflections about childhood, growing up, listening to the songs and reading the texts examined in these pages, as well as remembering scenes of death and grief and recollecting the dead through the cultural material associated with them. Some of these sequences are grafted onto the chapters in question, but in the last chapter, the critical and the expressive become more interwoven. At times, we wish or need to sing our grief, to write elegies and dirges for the dead. At other times, we want to understand death, to disentangle complex emotions, to rationalise what death means and what it does to the dead body and the living psyche. Art allows us to play with death, to explore the transgressive contradictions of grief, and in reanimating the dead we explore the counter-intuitive power of fiction or the revivificatory power of performance.

As I use the ideas of death, grief and reanimation to think about literary and theatre aesthetics, talking about ghosts and haunting, textual burial, the reanimation of forms, styles or movements, I will be articulating that link between art and the survival of the dead. Works analysed in this book use the metaphorics of death and reanimation to reflect on the need for new forms and 'living characters' (Chekhov, 1993a: 66), to find a language to express death's presence and the grieving process, and to memorialise the dead. From ghosts to memories, from elegies for the living to the return of the dead, from ballads to song fragments, the dead are reanimated in literature, theatre and performance in multiple ways. I will be trying to capture some of that multiplicity in my own critical and expressive languages of grief as they intersect with, undo, amplify or reconfigure one another.

Reanimating grief

In her memoir *Love's Work*, Gillian Rose tells the reader that she has terminal cancer. She anticipates the ways in which the announcement of her death might transform the reading process:

> I must continue to write for the same reason I am always compelled to write, in sickness and in health: for, otherwise, I die deadly, but this way, by this work, I may die forward into the intensified agon of living. (Rose, 1995: 71)

Writing has been a way of living. Her compulsion to write undoes the logic of dying, makes it generative rather than a waste. She will 'die forward', in a dynamic and life-affirming way. A few lines later, Rose notes how people react when they hear she is dying: 'For what people now seem to find most daunting with me, I discover, is not my illness or possible death, but my accentuated being; not my morbidity, but my renewed vitality' (Rose, 1995: 72).

This book echoes Rose when it argues that literature and theatre, performance, music and song make out of death an intense form of living, giving grief, loss and mourning a vitality, revivifying the dead in creative, utopian, expiatory and fantasmatic ways. The work of reanimation makes art out of loss, erecting memorials in writing, re-presenting bodies, acknowledging the ephemerality of the living and the permanence of the dying. Reanimation is about writing names in water (to echo the words on Keats' gravestone), leaving 'not a rack behind' (*Tempest*, 4.1.156; Shakespeare, 2016a: 3255), apart from the resurrections of art that come from reading and viewing, singing and remembering our griefs and our futures, with and without the dead.

In the next chapter, I will use uses classic scenes of reanimation to show how texts engage with death in literature and theatre from ontological, epistemological and aesthetic perspectives. In Chapter 2, I think about reanimation, performance and memory by exploring how the dead return to haunt the living via animals, objects and puppets in the work of the theatre company Complicite (*The Caucasian Chalk Circle*, *Mnemonic*) and of Romeo Castellucci and his company Societas Raffaello Sanzio. Chapter 3 stays with theatre, and metatheatre, to explore multiple forms of reanimation in relation to Shakespeare's *Hamlet* (1600), linking the text's thematics to live performance and the transition from theatre to literature in the form of Maggie O'Farrell's 2020 novel *Hamnet*. Chapter 4 uses Chekhov's plays *The Seagull* and *Three Sisters* to explore ungrievability, death and representation via the demise and return of forms of realism. Chapter 5 analyses Enda Walsh's work, especially in *The Walworth Farce*, as a transformative reanimation of Samuel Beckett's avant-garde aesthetics, woven through with reflections on how theatre stages or fails to stage death and grief. In Chapter 6, I link literature, theatre and music in James Joyce's short story 'The Dead' and Sally Rooney's *Beautiful World, Where Are You*, both of which prominently feature the Irish folk ballad 'The Lass of Aughrim'. Chapter 7 examines the ballad 'Finnegan's Wake' to reflect on scenes of grieving and revival in a range of cultural works from literature, television and song, using this material to exemplify the act of expressing my own grief through researching and reconstructing exchanges and fragments revolving around songs and acoustic memory.

These readings gravitate towards scenes of grief, encounters with the dead, and transitions between animacy and inanimacy, staging the difficulties of letting go, of believing our senses, of accepting the substitution of silence for words and of memories of the dead for the living vibrations of laughter. They are propelled critically by a desire for the stabilising qualities of knowledge but also seek out echoes and intensifications of grief. In a two-way process, this book is a search for ways of expressing the emotional and perceptual characteristics of grief and, at the same time, explores grief's impact on reading practices and on the processes of critical thinking and creative writing. Grief's temporality, its recursiveness and repetitions, assigns a key role to performance. Whether in theatre, as a critical metaphor or as an analytical category for exploring how grief is constituted, performance leads us to reflect on grief's dynamics and locations, on the social pressures governing it, and on the relationship between the internal, private emotions of grief and the public rituals of mourning.

1
Genealogies of grief: classic reanimations

I read the elegy in a hospital room after the death of my mother. She had always been afraid of storms and terror gripped her at the first claps of thunder. As children, we saw her, a usually indomitable figure, suddenly shed decades and return to a kind of childhood fear, her voice different, asking us to be quiet as she hid on the staircase, or, in an earlier home, in a now forgotten nook. We loved these quiet moments of thunder – we briefly had the upper hand – but we knew to tiptoe around. It made no sense to us, this astraphobia, this fear of noise – it couldn't harm us, and we would laugh about it. I chose this elegy for many reasons, because it was Shakespeare, because I was a literature and theatre academic, because its rhymes and couplets promised order in the midst of chaos, but also, perhaps mostly, because of the lines:

> GUIDERIUS. *Fear no more the lightning-flash.*
> ARVIRAGUS. *Nor th'all-dreaded thunder-stone.*

I sensed these lines would speak directly to my grieving siblings in the hospital room, that literature and theatre would offer a secret language to them, a code that would tap into their own childhood memories. It is only now, on repeat reading, that the phrase 'thunder-stone' stands out, glossed by Dyce as: 'Thunder-stone. The same as thunderbolt; both formed upon an erroneous fancy, that the destruction occasioned by lightning was effected by some solid body', and then, 'The thunderstone is the imaginary product of the thunder' (Dyce, 1904). I like the idea of literature and theatre, their ghosts and reanimations, as being 'imaginary products', that misprision which takes noise and insubstantiality to be solid things.

This chapter explores classic examples of reanimation in literature and theatre, partly to start constructing a genealogy of the concept and partly to think about recurring themes in the book: the presence of ghosts and theatre's propensity to play with the distinction between the living and the dead. It offers a series of snapshots of reanimation which are inevitably selective, drawn from Western literature and theatre and linked to my own trajectory as a reader and academic; works encountered in the context of school or university which are reconfigured by the subsequent grieving process. One of the main contentions of this book is that grief reorders the literary and cultural texts from our past reading repertoires, bringing a new framework to scenes of loss and encounters with the dead.

This series of foundational scenes of reanimation has been chosen because of their influence on subsequent artistic forms of reanimation, but also because they illustrate particular aspects of the concept in relation to the body, memory, voice and language. Though disparate in nature, moving between ghosts, fake deaths, miraculous resurrections and poetic elegies, each example captures a certain quality of grief: the difficulty of letting go, or the return of the dead as memory, unconscious projection, or visual or verbal hallucination.

Encounters with the dead in Homer, Virgil, Ovid, Greek tragedy, the Bible and Shakespeare are historical nodal points in the Western canon for how literature and theatre represent the grieving process. The chapter traces a trajectory from direct encounters with the object of grief in the form of ghosts or phantoms to more multi-layered episodes in which grief is a literary or theatrical device. Each of these scenes deals with how we conceptualise death itself as a phenomenon. Fittingly for a book emerging from the deaths of my parents, the chapter begins with encounters with parental ghosts in *Odyssey* and *Aeneid*, focusing on the missing body, as well as questions of language and voice. Classic accounts of the Orpheus myth in Virgil and Ovid convey the magical power of the poetics of grief as well as grief's strangeness, perhaps even its horror. Sophocles' *Electra* introduces a more analytical world in which a character returns from a pretend death, shifting the focus to language, narrative and rhetoric. *Electra* is representative of modes of literature or theatre which play with objects, double-takes, *coups de théâtre* and other devices to communicate grief's confusion. The chapter touches on the Christian resurrection narrative as a key cultural intertext for many later scenes of reanimation, such as *The Tempest* or 'Finnegan's Wake', focusing on Jean-Luc Nancy's reading of it as a resurrection *of* death, not *from* death.[1] The final part of the chapter reflects on elegies for false deaths in *Cymbeline* and *The Tempest*, scenes of grief predicated on miscomprehension, displacement and the proleptic effect of literature's enchanting memorials for the (only provisionally) dead.

Parental ghosts

Homer's *Odyssey*, Virgil's *Aeneid*, and Virgil's and Ovid's versions of the Orpheus myth all feature scenes of *katabasis*, episodes in which a living hero descends to the underworld and has a series of encounters with the souls or shades of the dead. Nicoló Benzi explains the recurrence of *katabasis* scenes in ancient Greek mythology and their defining characteristics:

> Heroes who perform a katabasis include Heracles, Orpheus, Theseus and Peirithous, and Odysseus ... katabasis, by its very nature, is seen as an extraordinary achievement .... Generally, katabaseis are performed to retrieve someone or something from Hades: Heracles Cerberus, Orpheus Eurydice, Theseus and Peirithous Persephone. (Benzi, 2021: 90)

Odyssey and *Aeneid* famously include encounters between the eponymous character and the ghost of a dead parent. In both cases, the emphasis is on the insubstantiality of the ghostly body and the realisation that the dead are ontologically different to us. Discussing *Odyssey*, Vayos Liapis explains that the Greeks had an 'embodied conception of the afterlife, in which a person's post-mortem existence is experienced in corporeal terms even when the dead are conceived as spectral replicas of their former bodies' (Liapis, 2021: 34). This duality is dramatised by the way the ghosts of the dead are mistaken for the living, even in the context of the underworld and its phantoms.

In *Odyssey*, the *katabasis* scene includes the encounter between Odysseus and the ghost of his mother, Anticlea, in Book 11, when he engages in a *nekyia*, a summoning of ghosts, after travelling to the edge of the underworld to question them about the future. Liapis suggests that in this scene:

> the earliest Greek description of a physical encounter in Hades between a living person and the dead, Odysseus converses with a number of shadows, all of which retain enough of the living person's physical features to be recognisable …. At the same time, however, they are phantoms, eidōla , "wraiths," or more accurately "likenesses" of the corresponding living persons, mere substitutes for the real thing. (Liapis, 2021: 34)

The spectres of the dead start appearing in a terrifying exhumation. When Odysseus tries and fails three times to embrace the ghost of his dead mother, she explains to him the difference between the living and the dead. It is at this moment of desired intimacy and longed-for touch, when the reanimated ghost could be at its most meaningful for Odysseus, that the reality of the schism between life and death, the powerlessness of ghosts and the consequent permission to grieve become apparent:

> So she spoke, and I wondered in my heart how I might clasp the ghost of my dead mother. Three times I sprang toward her, and my will said, 'Clasp her,' and three times she flitted from my arms like a shadow or a dream. As for me, the pain grew ever sharper in my heart, and I spoke and addressed her with winged words: 'My mother, why do you not stay for me when I wish to clasp you, so that even in the house of Hades we two may throw our arms about each other and take our fill of chill lamenting'. (Homer, 1919: 11, 204–13)

Odysseus's repeated attempts to embrace Anticlea underline his physical presence in contrast to the evanescence of the ghostly maternal body. As Susanne Turner suggests, Anticlea's 'ontological status is now so slippery it can only be described through things it is not' (Turner, 2016: 144). The attempted embrace resembles a childhood act of former touch and intimacy. The scene is ostensibly part of Odysseus's quest for knowledge about the future, but, Rachel K. Alexander argues, it also 'affirms the relationship between memory and mortality' (Alexander, 2022: para. 15); it is about a knowledge of the past, of death, and of what it means to grieve.

Anticlea's explanation of what happens after death is a curious articulation of the self-evident: that death is universal and that the body decays. What is notable is Anticlea's use of vivid images to convey the dissolution of the flesh and the ghostliness of the dead:

> So I spoke, and my honored mother at once answered: 'Ah me, my child, ill-fated above all men, it is not that Persephone, daughter of Zeus, is deceiving you, but this is the appointed way with mortals, when one dies. For the sinews no longer hold the flesh and the bones together, but the strong force of blazing fire destroys these, as soon as the spirit leaves the white bones, and the ghost, like a dream, flutters off and is gone. But hurry to the light as fast as you can, and bear all these things in mind, so that hereafter you may tell them to your wife'. (Homer, 1919: 11, 214–24)

Anticlea's words outline what happens to body and soul after death. She is explaining the phenomenon of death itself, giving an account of the decay of her own body, a linguistic affirmation of the lesson Odysseus has just learnt physically through the failed act of embrace. The visual, the haptic, the verbal and the vocal are all at play in this scene, even though they undermine each other: whose is this voice without a living body? How can this apparitional body exist without being touched? How can the voice survive in this incorporeal form? Odysseus cannot conceptualise his mother's death, or more precisely the fact that she could no longer be the living version of herself. Yet despite this block to understanding, the ghost of Anticlea tries to explain, amplifying the contradictions that characterise the act of grieving.

The scene is about Odysseus's growing knowledge of the nature of ghosts but also about the singularity of maternal death. It communicates the contradictory effects of grief, especially at the loss of a parent: the wish to reconnect with the dead, the difficulty of letting go, the hallucinatory quality of memory, the evocation of childhood and the desire to touch the living body again.

Anticlea's final words to Odysseus are a request to remember and pass on what he has seen, 'bear all these things in mind, so that hereafter you may tell them to your wife' (line 224). As Alexander notes, 'Anticlea suggests that the proper response to knowledge about death is to remember this knowledge in order to share it with one's beloved' (Alexander, 2022: para. 18). The encounter between the living son and his dead mother, the triggering of grief, also leads to the *production* of narrative. Discussing the visuality and visibility of the dead, Turner says that '[a]s Odysseus discovers here to his dismay, death transforms the dead into images, reducing them to representation' (Turner, 2016: 144–5). What he also discovers is his responsibility to transmit the knowledge and memory of the dead, these *images*, to others.

While Anticlea's body is visible but insubstantial, her voice remains. It plays a complex role in this scene because, at one level, the voice already occupies a space in between the bodily and the immaterial, merging the written, the textual and the performed. The human voice indicates singularity, presence, directness, but at the same time it is ephemeral, vestigial, an auditory memory. The voice is the body's signature, produced by the specific configuration of organs, lungs, larynx, mouth and tongue: it bears the imprint of an individual body, yet here it is produced by an apparition, a phantom. The ghost's voice troubles categories, disrupting any clear distinction between presence and absence. In Chapter 7, I explore the memory of voices in the grieving process by thinking about song fragments, accents and the trace of the voice in the act of laughter. In the scene with Anticlea, the maternal voice retains the explanatory function of a parent talking to a child, but in this case instead of teaching her son about the world and how to live in it, Anticlea is explaining death, the decay of the body and the phenomenon of mortality.

Aeneid

Virgil's *Aeneid* Book 6 includes a similar scene of *katabasis* to that in Homer's *Odyssey*, only this time the encounter is between Aeneas and the ghost of his father, Anchises. Unlike Odysseus's encounter with the dead, which occurs above ground, Aeneas descends into the stygian gloom, guided by the sibyl. I want to examine the collision between the physical and the insubstantial in Virgil's account, noting how the scene operates visually, in relation to the ontology of ghosts but also at the level of poetic imagery, and finally subliminally, at the level of the missing voice, the absent body in the text.

In a review of Seamus Heaney's translation of *Aeneid* Book 6, Kate Kellaway says:

It is a book about the impossibility of which we all dream – a reunion with people loved and lost. Describing the meeting between Aeneas and his father, [Heaney] is careful to ensure nothing distracts from the moment of their embrace, until the heart-rending resolution. (Kellaway, 2016)

Kellaway quotes Heaney's translation of lines 700–2:

> Three times he tried to reach arms round that neck.
> Three times the form, reached for in vain, escaped
> Like a breeze between his hands, a dream on wings.

The Loeb translation of these lines, by Fairclough, revised by Goold, has the following:

> Thrice there he strove to throw his arms about his neck;
> thrice the form, vainly clasped, fled from his hands,
> even as light winds, and most like a winged dream.
>   (Virgil, 6, 700–2)

The Latin text is as follows:

> Ter conatus ibi collo dare bracchia circum,
> Ter frustra comprensa manus effugit imago,
> Par levibus ventis volucrique simillima somno.
>   (Virgil, 6, 700–2)

The Latin words capture the incoherent dynamics of grief and the insubstantiality of the revenant: 'frustra comprensa', 'reached for in vain' (Heaney), 'vainly clasped' (Fairclough/Goold).

Notable here is the way the tension between living body and intangible soul/phantom/ghost is played out at the level of language. No English version can replicate the susurration of the sibilants in 'simillima somno', the airy 's' of the ghost-phantom escaping, the repeated 'm' consonant subliminally evoking the tangibility of the body (to say the words out loud needs the lips to open and close) as if trying to prevent the evanescent imago, phantom or memory from vanishing. This linguistic tension is picked up by the vivid poetic metaphor of 'winged dream', the vibrating of bird wings in contrast to the nebulosity of the dream. Body and soul, lips closing, breath escaping, are all heard and felt subliminally in these words. Heaney's translation uses a repeated 'ee' vowel sound ('like a br__ee__ze betw__ee__n his hands, a dr__ea__m …')

to express the tension between cohesion and dissolution, as if the words themselves are trying to cling together phonically while the soul of the dead is fleeing Aeneas's grasp and, by extension, comprehension or verbalisation.

As Pierre Bonnechere and Gabriella Cursaru say, '[t]he journey into the Beyond includes in addition a tension between life and death, mortal humanity and divinity, below and beyond limits' (Bonnechere and Cursaru, 2016: 2). There is more at stake in the act of *katabasis* than a quest for knowledge of the future. These scenes are about the transition to grief and the acceptance of the body-becoming-memory or image, escaping our embrace or touch. In the encounter between Aeneas and his father's ghost, poetry's phonic echoes, its sibilants and assonances, bind us to the sound-producing body and voice at the very moment the ghost-image of the grieved object, the permanence of the parental figure, dissipates like a 'dream on wings'.

Orpheus: repeating and expressing grief

Taken together, these scenes explore the difficulty of accepting the death and dissolution of the body. The ghost resembles the living person, continuing as memory, but the tangibility of the body has vanished. The desire for touch recurs, as does the voice, and in Virgil's poetry even the articulation of grief replicates at the level of sound the tension between the fleshly body and its afterlife as concept, memory and image. The voice lives on, an auditory hallucination, produced by the body but now uncanny and spectral. The three attempts at touch, three failed embraces, tell us about grief's dynamics, about the reiterative nature of the grieving process, its gradual comprehension of loss requiring this embodied, enacted form of knowledge.

Orpheus is also a figure who engages in a *katabasis*, yet the focus in the Orpheus myth is less on the ontology of ghosts and more on grief's expressive power. The Orpheus myth in versions from Virgil and Ovid links grief with poetry and desire. In the story, grief survives death, has transformative qualities, is enchanting and dangerous. Orpheus's journey to the underworld to search for his wife, Eurydice, acts out a fantasy of resurrecting the dead, but then reiterates loss all the more permanently. As Helen Sword observes, 'Orpheus embodies both the powers of art and the limitations of art – both the possibility of conquering death and the futility of the attempt. It is the very ambivalence of the myth he inhabits that accounts for its tremendous potency' (Sword, 1989: 408). Orpheus is punished for disobeying the gods. By looking back, he incurs a double death and second mourning.

In the *Georgics* (4, 453–527), Virgil emphasises the solitude and durability of Orpheus's grief:

> Orpheus, consoling love's anguish, with his hollow lyre,
> sang of you, sweet wife, you, alone on the empty shore,
> of you as day neared, of you as day departed. (Virgil, 4, 464–6)

When he visits the underworld, the souls of the dead gather to hear Orpheus's song. In a beautiful metaphor, the shadows, wraiths, those without light or substance, are suddenly imagined in the everyday image of birds fleeing winter rain, the strangeness of death offset by the imagery of the living creatures:

> The insubstantial shadows, and the phantoms of those
>   without light,
> came from the lowest depths of Erebus, startled by his song,
> as many as the thousand birds that hide among the leaves,
> when Vesper, or wintry rain, drives them from the hills …
>   (Virgil, 4, 571–4)

Orpheus's grief song reduces the underworld to stillness, causing Cerberus and the Furies to fall silent, almost as if it had become a painting. At the moment Orpheus turns back and loses Eurydice, her disappearance is captured in metaphors of liquid, shadow and smoke:

> 'Orpheus,' she cried,
> 'what madness has destroyed my wretched self, and you?
> See, the cruel Fates recall me, and sleep hides my swimming eyes,
> Farewell, now: I am taken, wrapped round by vast night,
> stretching out to you, alas, hands no longer yours.'
> She spoke, and suddenly fled, far from his eyes,
> like smoke vanishing in thin air, and never saw him more,
> though he grasped in vain at shadows, and longed
> to speak further … (Virgil, 4, 494–502)

Though it is Proteus who is famously able to metamorphose, the double death Orpheus witnesses also becomes ungraspable and intangible, negating the corporeal. Death and grief have the power to freeze the world into a numbed stillness, or to turn what is solid into shadows and smoke.

Orpheus's song charms the animals, woods and forests around him, giving them a kind of sentience, but his mourning is met with punishment. Yet even death cannot extinguish his threnody, as the head torn from his body continues to speak:

> the voice alone, the ice-cold tongue, with ebbing breath,
> cried out: 'Eurydice, ah poor Eurydice!'
> 'Eurydice' the riverbanks echoed, all along the stream.
>   (Virgil, 4, 525–7)

Orpheus's mourning song not only survives death, orchestrating inanimate objects and trees so that they listen to his keening; it also survives his own death, receiving an answering echo from the landscape.

Joseph Roach thinks about the Orpheus myth in relation to performance. He analyses it in terms of forwards and backwards movement (in time and space), presence and absence, the poet at risk of destruction and the survival of art after death:

> [Orpheus's] body violently dismembered and its pieces scattered, the poet's severed head still sings beautiful laments for his lost love, filling her absence (and his own) with his song. The dark beauty of that fate figures the perils of looking back too soon and moving on too late, but it also immortalizes Orpheus as the heroically embodied singer-poet, the avatar of both literature and performance. (Roach, 2010: 1084)

Orpheus thus becomes the embodiment of the power of elegy, generated by grief. The way in which his poetry charms inanimate objects speaks to the magic power of grief, which finds echoes in the world around it, its intensity giving objects and stones a testamentary eloquence. Orphic song, poetic elegy, the evocatory performance resuscitate the dead in memory with powerful force.

Maurice Blanchot's influential reading of the myth in 'The Gaze of Orpheus' expounds a theory of the genesis of the work of art using metaphors of hiddenness, obscurity and veiling. In Blanchot's analysis, the Orpheus myth is an allegory of the perils of the creative process. Blanchot focuses on the moment when Orpheus, leading Eurydice from the underworld, prematurely turns back to look at her, thereby losing her forever. Sword calls the backward glance 'enigmatic' (Sword, 1989: 408) and it remains puzzling why Orpheus's gaze should have such disastrous consequences. For Blanchot, Orpheus is caught in a double bind, where looking at Eurydice is a betrayal, but not looking would also be a denial of the impulse to embrace art's secret power and hidden beauty:

> And, of course, by turning toward Eurydice, Orpheus ruins the work, which is immediately undone, and Eurydice returns among the shades. When he looks back, the essence of night is revealed as the inessential. Thus he betrays the work, and Eurydice, and the night. But not to turn toward Eurydice would be no less untrue. Not to look would be infidelity to the measureless, imprudent force of his movement, which does not want Eurydice in her daytime truth and her everyday appeal, but wants her in her nocturnal obscurity, in her distance, with her closed body and sealed face – wants to see her not when she is visible, but when she is invisible, and not as the intimacy of a familiar life, but as the foreignness of what excludes all intimacy, and wants, not to make her live, but to have living in her plenitude of her death. (Blanchot, 1982: 127)

For Blanchot, Orpheus's desire to look at Eurydice creates the space for poetry and song because it results in her permanent absence through death. Poetry, elegy and songs of mourning are a result of Eurydice's return to the underworld. As Lynne Huffer says, 'Blanchot's project in *The Space of Literature* [is] to describe the operation through which the negativity of loss opens toward a promise of poetic communication' (Huffer, 1998: 176). For Blanchot, '[w]riting begins with Orpheus's gaze' (Blanchot, 1982: 131). Eurydice embodies a complex conceptual space that literature is reaching towards, as Sally M. Silk suggests in her reading of Blanchot: 'Orpheus's gaze ... creates its own literary space. The desire that makes him turn to see Eurydice and thus lose her comprises the potentiality of the literary work embodied in the convergence of art, desire, and death' (Silk, 1994: 542). This is a space of transgression and failure, of embodied presence and spectral absence, the space of a powerful poetics structured through death, grief and desire.

The gaze itself signifies impatience, the privileging of visibility, the desire to verify the transition from ghost to living being just at the moment of exit from the underworld. It represents a desire to know and the rejection of doubt, a loss of faith and an act of disobedience all at once. This tender act of human emotion is the scene of a redoubling of death and the reiteration of grief, locking it into permanence. The revenge is disproportionate, violent and unforgiving, reasserting the logic of the myth structure and the power of the world of the gods, myth and magic. The successful gaze would endanger poetry and song because it would substitute visual pleasure and fulfilled desire for absence, loss and grief. Yet the loss-producing gaze is the song's guarantor. Thus, Orpheus as poet redoubles his poetic power by experiencing a second, permanent loss and renewed mourning.

For Ovid's version of the myth, Orpheus queers desire and disrupts gender categories. In the introduction to his selections from Ovid, Ted Hughes says *Metamorphoses* is about how 'bodies had been magically changed, by the power of the gods, into other bodies' (Hughes, 1997: vii). This change, it is worth adding, is not necessarily into other *living* bodies, but sometimes into other, postmortem, forms of the same body. In *Metamorphoses* Book 10, Orpheus's grief leads to thwarted relationships with women, as it does with Hamlet, whose grief is criticised by Claudius for being 'unmanly' (1.2.94; Shakespeare 2016b: 1771). Ovid uses Orpheus's mourning dirges to sing songs of queer desire:

> From Jove, O Muse, my mother—for all things yield to the sway of Jove—inspire my song! Oft have I sung the power of Jove before; I have sung the giants in a heavier strain, and the victorious bolts hurled on the Phlegraean plains. But now I need the gentler touch, for I would sing of boys beloved by gods, and maidens inflamed by unnatural love and paying the penalty of their lust. (Ovid, 10, 148–54)

Orpheus's deathsongs feature the queer encounters of Jupiter and Ganymede, Apollo and Hyacinthus, before touching on a number of other doomed infatuations, including Venus and Adonis.

Ovid tells us about Orpheus's second visit to the underworld, this time occasioned by Orpheus's own violent death, in which he reunites with the shade of Eurydice, caught between life and death, ghost and living body, on the threshold of reanimation:

> The poet's shade fled beneath the earth, and recognized all the places he had seen before; and, seeking through the blessed fields, found Eurydice and caught her in his eager arms. Here now side by side they

walk; now Orpheus follows her as she precedes, now goes before her, now may in safety look back upon his Eurydice. (Ovid, 11, 61–6)

In Ovid's version, Eurydice and Orpheus, finally united in the underworld, mime the choreography of loss, rehearsing the catastrophic moment of their earlier separation, caught in an eternal performance. They shift between walking side by side to walking one after the other, re-enacting the death-bringing look that leads to Eurydice's second descent. The poet conjures up the figures of Orpheus and Eurydice reunited in the underworld, their ghostly walk, in the poet's textual reanimation of them in death, oscillating between a lateral mutuality and an acting out of their traumatic separation, a ritual of rupture and repair.

Sophocles' *Electra*: grief's 'perceptual chaos'

These ghosts, revived phantoms and second deaths communicate grief's strange, disruptive quality. They map patterns of separation and reunion, the recognition of death's impact on the body, the endurance of the living person in memory, and the translation of these powerful affects into the language of poetry or reparatory choreographies. The Orpheus myth gives grief a supernatural quality, so forceful that a disembodied head continues expressing its emotion, or inanimate objects reflect its eloquence, moved to sentience.

In Sophocles' *Electra*, the focus shifts from the conceptualisation of death, and the links between death, absence and poetry, to epistemological questions about meaning, context, the genuine/fake and the operations of rhetoric. Sophocles' *Electra* contains scenes of grieving, a central character returning from the dead, and an encounter between a living person (Electra) and the object of their grief (Orestes). Electra is in prolonged mourning for her murdered father Agamemnon and is waiting for her brother Orestes to return to exact revenge against their mother Clytemnestra. In Sophocles' play, Orestes, in disguise, reports to everyone, including Electra, that he has died. Electra's lament for her dead brother is cut short when he slowly reveals that he is in fact only pretending to be dead, and that he is ready to take his matricidal revenge on Clytemnestra.

Once the deception is exposed, the play continues with the rest of the revenge cycle.

Sophocles' *Electra* creates a space for scepticism, self-doubt and self-performance. By playing with grief, Sophocles shifts our understanding of grief's dynamics beyond painful lessons in mortality and the ontology of ghosts to focus on the link between grief and narrative, the construction of grief through language and performance, and the role of perception in shaping grief's affects. As Mark Ringer suggests:

> *Electra* is a tragedy that is about tragedy, a play that draws the audience's attention to its own theatricality. The play's metatheatrical resonances explode conventional notions of closure and compel the audience to perceive duality almost everywhere within the dramatic action. (Ringer, 1998: 128)

The question of how to mourn is crucial in the play, as are attempts to regulate grief, a strategy that acknowledges grief's disruptive force. At the outset, Sophocles' *Electra* seems to be about the alienating effect of excessive mourning. As with *Hamlet*, disproportionate grief is a threat to systems of power. *Electra* explores how grief is associated with the unruly feminine and becomes a sign of female otherness.

Two key scenes encourage us to think about the linguistic composition of grief. Delivering the fake announcement that Orestes has died, the Messenger gives a long account of his death (Sophocles, 1995: 700–60). Since there is no death – this is just a textual performance – the critical distance this knowledge provides allows us to stand back and analyse how the requisite emotion is constructed in the speech. From the point of view of the revenge plot, grief at this point in the narrative has to be convincing, and we experience the uncanny doubleness of knowing there is no death, yet feeling the emotional power of its evocation nonetheless. The play here foregrounds its metatheatrical exploration of fiction by exposing literature's fabrications: what is being staged is the power of fiction, the double status of theatre, its ghosting of the real in ways both uncanny and troubling. The Messenger's speech communicates the power of language to create alternative realities, to turn the living into the dead, to transgress on grief in order to create plausible fictions.

The second scene to draw attention to the collision of the real and the fabricated is the extended recognition scene between Orestes and Electra, in which a living character pretending to be dead gradually reveals that they are in fact alive. In it, Orestes breaks the news of his own reanimation to Electra, even though she is apparently holding an urn containing his ashes:

> ELECTRA. It [the burial] does [concern me], if it is the body of Orestes that I hold here.
> ORESTES. It is not Orestes, except in pretence!
> ELECTRA. But where is the tomb of that unhappy one?
> ORESTES. There is none; a living man does not have a tomb!
> ELECTRA. What did you say, young man?
> ORESTES. All that I say is true!
> ELECTRA. Then is the man alive?
> ORESTES. If I am living! (Sophocles, 1995: lines 1216–23)

The exchange shifts between hypotheticals and requests for empirical evidence, evasive statements like 'If I am living!' (line 1223) betraying a desire to occupy this duality between grief and the return of the dead, between absence and presence. Overall, the scene marks the tricky transition between fictional and real, between an end to grief and the start of revenge.

The scene's topsy-turvy reversals demonstrate how the playfulness of theatricality captures some of the manifestations of grief: the difficulty of accepting death, the desire for the deceased to return, their reappearance as image, memory or evocation. In the scene, the weight of Electra's grief is conveyed by her reluctance to relinquish it. In this way, *Electra* articulates grief not through poetry and elegy, but through reversing and theatricalising it, all the more powerfully suggesting that the experiences of grief may escape texts and representation, remaining communicable only as the antithesis of these playful versions and inversions of genuine grief.

At the centre of *Electra's* metatheatre of grief is an object, the funeral urn, which, even in the context of the playworld, is nothing more than a theatrical prop. The urn embodies the power of theatre to reproduce painful emotions, but also represents a comic absurdity in this context. Both the same and different to the real object of mourning, a container of death and the cremated body, the very epicentre of loss, is now a plot device, disrupting the authenticity of grief by its known falseness, turning a scene of bereavement into a kind of textual detective story about the intricacies of plausible plotting. It is daringly visible before Orestes reveals he is still alive, a kind of limit-object testing the ingenuity of the fictional. For Ringer, the urn is a symbol of the ways art condenses and compresses complex issues: 'The urn compacts the fictitious corpse into a little room, much as the art of tragedy compacts into a small performable space the crises of existence' (Ringer, 1998: 187). To that extent, the urn acts as a metonymy for the play as a whole.

Electra thus articulates grief as a series of double-takes and displacements. Ringer calls the effect of these plot twists 'perceptual chaos' (Ringer, 1998: 192). *Electra* undoes the grandeur of ghosts and the poetics of grief songs. Instead, we are in a world of doubleness and reversals, in which death is not located where we think it is (the urn) and where grieving takes unpredictable forms. *Electra* creates and undoes grief and mourning, posing complex questions about the relationship between the fictional and the real. What results is a sense of the (cunning) power of theatre to depict scenes of death and grief, and at the same time a kind of autocritique of theatre because of the way in which it displaces grief's affects, or mobilises them. Grief is thus communicated through its non-presence, and the space for death is constructed by the fact that death in the text is evaded, pretended and performed.

Christian resurrection: death's afterlife

The Christian resurrection looms large over later episodes of reanimation in literature, theatre and performance, as well as other art forms. As with scenes of reanimation discussed earlier, the tension between physical presence and spectral absence, between the status of the body and its disappearance are central themes.

Resurrection, reanimation and touch are closely associated with one another. In the Ashmolean Museum in Oxford, Giuseppe Maria Crespi's (1665–1747) painting 'Noli Me Tangere' depicts the moment in John 20: 15–17 (King James version) in which the resurrected Christ meets Mary Magdalen, who has come to visit his tomb after his crucifixion, only to find it empty. Like the intangibility of the summoned ghost in *Odyssey* and *Aeneid*, but going a step further, the reanimated Christ issues the explicit order 'noli me tangere', 'do not touch me', in St John's Gospel, v. 17, 'Jesus saith unto her, Touch me not; for I am not yet ascended to my Father: but go to my brethren, and say unto them, I ascend unto my Father, and your Father; and to my God, and your God' (King James version).[2]

Crespi's painting is one in a long series of depictions of this biblical scene in Western Christian iconography and painting. Works by Fra Angelico, Fra Bartolomeo, Titian, Correggio and Hans Holbein the Younger, among others, depict the moment when Christ says 'noli me tangere'. The impulse to touch, the gesture to re-establish contact with the flesh, is repudiated in the phrase, suggesting that a reconnection with the physical will block the ascent of the body to heaven. This key transitional moment, not between life and death but between death and resurrection, exerts an uncanny fascination because it entails a rejection of the body and the intimacy of touch/embrace.[3]

In his discussion of the Western tradition of paintings representing the 'noli me tangere' scene, Jean-Luc Nancy interprets the resurrection narrative, particularly as depicted in Western painting, as a revival not of the dead, nor a return of the living, but a resurrection of death itself: 'It is the glory at the heart of death: a dark glory, whose illumination merges with the darkness of the tomb' (Nancy, 2008: 17). In Nancy's analysis, the resurrection confronts us with the permanence of death, thus becoming a metaphor for knowledge of the unknowable. In Nancy's words: 'The resurrection is not a resuscitation: it is the infinite extension of death that displaces and dismantles all the values of presence and absence, of animate and inanimate, or body and soul' (Nancy, 2008: 44). The resurrection is the undoing of the rational: the repeated paintings of the scene are testament to the desire to view it from different angles, to understand the impossibility of the encounter and to signal its seriality (the 'infinite extension' Nancy mentions).

Just a few lines later in St John's Gospel, we learn about 'Doubting Thomas', who insists on verifying Christ's wounds by inspecting the laceration in his side with his hand. This curious moment, denying Mary Magdalen's touch but permitting the sceptical Thomas to explore his wounds, allows Thomas to test Christ's living body at the moment when Christ will abjure the body's pains (and pleasures). The wound itself becomes highly symbolic, even eroticised. Reanimation, for Christ, is both a deeply material and corporeal act and one which turns the body into a sign, a metaphor, thus denying its physicality.

Christ's death and resurrection underpin many subsequent scenes of reanimation. As I discuss later, the wake in Irish funeral traditions was viewed as a threat to the effacement of the body in Catholic death rituals because of its emphasis on intoxication and sexual desire (it was a space for celebration and erotic play). The ballad 'Finnegan's Wake', in particular, discussed in Chapter 7, proposes a whole series of inversions of Christian dogma, a baptism with whiskey (not with purifying water), a fake death and a comical resurrection.

Shakespeare's elegies for the living

For Nancy, resurrection scenes are about death as a permanent presence that defines the ontology of the living. Shakespeare's plays include numerous false deaths and theatrical reanimations, scenes in which characters thought to be dead are revealed to be alive. The two elegies examined below are scenes of apparitional grieving, mourning without a body. While the action of Orestes in *Electra* demonstrates theatre's doubleness, and death and grief become intricate plot devices, in Shakespeare, the creation of elegies for the not-really-dead pushes the poetic act further, so that the articulation of grief exceeds the plot function of the event. Grief both contributes to and interrupts the narrative arc of these plays, operating as a theatrical device and at the same time a powerful elegy for the dead. I focus on two famous elegies in *Cymbeline* and *The Tempest*, respectively.

Cymbeline's 'Fear no more the heat o' th' sun' (4.2.257–80; Shakespeare, 2016c: 3093–4) is pronounced at the apparent death of Imogen. Her two half-brothers, Guiderius and Arviragus, alternate the verses, then take individual lines, before both reciting 'Quiet consummation have,/And renownèd be thy grave' (Shakespeare, 2016c: 3094). The elegy aligns the brothers with one another, until reciting the words in unison brings their grief into synchronicity. The elegy, part-poem, part-performance, highly emotional but based on the false premise of Imogen's death, evokes the dangers and travails of living, from natural disasters to the violence of tyrants, while also incorporating Shakespeare's typical concern with transience, in this case the ephemeral nature of science, knowledge and learning. As the verses are broken up into lines, the elegy moves towards the supernatural: witchcraft, ghosts and the undead appear, while the couplet at the end touches on the finality of the grave. The elegy takes us from the macrocosmic to the location of the burial place, from the fantastical, via the climatic, to the here and now of grief and loss.

The elegy operates at several levels simultaneously. It is an elegy for the dead, a literary text, a text for performance and a plot device in a piece of theatre, predicated on a false death and future reanimation. That is to say, it embodies all of these functions and more, which merge in the text. At the same time, it creates a complex emotional resonance around the idea of fiction and the pleasures of theatre, a space to express utopian desires for death's temporariness and the reanimation of the dead. The elegy's expressive power derives precisely from the impermanence of the death it commemorates; it is premised on a future disavowal of death. Dramatic irony augments the poetic eloquence of the text. As an expression of grief, it circulates between the fictional contrivance of the play's plot structure and the experience of grief in the real, co-existing in these worlds. The thought that this is a temporary grief gives the words a duality, overlaying them with the sense that this grief's eloquence might only be possible through the displacements of fiction, theatre and their enchanting reversals. Seeing grief through the refracting prism of the poetic does not misrepresent or falsify grief; instead, it conveys the idea that it might only be verbalisable through fiction and theatre's distorting lenses, and furthermore that the other side of this eloquence might be a stuttering disintegration of language into a very different poetics of grief around ineloquence, gaps and the inexpressible.

Turning to another Shakespeare play, *The Tempest* starts with Prospero's magical conjuring of the storm that leads to multiple false deaths and subsequent mourning songs. These include Ariel's song to Ferdinand, who is 'weeping again the king my father's wrack' (1.2.389; Shakespeare, 2016a: 3227):

> Full fathom five thy father lies,
> Of his bones are coral made;
> Those are pearls that were his eyes;

> Nothing of him that doth fade,
> But doth suffer a sea-change
> Into something rich and strange.
> Sea-nymphs hourly ring his knell.
> Hark, now I hear them, ding dong bell. (1.2.395–401;
>   Shakespeare, 2016a: 3227)

In the song, Shakespeare transforms the decaying body into a beautiful textual object, the imagined corpse of Ferdinand's father seen as a cluster of coral and pearls, rare and valuable substances created by the organic transformation of the sea. The drowned body ('father') beneath the water is given a consonantal correspondence with its location ('full fathom five'), as the 'f' sounds align and reinforce one another. Bones and coral seem to interpenetrate and invade one another through the unstable grammatical number of the 'are' in the line, 'Of his bones are coral made' (1.2.396; Shakespeare, 2016a: 3227). Decaying and dissolution are figured poetically as a 'fading' process, as would happen to a picture, to material or a memory, so that the horror of the corrupting body is displaced onto an image of recollection rather than the abject materiality of the corporeal.

The transformation into 'something rich and strange' both embellishes the oceanic decay of the corpse and exposes it to a magical metamorphosis, enacting through words the sea-change that only literary language can bring about, in contrast to the actual bodily corruption of drowning. The sea-change is poetry, a kind of mesmerising hypnosis, a magical effect on the senses that Ferdinand acknowledges is something that calms the fury of the waters as well as the painful grief, the passion (etymologically 'the suffering'), he feels at the death of his father.

The Tempest reverberates with images of failed deaths and mourning, scenes of reanimation in which those who were thought to be dead, father and son, are found to be alive. In the final act of the play, Prospero gives up his power to revive the dead, by which is meant both the ability to create enchanting fictions and the capacity via Ariel to control the elements and to create the illusion of loss. His speech at the end of the play specifically refers to the ability to raise the dead and his decision to abandon it:

> ... graves at my command
> Have waked their sleepers, oped, and let 'em forth

> By my so potent art. But this rough magic
> I here abjure. (5.1.48–51; Shakespeare, 2016a: 3259)

In both *Cymbeline* and *The Tempest*, the elegies are complex poetic acts, celebrating the body's removal from physical and emotional pain as a result of death, and then the body's transmutation into an object of textual beauty. They are elegies for the dead, but shaped by the reader's knowledge that the objects of the elegy are still alive, and that they will be reanimated as the play unfolds. They are plot devices but also stand-alone acts of poetry, part of a narrative structure yet also detachable from it, to be read and understood as simultaneously genuine and fictional, grieving for the dead, but conjuring up fantasies of reversal and survival that testify to the enchanting power of art. The text creates space for the expression of grief through the suspension of the real death that would occasion it, or at least the knowledge that the poetic grief song is underscored by a future textual reanimation. In terms of the plot of the play, the grief elegy is superfluous, taking up too much time, distracting us from the dramatic events and the twists and turns of the intricate plot. Thus, the grief elegy works through interruption of the plot sequence, a linguistic stalling of the linear progression of the play form. The grief song with its verbal intricacy is liberated by the fictional and future reanimation of its object, creating space for grief as a disruption, distortion or arresting of flow, rhythm and time.

Conclusion

This chapter has looked at classic scenes of reanimation to explore different types of encounter between the living and the dead in literature and theatre. The ghost or phantom in Homer and Virgil evokes the ongoing presence of the dead in memory and the difficulty of grasping death. These encounters with ghosts are about understanding the changed ontological status of the dead in relation to the living, particularly in relation to the body and the voice; they also expose the limits of ontologies that revolve around animacy and inanimacy by showing the evocative power of the image, the voice and memory. The Orpheus myth in Virgil and Ovid conveys the enchanting, at times supernatural, reanimating power of grief, as well as grief's recursive quality, its repetitions and after-effects, its departure from comprehensibility and rationality, and failed or broken reanimations (the singing head being the most powerful example of this). In Sophocles' *Electra*, doubleness, theatricality and the limits of fiction are woven into the expression of grief. The play is about knowledge and narrative, showing us real and performed grief, demonstrating how death is a painful phenomenon but also generates puzzling narrative and textual encounters. In the Christian resurrection narrative, following Nancy, the resurrection signals the presence of death in our lives, that sense of mortality that Kennicott refers to in discussing the death of his mother (Kennicott, 2020: 10). Finally, in *Cymbeline* and *The Tempest*, elegies for false deaths expose the duality of art, its creative eloquence constitutive of our very articulation and perception of grief while simultaneously distancing itself from some of grief's inarticulacy, gaps and silences.

This classical archive of grief reanimates the dead in multiple ways, visually in the forms of ghosts and phantoms, through plot detours and reversals, and via powerful elegies for the dead which are then invalidated by the return of the living subjects. Reanimations rationalise and materialise our fleeting, fragmented memories of the deceased. They revive the dead in fictional form as coherent ghosts that differ so much from the intermittent ways in which the dead return to us as we grieve. Yet via these reanimations, we negotiate the challenges of articulating our loss, acting out allegories of reconstruction and disappearance, finding expressions of grief in the enchanting revivals of literature and theatre while conscious of their failure to map an affect which often revolves around absence and negation.

In the next chapter, I look at moments of enchantment in theatre known as *coups de théâtre* in order to think about animacy and inanimacy, picking up on questions of the materiality of the body, the uncanny displacements and double-takes of grief and the 'perceptual chaos' of animating objects.

Notes

1 Christ's resurrection which puts the status of his body in doubt contrasts with that of Lazarus in John 11: 1–44 (King James version) in which mourners fear the smell of the decaying corpse when told by Jesus to open Lazarus's tomb after four days. Lazarus's reanimation is a very physical one, restored to corporeal life, rather than the transitional body of Christ soon to ascend to heaven.
2 Peggy Phelan discusses the 'noli me tangere' and 'Doubting Thomas' episodes in *Mourning Sex: Performing Public Memories* (London: Routledge, 1997), pp. 27–37.
3 In Greek, the phrase translated as 'noli me tangere' is in the present continuous, suggesting not the preclusion of a simple, singular touch, but the request for the termination of a lingering embrace (the difference between 'do not touch me' and 'stop touching me').

2

Animate objects of mourning

We spent a lot of time in cemeteries, edging between the plots in a series of wide-legged, beam-balancing right angles and perpendiculars, trying not to tread on the dead, as if their ground might suddenly give way. In the memory album of the past, flicking through the childhood sections, a white marble headstone looms large, scandalously displaced from its moorings, black words added in defiance. I'd call this episode in the family drama 'graves and ancient grievances'. In Baltyboys, I encountered my name, a twelve-year-old visitor at my own graveside, and then years later, added again, as if the dead me's were multiplying. In Temple Boden, we found the white headstone monument once more, adjacent ones becoming the new pieces of the jigsaw of your past. As a composite acoustic soundtrack to such scenes, I still remember the sound and the actions of the men cleaning the headstones, the rhythmical swooshing of the brushes against granite. Even today we search for the brand of bleach they said they used, the only one that did the job without damaging the stone, but they told us not to tell anyone what it was.

In this chapter, I use the phenomenon of the *coup de théâtre* to offer some more general theoretical perspectives on reanimation, establishing the links to grief and the way acts of reanimation in art create utopian spaces of reparation and restitution. The chapter thinks about performance as memory, the memory of performance or moments of performance, rather than memory as a theme or motif in a piece of theatre, and it looks at reanimation in relation to objects rather than in terms of ghosts, theatrical characters or metatheatrical reimaginings.

I investigate four examples of sudden magical or enchanting moments in performance, exploring how they are constituted in relation to processes of memory, grief and mourning. The companies discussed are the UK's Complicite, led by Simon McBurney, Russia's Formalny Theatre and the Italian theatre company Societas Raffaello Sanzio, whose director is Romeo Castellucci. I suggest that these *coups de théâtre* act as mnemonics of grief as well as embodying some of the uncanny doubles of the mourning process characterised by the shift from animacy to inanimacy, from subject to object. By transforming objects in performance, the *coup de théâtre* often evokes death and grief while at the same time allowing us to articulate anxieties and desires around loss and mourning. Drawing on Freud, I explore the idea that these theatrical moments linger in memory as uncanny substitutions, embodying something fundamental about theatre and its ontology as ephemeral and fragmentary, yet reiterative and reanimatory.

Enchantment is a useful concept for thinking about reanimation in theatre. It helps us reflect on the changing status of the object in the *coup de théâtre*. By destabilising rational modes of understanding, the *coup de théâtre* enters into the temporality of death and mourning, as objects occupy dual ontologies, both living and inanimate, literal and metaphorical. The *coup de théâtre*, the chapter suggests, is a point in performance in which perception and memory, the visible and the conceptual, converge, and in which the permanence of death is troubled by the reanimating effect of theatre.

Unforgettable moments in performance

A horse, a chair, autumn leaves, a small child – animal, item of furniture, vegetal matter, human being; four familiar things that become integral to the unforgettable moments of performance under discussion. I explore why these *coups de théâtre* have remained such powerful memories in my mind and, in the process, reflect on different modes of engaging with acts of theatre which enchant, seduce or elude us. I ask what role theory (or theoretical thinking) can play in understanding the 'magical' and ephemeral effects of performance, and reflect on how these moments are linked to death and mourning, both thematically and affectively. My analysis acknowledges and celebrates the role that subjective experience plays in the way these events persist as formative memories of performance, avowedly reading them through the lens of my own experience of grief and mourning, linking the *coup de théâtre* to the *coups*, or blows, of death and bereavement which frame the period between viewing them for the first time in performance and writing critically about them.

The first *coup de théâtre*, taken from my own personal archive of such scenes in performance, comes from Societas Raffaello Sanzio's *Giulio Cesare* (1997), an adaptation of Shakespeare's *Julius Caesar*, directed by Romeo Castellucci. The *coup* in question involved a live horse being brought onstage early on in the performance. This occurrence became an occasion for self-questioning: why was this moment so shocking and surprising? Why should the presence of the real horse in the sphere of representation cause such disruption to the theatrical world of signs? Why is the real object, the live horse, so unexpected in this context? The second comes from Complicite's *Mnemonic* (1999) devised by the company, featuring the transformations of a chair from object to human to dead body. The third comes from Formalny Theatre's *School for Fools* (2001), directed by Andrey Moguchiy, based on the 1976 Russian novel of that title by Sasha Sokolov about a young boy sent to a school for children with mental disabilities. Whereas in Castellucci the real horse is implicitly replacing a theatrical horse, a puppet or mechanically animated one, here, the *coup de théâtre* involves the more explicit transformation of an object. At one point, autumn leaves, scattered around the performance space, are swept into a pile and suddenly, as if by magic, become a freshly dug grave in a cemetery. The theatrical object (the leaf) goes from being a generic signifier of autumn and decay, via a performative gesture – someone sweeping up – to embody death, loss and grief. In the final example, from Complicite's *The Caucasian Chalk Circle* (1997), directed by McBurney, an apparent puppet is revealed to be a live human child. The moment of transformation is all the more surprising because of the length of time spectators have seen the actors manipulating what we thought was an object. Once again, the *coup* operates through substitution, but in this case one that was in place from the beginning of the performance, bringing ideas of deception, delusion and pretence into the equation.

In each of these *coups de théâtre*, the relationship between the living body and the body as object, becoming-object or as dead or absent object is central. Theatre theorists have explored how objects in performance can be used in multiple different ways: the object can be itself, represent itself, represent something else or be used in a non-representational way. Patrice Pavis provides us with a list of the different uses of theatre objects, ranging from the naturalistic, pragmatic, aesthetic or poetic, functional, ready-made, found, poor and so on (Pavis, 1998: 239–40), while for Alice Rayner, objects 'can expand into meanings as signifiers with historical attachments and concepts, or contract into aesthetics as form, surface, and texture' (Rayner, 2006b: 101); they can be 'symbols of other things, like an abstract concept ... or they can contract into something close to pure image' (Rayner, 2006b: 101). These examples catalogue the symbolicity of the object in performance, its protean quality, its ability to metamorphose, to become a symbol, to revert to its material self or to represent something entirely different, even the very absence of the human and the animate. Building on Rayner's ideas, this chapter will suggest that in the *coups de théâtre* I am bringing together, it is the object's shift between the literal and the figurative, either visibly or conceptually – establishing the *both/and* rather than the *either/or* of the theatre object's ontology – which alters our perception of the object in performance and creates moments of theatrical enchantment.

It is this shift between *both/and* in relation to animacy and inanimacy which anticipates the explorations of different forms of reanimating grief in later chapters as living beings become objects or symbols, as human bodies become static theatre metaphors to be reanimated by the energies of performance, or as dormant memories of the dead are revived by a song or a musical fragment.

Enchantment and the 'hermeneutics of suspicion'

In each of the four cases I discuss, the *coup de théâtre* produces a magical, enchanting moment of theatre, a counter-intuitive occurrence, one that produces emotions of wonder and surprise, as well as curiosity and self-questioning. Enchantment is a term which has had a lot of critical attention recently. Critics like Jane Bennett, Rita Felski and others have used it to launch a critique of rationalism in the context of cultural and aesthetic analysis. In this context, it allows us to think about the *coup de théâtre* in relation to the non-rational, the sensory and the corporeal in performance. Rather than trying to explain away the magical effects of the *coup de théâtre*, the critical concept of enchantment lets us be *carried away* by it. For Felski, enchantment challenges 'the hermeneutics of suspicion' in literary theory, the impulse 'to purge [literature] of its enigmatic and irrational qualities' (Felski, 2008: 54). Felski glosses 'hermeneutics of suspicion' as 'the name usually bestowed on [a] technique of reading texts against the grain and between the lines, of cataloguing their omissions and laying bare their contradictions, of rubbing in what they fail to know and cannot represent' (Felski, 2011: 574). Establishing the poetics of enchantment is a way to question the tendency of literary or critical theory to try to explain (away) or expose art's conundrums. This validation of enchantment is particularly apt for theatre as an artistic practice that relies on bodies and space, since, as Felski says, '[o]nce we face up to the limits of demystification as a critical method and a theoretical ideal ... we can truly begin to engage the affective and absorptive, the sensuous and somatic qualities of aesthetic experience' (Felski, 2008: 76).

The *coup de théâtre is* enchanting: that is why we remember it long after the event. In other terms, it 'casts a spell', a 'magical' transformation that we cannot explain easily in logical terms. For Bennett, enchantment is a particularly physical, sensual experience: '[e]nchantment includes ... a condition of exhilaration or acute sensory activity. To be simultaneously transfixed in wonder and transported by sense, to be caught up and carried away – enchantment is marked by this odd combination of somatic effects' (Bennett, 2001: 5). Felski likens this transformation to altered states of consciousness: '[e]nchantment is soaked through with an unusual intensity of perception and affect; it is often compared to the condition of being intoxicated, drugged or dreaming' (Felski, 2008: 55). Enchantment, in other words, is a term that brings us back to the bodily experience of art or theatre, to the sense of wonder it generates; it is not aimed at discounting theory or critical investigation altogether, but at operating dialectically with them. Enchantment, one could say, forces explanatory forms of theory to go back to moments of experience as they are felt perceptually and visually; in the case of theatre, the effect of this is to preserve the productive confusion and affective vertigo generated in live performance.

In the *coups de théâtre* in this chapter, enchantment derives from a scene of transformation or substitution. Central to each scene is the role of the object and the way in which the boundaries between the living and the non-living are blurred. In each one, the event generated a shock of recognition and a desire to understand which made the *coup de théâtre* compelling and memorable. This analysis is interested in the tensions between the pleasure of a theatrical memory and the impulse to explain its logic, reckoning with the possibility that the memory depends on its inexplicability and that this enigmatic resistance to theorisation might be linked to other forms of loss of meaning, in particular the experience of grief. My attraction to these moments of performance, their designation as exemplary *coups de théâtre*, is shaped by the way they help me conceptualise death and mourning, their enigmatic quality opening a space for such projections of affect.

Context of the term *coup de théâtre*

The OED connects the primary meaning of enchantment with magic or sorcery, before citing the word's figurative links with something overpowering or that creates a '(delusive) appearance of beauty' (OED). The reference to 'delusive' here is relevant to my analysis of these *coups de théâtre*, which often involve a feeling of deception, a self-consciousness about our own willingness to be enchanted. We return to a moment of theatrical enchantment as if spellbound, unable to explain its hold over us. It is disorienting: '[a]esthetic enchantment', says Felski, 'leads inexorably to ontological confusion, to a disturbing failure to differentiate between fact and fantasy, reality and wish fulfilment' (Felski, 2008: 53). This confusion, I suggest, energises memory and generates the impulse to try to comprehend what we have seen. As Paul Ricoeur puts it, '[e]nigma does not block understanding but provokes it' (Ricoeur, 1970: 18), precisely because it forces us into other relationalities with the artistic object than simple quests to expose and scientifically dissect it.

The *coup de théâtre* has historically been associated with the sensational, the unexpected or the sudden, and was especially criticised as a phenomenon during the Enlightenment rationalism of the eighteenth century onwards. The OED defines a *coup de théâtre* as 'a sensational turn or action in a play' and, by extension, 'any sudden sensational act', while French dictionaries put the emphasis on an 'unexpected event' ['événement inattendu'] (Larousse) or a 'sudden reversal' ['brusque retournement'] (Robert). Two of Aristotle's key components of tragedy in *Poetics*, *anagnorisis* (recognition) and *peripeteia* (reversal), can be viewed as different forms of *coups de théâtre*, one focusing on character, the other on plot (Halliwell, 1987: 38). For Aristotle, an unexpected event explicable in relation to the preceding plot was a key element of the highest form of tragedy. The *coup de théâtre* was a crucial component of the tragic play, but only if it was logical and plausible.

The earliest use of the phrase 'coup de theatre' (used without accents) cited by the OED is in a 1747 letter by Horace Walpole. Edward Gibbon employs the phrase 'Quel coup de théatre [sic]' figuratively in his French-language *Essai sur l'étude de la littérature* in 1762 in the course of a discussion of Virgil's *Aeneid* (Gibbon, 1762: 45). For specifically theatrical uses in English, we can turn to *The Critical Review* edited by Tobias Smollett in 1769, where we find the phrase 'a happy coup de theatre', without accents, used as part of a discussion of the final act of John Hoole's play *Cyrus* performed at the Theatre Royal Covent Garden in 1768. Edward Taylor uses the phrase, again without accents, when talking about Voltaire's 1748 play *Semiramis*, in 1774 (Taylor, 1774: 116).

In the French-language context, one of the most notable figures to explore the term early in its existence is Denis Diderot. Peter Szondi quotes Diderot's definition in the *Entretiens sur le fils naturel* (1875 [1757]) of the *coup de théâtre* as 'an unforeseen event [*"incident imprévu"*] which finds expression in the action and which suddenly alters the circumstances of the characters' (Szondi, 1980: 328). Szondi explains that the *coup de théâtre* was objectionable to Enlightenment figures like Diderot because it did not embody the logical or scientific; instead, 'it is perceived as untrue, as merely theatrical, that is to say, created exclusively in response to the needs of the theater' (Szondi, 1980: 328). For art critic Michael Fried, Diderot 'urged playwrights to give up elaborate *coups de théâtre* (surprising turns of plot, reversals, revelations), whose effect he judged to be shallow and fleeting at best' (Fried, 1980: 78).

Unlike writers who have seen the *coup de théâtre* as merely a plot twist or dismiss it as a piece of shallow theatricality for its own sake, I want to explore their fascination, arguing that the *coups de théâtre* being discussed constitute themselves ontologically through absence, by recurring in the memory, inexplicably, and by evoking the enigmatic and the unreasoned. These *coups de théâtre* are points of convergence for complex issues around materiality in performance. I actively adopt a way of thinking about theatre which combines memory, affect, autobiography and performative criticism, in line with the mixing of the expressive and the critical in the book as a whole. The perceptual disruption of *coups de théâtre* acts as an opening into more affective and performative modes of writing that help me understand the simultaneous need to understand, analyse and perform grief.

Castellucci's horse

Speaking of a Dublin performance of *Giulio Cesare* in 1998, Michael Billington called it:

> an Artaud-like meditation on themes within Shakespeare's play: rhetoric, power, violence, apocalyptic visions … Castellucci bombards us with strange images and cacophonous sounds: suspended statues, industrial detritus, a real horse, toy animals, the sound of distant trains or a needle scratched across a record. (Billington, 1998)

The production was indeed notable for its 'strange images': the use of an endoscope to project live video material of an actor's throat and larynx onto a cinema screen; outsized or ageing, naked human bodies; ritual washing; industrial, mechanical soundscapes; a live horse, and a horse's skeleton. Lighting, sound and bodies all formed a distorted symphony of ritualised actions in the production, placing the accent on rhythms and ear-splitting sounds, on unusual, disturbing presences in penumbral darkness, both human and animal.

For Nicholas Ridout, the real horse onstage was 'dragged into the world of signs' (Ridout, 2006: 105). He examines the production as part of a wider project to think about the 'confusion of attraction and repulsion, compulsion and disappointment … experienced in the modern theatre' (Ridout, 2006: 3). In his analysis, the live horse contrasts with the other human and animal presences in the performance. Using Ridout's terms, it can be argued that the horse's 'attraction' derives from the degree to which it questions the idea of theatre as a safe space of mimetic representation; it is a *theoretically* fascinating presence, a critical *coup de théâtre*. Its 'disappointment' comes from the fact that it remains, simply, a horse, however much we *drag it* into our theorisations of what it is doing onstage.

As soon as an object or an animal is framed theatrically, it is contaminated by the theatrical, even if it occupies a purposefully liminal position in relation to the real (such as an object accidentally incorporated into a performance). Yet in the case of Castellucci's horse, mimesis is under attack as the horse is, obviously, physically, and unpredictably, real. As Daniel Mesguich argues, 'the real horse in theatre is both a horse and the metaphor of a horse (of a real horse)' (Mesguich, 2006: 18; my translation), that is, simultaneously real and figurative, representative of itself, figurative in its connotations and, in Castellucci's production, a violent attack on theatre's representational aesthetics. In *Giulio Cesare*, the horse is out of place; it feels obscene to theatricalise and aestheticise it; one fears for the well-being of the animal. It brings an alternative modality of being into the frame of performance and, in fact, crystallises the contingency of performance, the possibility that things may go wrong, that material things will not *follow their script*. The horse, then, becomes the vehicle for theorising theatre's liveness and a mechanism for destabilising its safe fictionality, what Anne Ubersfeld calls its 'denegation', or repudiation, of the real (see Ubersfeld, 1981: 311–18). Pavis translates 'dénégation' as 'denial' and calls it a 'term from psychoanalysis that refers to the process which brings to consciousness repressed elements that are denied at the same time' (Pavis, 1998: 93) before explaining that denial is '[t]he experience of theatrical illusion, accompanied by the feeling that what one is observing does not really exist' (93). It brings the outside of the theatre, the opposite of the human and the antithesis of the aesthetic consciousness, into the framework of performance. It simultaneously operates as a metaphor of a range of concepts, and of itself; indeed, it acts as the risk of the undoing of metaphor in the moment of performance.

In this case, the presence of the horse does not mean that the fictional has become real but that the theatre has made use of the real to expose its own fallacious categories of self-definition. The horse replaces the putative theatre object (Castellucci could have used a puppet horse, any other object standing in for a horse, or a mimed or choreographed horse), takes on the attributes of a theatre object (it cannot avoid this) and yet repudiates this categorisation (one is always conscious of its presence as a real, live horse). Even though the horse is operating within a representational network – the frame of theatre – it risks disrupting that framework at any time by doing something unpredictable, exposing the contingency of performance usually governed by rehearsed control.

Crucially, Castellucci's horse redirects our attention from the ontology of theatre to its epistemology. In destabilising categories of objecthood and fictionality, it prompts us instead to question how such concepts are defined. As Rayner suggests: '[b]oth real and alienated, the status of the objects is not a matter of ontology but of perspectives and positions relative to the subject that are constantly in transition' (Rayner, 2006b: 191). The horse's role is not to get closer to the real, but to help us rethink how we categorise it as a theatrical presence (real and/or representation of the real). It does this because the live animal cannot be contained by the frame of representation. Consequently, the horse draws attention to the frames themselves, questioning how the real and the aesthetic are defined, intersect and undo one another.

In Castellucci's *coup de théâtre*, the horse is a negation of the aesthetics of representation. Since a real horse replaces a theatrical one, the *coup de théâtre* risks undermining theatre's mimetic power. Yet a second stage of reflection negates this negation when we see that the *coup de théâtre* captures the affective pleasure of the disruption only *because* it occurs within the framework of performance. Without theatre's propensity to represent the real, the horse returns to its non-theatrical presence. The *coup de théâtre*, then, is an embodied moment of thinking about theatre which oscillates between the theoretical and the non-theoretical, the horse-as-metaphor and horse-as-live-animal. Suddenly, the live horse, occupying the mimetic space of a prop, acts in a way which reanimates it, turning the space of representation into a space of absence, a space for the death of the real, which the presence of the living horse momentarily reverses.

Stages of transformation: McBurney's chair

Turning to Complicite's *Mnemonic*, a crucial moment of enchantment in this production relates to the different forms a chair, belonging to the director Simon McBurney, takes in performance, and specifically its reanimation as a puppet to play the role of the iceman in the devised piece. As Oliver Reynolds observes in the *TLS* review of the 1999 production, 'when the cast animates the chair … such moments are touching and theatrical' (Reynolds, 1999: 18). The stage directions for Scene 33 in the text explain further:

> *Over the following text, the chair slowly becomes the puppet of the iceman. The rest of the cast come around the table and take the puppet. It has a stick and its face is a pillowcase. … The Iceman leans against the bed. … He falls to his knees, his head falls against the stone. … The puppet by now is lying on the stone. The only movements are its final breaths. The company slowly retreat from the body.* (Complicite, 1999b: 63)

This *coup de théâtre* is a more explicit encounter with death and grief, acted out through the complex metatheatricality and encoded autobiography of the scene in question. Here again the object moves between animacy to inanimacy, questioning the mimetic process through the re-establishment of the banal object, but also overtly enacting the desire for the *coup de théâtre* to bring the dead back to life again, even if ephemerally.

Liliane Campos observes of Complicite that 'the chair is to the company what the flying horse was to Bulgakov, the embodiment of art's freedom and its ability to escape from naturalistic constraints' (Campos, 2014: 176), noting how they use objects and props with 'semiotic versatility' (180). This is true of the chair in *Mnemonic*, since early in the piece McBurney tells us about the link between the chair and his dead grandfather, the object consequently primed by association with autobiography and loss: 'So, for example, perhaps

I thought about my father because this chair was his. I *know* it. He sat on it. And so did my grandfather' (Complicite, 1999b: 5; italics in original). The chair also serves as an intertextual mnemonic of previous Complicite productions (most notably, the 1997 production of Ionesco's *The Chairs*). In Ionesco's play, the empty chair replaces the missing human body, and chairs gradually fill the stage to symbolise the absurdist delusions of the central characters, Old Man and Old Woman (they also function as a bleak allegory of theatre's attachment to creating the non-real).

During the performance of *Mnemonic*, the chair stands in physically at times for the prone, frozen body of the five thousand-year-old iceman: its arms and legs are disarticulated to make it look humanoid, and scientists observe the chair through ad hoc frames as if viewing a specimen on a table. However, its most powerful incarnation is when the company puppeteer the chair collaboratively so that it becomes the living body of the iceman as he makes his final journey before his solitary death, 'weaving together … narrative threads through verbal and visual parallelisms' (Campos, 2014: 182). The Complicite performers dismantle the chair in the process of turning it into a humanoid puppet, its hinged legs transforming it from a four-legged item of furniture into a human body. The performers collectively act as its puppeteer, each holding a limb or supporting the chair-puppet iceman's head, and they animate the disarticulated chair by having it mimic a human walking motion, replicating a human being's gait and breathing with stunning observational verisimilitude. The object becomes a puppet becomes an ancient iceman taking his last journey, and we watch entranced as its breathing slows and it reverts back to its object-state at the end of the sequence.

What was memorable in this *coup de théâtre* was the apparent sentience of the chair-object-puppet; the mimetic accuracy of its wooden components (the chair-as-iceman actually seemed to be breathing) was emotionally painful but theatrically and visually pleasurable. The chair-object had been brought to life to enact the death of the body it was representing, returning at the end of the sequence to its initial state as object (and allowing the body and the chair-object to converge in material terms at this point). The enchantment of this *coup de théâtre* occurs because the chair-object transformation works on several levels simultaneously. It embodies the polysemy of the theatrical object in performance, performs the transition from animacy to objecthood, and acts out the thwarted desire to use theatre to do something impossible and counter-intuitive: to revive the dead.

We have so far noted an example of theatre where a real horse disrupts the categories of theatrical and real. In this case, the chair acts as simultaneously real and fictionally framed, both metaphor and literal chair, a challenge to the relationship between figure and referent. The real becomes the fictive presence of the real within the framework of the performance, both material and spectral, both concept and actuality. As Complicite's chair lies still after the iceman has died, it is 'in between' states, both object and body, chair, puppet and representation of corpse, now also overlaid palimpsestically with the death narrative it has just enacted. In both cases, the shift between states produces a doubleness, or more precisely a potential for plural ontologies: chair, mnemonic of loss, theatre object/prop, puppet, iceman, scientific specimen, and so on.

From negation to gesture

In the *coups de théâtre* examined above, the transformations have been overtly spectacular: the real horse supplants a theatrical one; the real chair transforms into a multiply animated, mimetically uncanny human body. But the *coup de théâtre* can also operate through minimal shifts and, in the following example, it is less the object that remains as memory but the transitional point between its two states. In this analysis, I trace the way in which the transformation of objects in a production is displaced onto a performative gesture to create a *coup de théâtre* whereby a movement operates to mobilise our perception of the expressive power of objects in transition.

In 2001, at St Stephen's Church as part of the Aurora Nova collective at the Edinburgh Fringe Festival, Russian company Formalny Theatre performed their production *School for Fools*. Reviewing the show in 2002 at the Barbican, Lyn Gardner noted that 'the schoolroom and [a] flat's living room are full of fallen leaves' (Gardner, 2002) and that this 'magical piece of theatre takes you into a theatrical world where naturalism and expressionism, realism and surrealism sit side by side' (Gardner, 2002). The *coup de théâtre* occurred when, at one point, an actor was sweeping dead leaves scattered across the stage that gradually formed into a pile. Suddenly, as the pile of leaves accumulated, the scene shifted, and it became apparent that the character was now at someone's graveside, and the pile of leaves represented a fresh grave in a cemetery. Describing the transition from scattered autumn leaves to the graveside scene in such simple terms cannot capture the sudden perceptual shift from an everyday moment and gesture to a powerfully emotive encounter with grief.

The sequence led to self-questioning about perception, a double take during which scattered leaves suddenly, inexplicably, become a grave and the viewer feels stunned by this quick transformation into a deeply affective scene of grieving. As one's reflections moved along the plane of language, one reflected on the nature of the theatrical effect and its power to enchant: whether it is because leaves on the ground connoting autumn and decay are linked metaphorically to the dead body, or that the fragile objects suddenly becoming so substantial and evocative of loss is a powerful moment of conceptual vertigo. Yet these attempts at understanding the force of the moment can only be verbally *expressed* sequentially and retrospectively, though they may have been felt instantaneously at the time of viewing. What was enchanting about this *coup de théâtre* is the convergence of different poetic, visual and other performance connotations in a theatrical sequence, but also the scene's reversibility, whereby the grave could just as quickly be disassembled and return to its previous form as scattered leaves, or even change once again into something else entirely.

In the case of Formalny Theatre, once again at the centre of the moment of enchantment is the shifting state of an object, here from scattered multiples (autumn leaves) to a singular other object (the fresh grave), different in density and signification, suddenly precipitating what were vague associations generated by the first objects into a more direct embodiment of grief. What the transformation signals is the absent body of death and the forcefulness of the grief behind the unanticipated intrusion of the site of the grave, effected by a human gesture that sweeps us into a scene of mourning. A gesture of the everyday living and moving body switches us into a contemplation of the still, inanimate body of the dead. Here, the gesture itself becomes the focus of attention. It is an everyday action that captures the ephemerality of theatre and the way the full force of loss returns during the grieving process in minor, unforeseeable ways. The sequence disrupts linear temporality as the fleeting human gesture ushers in the permanence of death. When the *coup de théâtre* recurs, in memory, it does so as the gesture itself.

As with Castellucci's horse, the leaves in this sequence enter into a symbolic system. In Castellucci's case, this results in bathos, whereby a live horse short-circuits the interpretive process and displaces theatrical aesthetics by the sheer physicality of its animal presence. Not enmeshed in the theoretical itself, remaining outside, it exposes the potential inadequacy of any act of critical, verbal theory that tries to capture theatre's power. For Formalny, the leaves activate a chain of association from liveness to decay and then death that the gesture of the sweeping human body erases, substituting a traceless kinetic memory for those tangible objects. Both the leaves and the grave are replaced by the gesture, which disappears without trace except *as* a memory of performance, a kink in time figuring the permanent immobilisation of death and its uncanny return as a mnemonic movement.

Thus, the gesture, in its painful insubstantiality and its afterlife as (performance) memory, communicates something specific about the mnemonics of grief. The gesture, here, captures that element of mourning that is the untraceable but devastating memory of death's insistence: the reappearance of grief not as theatrical image, poetic text or object, but through the unpredictable kinesis of loss. In the performance, the sweeping gesture produces a scene of grieving, and it sensitises us to the ways in which movements, gestures and corporeal choreographies form the materials evocative of grief as surely as words, images, or other recollected events or encounters with the dead. In this case, the ephemerality of the mnemonic, a performed gesture as part of a piece of theatre, ties in with grief's connection to the transience of the human body and of our memories of loss.

Complicite: unveiling the real

The *coup de théâtre* challenges what we think we know about theatre, enchanting us into engaging with performance beyond the desire to explain and theorise its mechanisms. It calls into question our wish for a certain form of definitive knowledge and, at the same time, asks us to think poetically about the in-between, about the evocative power of the gesture and about the subjective affinities that we bring to our readings of moments of performance. In Complicite's *The Caucasian Chalk Circle* from 1997, the *coup de théâtre* similarly confuses the distinction between live body and theatrical object, between the visible and the hidden. Instead, it opens up a conceptual space in which to explore the limitations of explanatory theory and asks us to bring new perspectives to our engagement with the force and resonance of acts of theatre.

As Paul Taylor says in his review of the original production at the National Theatre: 'Complicite once again create theatrical magic with the simplest of means' (Taylor, 1997). In the production, Grusha's child is performed by a puppet. It has been animated by actor-puppeteers throughout the performance, and we are invited to admire its mimetic realism – it looks like a real child, creating that uncanny sense we experience when we see puppets acting convincingly as humans. Freud explains this uncanniness when he says that 'we have particularly favourable conditions for generating feelings of the uncanny if intellectual uncertainty is aroused as to whether something is animate or inanimate, and whether the lifeless bears an excessive likeness to the living' (Freud, 2003: 140–1). By extension, the manipulated puppet becomes a metaphor for the fictional child in Brecht's play who is subjected to adult conflict and violence. At a key moment, as the puppet is being fought over, suddenly a live child is unwrapped from inside the puppet and walks around on its own. The point at which the object becomes animate, where the puppet child becomes a real child, is an enchanting *coup de théâtre*; the object has become a non-object and we as audience members have been pleasurably deceived all along.

How do we reconstruct the affective impact of this *coup de théâtre*? In the first instance, there is the feeling of duplicity at not knowing when the substitution was made and how it went unnoticed. This is accompanied by the retrospective concern about the live child being subjected to the vigorous manipulations of the adult actors, that it could have come to harm; the 'puppet' has been thrown about, fought over and pulled physically in different directions. The *coup de théâtre* brings with it a sense of delusion (recall the OED definition of enchantment and its link to delusion earlier) in which the spectator becomes complicit in the driving desire for mimetic performance and, allied to it, are both disappointment and attraction, to echo Ridout's terms. Disappointment occurs when the puppet is substituted for a truer, less virtuosic real, but is accompanied by attraction to the exposure of our investment in the skill of the puppet's manipulations. Thus, this double attack on theatricality plunges us into a moment of fundamental doubt about theatre's relation to the real.

The unveiling of the real child within the puppet enchantingly reproduces what we already felt about the uncanny mimetic realism of the puppeteering: how lifelike it was. Substituting the real child runs the risk of a certain theatrical redundancy: how like a real child was this real child! Within the frame of Complicite's physical theatre and choreography, the child operates as a vector for the company's transformative use of objects, in which body and object are exchanged or prosthetically linked. As Tomasz Wisniewski points out, Complicite often use fragments to form bigger pictures (Wisniewski, 2016). Here, the introduction of the real child undoes this tendency towards coherence by disrupting the virtuosic mimesis with the presence of the real. Thus, in a similar way to Castellucci, the referent collapses back into the object of representation and radically destabilises the mimetic process.

For Freud, such a moment is uncanny not primarily because of the puppet's sudden animacy, but because it creates a sense of doubleness. The real child is a double of the puppet child, and vice versa. In Freud's account, the existence of the double goes from being a denial of death, 'an assurance of immortality' (Freud, 2003: 142) in early religions or the primary narcissism of childhood, to becoming 'the uncanny harbinger of death' (Freud, 2003: 142). When added to the uncertainty about the animacy of the puppet and the way the *coup de théâtre* recurs as a repetitive memory – enchanting, asking to be theorised but resistant to explanation – then we can see this scene, as with the preceding ones discussed, fulfilling the conditions for Freud's uncanny. I situate the desire to return to the *coup de théâtre*, its fascination, in relation to Freud's discovery 'that anything that can remind us of this inner compulsion to repeat is perceived as uncanny' (Freud, 2003: 145).

However, the transformation in Complicite's *The Caucasian Chalk Circle* is both evocative of death, in Freudian psychoanalytical terms, but also produces a feeling of theatrical pleasure, or enchantment, precisely at the moment when the living reality of the puppet/child is reasserted. As with the bathos of Castellucci's horse, Complicite's bathos comes from the way the real child threatens the virtuosity of the puppet performance by asking what purpose the realistically operated puppet serves beyond theatrical enchantment. The *coup de théâtre* provokes a sense of bathos when it undermines our wonder at the theatrical virtuosity of the puppet. However, this feeling is soon replaced by a further sense of enchantment when we realise that the use of the live child is a theoretical act that highlights the preceding virtuosity, while still questioning its theatrical purpose. The pleasure we feel at the uncanny substitution seems to give the *coup de théâtre* a (reparative) logic of its own.

It is striking that the reappearance of the live human child out of the representational form of the puppet evokes an association with death when, as I mentioned above, it should ostensibly be about revival and reanimation. But as Freud suggests, uncertainty about animacy signals a return of the repressed anxiety about the stability and permanence of the dead. In theatrical terms, the appearance of the live child demonstrates the idea that theatre is conventionally premised on the absence of the object. Drawing our attention to the theatricality of the (apparent) puppet replaces that absence with the actual presence of the live child. However, this gesture is in fact a double encounter with the absence of the object of representation, an absence made all the more acute because it is enacted through an excessive and enchanting performance of *presence* and *liveness*. This substitution, instead of reversing the sense of absence, duplicates it: the live child is now imitating the live child that was pretending to be a puppet imitating a live child, and therefore the *coup de théâtre* ends up expressing all the more eloquently an impossible attempt to recapture the lost object.

Theatricality and enchantment

In Castellucci's case, the live horse might be read as a general critique of theatre: we are asked to contemplate it and potentially conclude that theatre seems fake compared to the horse's powerful beauty and presence, its existence outside the denegated, safe realm of theatre aesthetics. All of our theoretical projections onto it dissolve in the materiality of its existence. In the case of Complicite's *The Caucasian Chalk Circle* puppet replacement, critical analysis of the moment risks turning enchantment into a sense of theatre's superfluity: why represent the child with a puppet when a real child represents itself *so much more effectively*? Yet it is the playful staging of the possibility of superfluity that in fact reinforces the moment of enchantment. The puppet as object is replaced with a non-object in the form of the child, but the child retroactively confirms the puppet's mimetic realism while at the same time defamiliarising it in a double gesture.

The recurrence in memory of the *coup de théâtre* as an obsessive, unresolved scene of performance acts out its originary uncanniness via a compulsion to repeat, a drive to theorise and rationalise the moment of enchantment. Coupled with that is the recognition that theorising will never be able to exhaust this moment of uncanniness because it relies on non-rational foundations (the possibility of reanimating the dead).

The resistance to understanding, or, the murder of enchantment

I have been pointing out how moments of enchantment operate through object transformations. Beyond this, we have seen that objects can be doubled, disappearing and reappearing, acting out processes of grief and the failure of theatre to bring the dead back to life in anything but a pleasurably ephemeral way.

Returning to these *coups de théâtre* brings with it anxiety that writing will verbally contaminate the complex sensorium which has situated these performative moments as visual memory, affective sensation and enchantment. Can theatrical enchantment be analysed? Can the *coup de théâtre* be explained without being destroyed? Discussing an image from Pina Bausch's work, Rayner notes the way the company 'created an image-object in motion … repeated it long enough to be perceived and reperceived and still not "understood" or signified (and hence murdered)' (Rayner,

2006b: 190). It seems that these moments continue to resonate precisely because they temporarily suspend the analytical frameworks we apply to theatre, and call for different categories of perception to replace them. At the same time, what remains is the desire to verbalise the memory, to undo the epistemological knot they represent. Working out their impact is an attempt to recapture that sense of disorientation, of vertiginous falling outside analytical categories and the substitution by another mode of perception. This is bound up with the fact that the moment is over – its ephemerality – and that it operated visually, through objects and their afterimage, in ways which intersect with language but also resist translation into the verbal. Attempts to communicate the moment to others run the risk of bathos, while theoretical attempts cannot capture the synchronic convergence of affect and perceptual disruption that they bring about.

Yet at the same time, what prompts these *coups de théâtre* to endure in memory is the degree to which they persistently ask us to make sense of them. As Rayner suggests, to understand such moments of theatrical enchantment may be to murder them. But these uncanny scenes, thematically and structurally haunted by the dynamics of death, also mimic the grieving process; as the dead resurface in memory, so the inexplicable but enchanting moments of performance come back as ghosts from our theatrical memory.

Conclusion

Theatre and performance, in ways exemplified by *coups de théâtre*, serve to undo strict binaries such as those between material and the apparitional, the living and the dead, the body and the object. In doing so, they allow us to explore unconscious processes and anxieties around death and grief, the coming to terms with loss, and death's painful transition from animate to inanimate.

The theatrical enchantment and theoretical pleasure of these *coups de théâtre* relate to the insistence of loss and the obsessive return of the dead to memory, which they activate. Underpinning each of these scenes is the banality, the hidden familiarity of loss, which are hallmarks of the experience of grief and mourning. Freud in *The Uncanny* suggests that '[i]t may be that the uncanny ["the unhomely"] is something familiar ["homely", "homey"] that has been repressed and then reappears, and that everything uncanny satisfies this condition' (Freud, 2003: 153). This insists itself into performance via self-consciousness, bathos, absence, the return of the same (the lost object; the pre-loss self) which the 'grieving self' perceives as totally different, as impossibly transformed from before and after the blow of death. The dramaturgy of these *coups de théâtre* shows us the same object becoming different to itself, gaining a double ontology caught between animacy and inanimacy, sometimes embodying both states at once. These theatrical objects can even be displaced along signifying chains by ephemeral performance events: the simple human gesture of sweeping a leaf along the ground. That sweeping gesture might be seen as the epitome of the *coup de théâtre* in what it says about loss, death and grief: it is something that disappears, tracelessly, but reappears with such profound, grief-inducing force in memory that its emotional toll cannot be reckoned. For, in the end, these *coups de théâtre* enchant us with a theatricality that helps us think through the sudden transformations and contradictory emotions associated with death, but also powerfully capture the sense of cognitive and perceptual disorientation that accompanies the experience of loss and grief. Grief's disorientation is allied with theatre's enchantment, allowing us via performance to see grief's uneven dynamics, its temporal twists, moments of revelation, and transitory acts of creation and reconstruction that undo themselves as we move between our confrontation with the absence of the dead and their serial return to the mind and memory of the living.

3

Grief, fiction, passion

Climbed over the gate into my uncle Billy's field in Ireland with J (9) and K (7) last Sunday. We tramped over to the far stone wall, me phoneless for the first time in weeks, the kids bounding along, cavorting with energy. Told them the next field was Mary Theresa Mc's, confirmed that yes, she was related to us, but several generations back ... what an oddly chaotic, amorphous and fragmentary view of family relations children of that age have. We came across an animal's skull, expecting a sheep – I pointed out the antler, and one of the children asked where its body was, and I said I didn't know but maybe the foxes took it. They seemed ok with that possibility. And then I told them about the flint-grey evening twenty years ago in the pouring rain under a bruised belligerent sky when, with my sister, sodden by the relentless rain, we dug a one-foot-cubed grave for a lamb that had died, its fragile body already stiffening in rigor mortis, the sound of the shovel striking the granite, reverberating, it seemed, before the next, more satisfying, squelch as it connected with the mud, and somehow the conjunction of light and rain and sky and this mini-burial displaced the chasm that had in the days prior been opened up by the sudden death, the wake, the dream-nightmare funeral of our father, and all I can remember of that time is this secular funeral ritual in miniature, and in fact even that's gone apart from the auditory memory of the sounds of the shovel, and now a deer skull with one antler without a body is all that remains of any of it.

Wrestling with the ghosts of the past can involve new encounters with literary and theatre texts that once seduced, captivated or confounded us. *Hamlet* is a text which haunts readers, its uncanny power resurfacing unexpectedly via words and phrases which have become common currency in the English language. This chapter explores *Hamlet* thematically and intertextually in relation to grief and mourning, especially the role of the dead father, thinking about textual revivals, the magic, mercurial text reanimated by each new performance, reading, rewriting or intertexual echo. In *Hamlet*, the dead return as ghosts, memories and skulls, in the form of narrated characters, and in the context of metatheatrical performance. By viewing the play's further reanimations via stage productions and a novel based on the events around its composition, grief at the death of a young child, the chapter argues that the play is ontologically constituted as a series of reanimations. In addition, critical readings across time return to *Hamlet* obsessively, as writers and theorists like Freud, Lacan, Greenblatt and Maguire show, reanimating the text by adding their interpretive and reflective voices to the work. The text propels these myriad reanimations through its meditations on death, its scenes of grieving and its philosophising about mortality.

Hamlet is a play about grief – more precisely, it stages the failure to act on grief, or to perform mourning properly. As Laurie Maguire puts it:

> [in *Hamlet*] the rituals of mourning, which should surround death and comfort the living, are maimed. The mourning period for Hamlet Sr is terminated incongruously by Gertrude's remarriage; Polonius has an 'obscure burial' ... Ophelia is denied full Christian burial. Hamlet, Ophelia and Laertes wander through the play suffering a grief that is denied the mediated outlet of full mourning. (Maguire, 2002: 74)

Maguire's analysis aligns with Jacques Lacan's view of *Hamlet* as a play of desire, mourning and the scene of the crime. For Lacan, '[t]he work of mourning is first of all performed to satisfy the disorder that is produced by the inadequacy of signifying elements to cope with the hole that has been created in existence, for it is the system of signifiers in their totality which is impeached by the least instance of mourning' (Lacan, 1977: 38). Mourning in this analysis has a reparative function: it addresses a hole, a tear or gap. Lacan suggests that in myth and folklore, ghosts appear to fill the gap in the real that is not satisfied by adequate mourning, in *Hamlet's* case as a result of the unsolved crime. Lacan sees *Hamlet* as being dominated by unfinished or incomplete mourning. As he suggests: 'Nor can we fail to be struck by the fact that in all the instances of mourning in *Hamlet*, one element is always present: the rites have been cut short and performed in secret' (Lacan, 1977: 40).

The play is about the reanimation of the dead and scepticism about their continuing presence, as Maguire indicates: 'it undoes ontological binaries, for the ghost disturbingly frustrates neat antitheses of life/death, presence/absence, agency/inauthority. Thus, the disequilibrium that Hamlet negotiates is not good versus bad but dead versus alive' (Maguire, 2002: 74). It features ghosts both visible and invisible and a human skull as a mnemonic of childhood, bodies intangible and material, psychic projections and physical remains. In this play, the body dissolves, haunts and smells; the stench of mortality, the decay of the flesh are juxtaposed with the peregrinations of the unquiet soul in torment, the projection of the mind caught in purgatorial limbo. When real characters die in quick succession at the end of the play, their deaths feel farcical and parodic compared to the theatrically performed deaths we have already encountered.

Hamlet's expressions of grief and his failure to make the transition to mourning are bound up with his insistent reflections on his own mortality, the self-destructive dimension of the grieving process which turns mourning into melancholia, in Freudian terms. As Freud explains, mourning and melancholia have many things in common. Yet while mourning is a conscious state, melancholia is associated with a more unconscious object loss. Trying to situate *Hamlet* between mourning and melancholia is difficult if we recognise Freud's words: 'In mourning it is the world that has become poor and empty; in melancholia it is the ego itself' (Freud, 1953: 246), since Hamlet, as a character, is full of wit and wordplay which seem to transform his melancholia into language creation. Freud's argument that self-destruction and revolt are bound together in the split subject of melancholic narcissism captures the division in Hamlet between self-critical soliloquies and the verbal liveliness of his interactions with others.

Philosophising about death, making it a metaphor or a pun, distracts Hamlet both from confronting his own grief and from acting on his ghost-father's call for revenge. Punning on death is the mark of an obsession, and making a piece of theatre to reveal a crime, the famous 'Mousetrap', is another way to avoid the material reality of mortality encountered most directly in the graveyard scene. As Stephen Greenblatt suggests, 'If there is any release for Hamlet from his obsession [with his father's death] – and it is not clear that there is – it comes from an unflinching gaze at a skull, the skull of the jester Yorick, but also, by extension, his father's skull and his own' (Greenblatt, 2016: 1758).

Hamlet, 'remember me'

Hamlet reanimates the dead in multiple ways. The first relevant event in the play is the return of Hamlet's dead father in the form of a ghost. As Maud Ellmann says:

> In the case of *Hamlet*, the father's murder has occurred before the tragedy begins, unwitnessed and unverifiable. Yet this death which never literally *takes place*, is *represented* time and again, by the dumb show and the mousetrap, by the testimony of the ghost, and by the carnage which completes the tragedy … (Ellmann, 2004: 85)

The Mousetrap and the scenes just before it present us with different versions of the grieving subject. The First Player recites a scene from a play about the death of Priam, King of Troy, producing the external appearance of grief that sets the philosophical prince thinking about the fictional and the real, performed grief and experienced grief. This will lead Hamlet to write his own play enacting his father's murder, bringing him back to life theatrically in order to stage his death as a way of exposing his murderer's guilt. Ellmann explores the links between ghost, words, and theatre, when she says:

> … ghosts are the visions which arise when words have failed to purge the agony of loss. Moreover, a theatrical performance is a text incarnate which embodies written words in living voices. … To perform a play is therefore to revive the dead, since every actor is the phantom of a script, as each performance is the afterlife of writing. (Ellmann, 2004: 88)

If '[t]o perform a play is therefore to revive the dead', what is Hamlet doing when he writes his own version of the scene of the crime? What form is his grief taking? Perhaps acting out a desire to grasp death, which is also a complex deferral of that confrontation: theatre as evasion, grief in the form of delayed encounter with the reality of death. This metatheatre of mourning reveals some of grief's dynamics, its swerving, veering quality, its repetitions, the way it makes us question the real, reframing it as memory in performance, memories recollected and rescripted under the sign of grief.

In the graveyard, there is no room for ghosts because the remains of the dead are everywhere visible and present to the senses. Hamlet learns that the skull being handled belongs to his childhood jester, Yorick. The transience of living, the decaying body and the durability of memory are all figured in the *memento mori* of the skull, this anti-ghost object which is the very antithesis of the living body, alongside words that reanimate the dead through memory and touch.

The juxtaposition in the play of the 'real' ghost, the father as memory, the theatrical character-father in the Mousetrap, and the material finality of Yorick's skull (with Yorick as father-substitute) prompts us to think about the different ways the dead haunt us and the various injunctions the dead impose on us. King Hamlet's ghost famously calls on Hamlet in 1.5.27 to '[r]evenge his foul and most unnatural murder' (Shakespeare, 2016b: 1780), imposing a filial duty which Hamlet will spend the rest of the play grappling with.

Grief asks things of us, requires us to prove ourselves. At least twice in his first speech, King Hamlet's ghost raises the possibility that his son will fail to act. At 1.5.33–5, the ghost says: 'And duller shouldst thou be than the fat weed/That roots itself in ease on Lethe wharf/Wouldst thou not stir in this' (Shakespeare, 2016b: 1781). Later in the ghost's speech, the injunction to revenge is couched in a conditional, 'If thou hast nature in thee, bear it not' (1.5.81; Shakespeare, 2016b: 1782), and the ghost warns Hamlet of the risks involved: 'Taint not thy mind, nor let thy soul contrive/Against thy mother aught' (1.5.85–6; Shakespeare, 2016b: 1782). This is no simple act of revenge in response to murder. According to the ghost, Hamlet will run the risk of inactivity, the corruption of his mind and aggression towards his mother – all of which, it turns out, come to pass. If the confusion of grief has fantasised this ghost-figure – this revenant of revenge – into existence (something Hamlet himself thinks is possible, emerging '[o]ut of my weakness and my melancholy' (2.2.520; Shakespeare, 2016b: 1800)), it has also manifested the differences between father and son, the father's uncertainty about the son's resolve.

Grief entails contradictions, its mandates enigmatic and baffling. The ghost's final words in the speech, 'remember me' (1.5.91), are strange and confusing. As Maguire argues:

> 'Remember me', pleads the ghost of Hamlet Sr, his last words in Act I before he returns to purgatory. But what does it mean to 'remember me' in *Hamlet*? Hamlet receives the instruction as a call to action, a not unreasonable interpretation given the ghost's explicitness …. 'Remember me' might more usefully function as a verbal memento mori, a reminder to value the living and to seize the day …. (Maguire, 2002: 69)

Hamlet immediately meditates on the phrase, even writing it down (as if speech might be as insubstantial as the ghost, and writing the only way to memorise its words). 'Remember' has the sense of 'recollect', but also, as the OED states, '[t]o put together again, reverse the dismembering of' (v.2). The word comes from Anglo-Norman and Old and Middle French, and appears in Chaucer, with linked meanings around recollect, call to mind, recall, retain in memory. 'To include someone in a will' and 'to commemorate' are also intimated here. Spoken by a ghost, a disembodied presence, first silent, then communicative, the sense of reassembling something into fleshly existence – to recorporealise, reanimate – is equally present in the phrase.

The very grammatical status of 'Remember me' is hard to pinpoint because it sits uneasily between imperative and a request for elegy. In any case, it launches a set of reflections on grief, loss and mourning. What does it mean to be asked to remember a father who has recently died? How could one *not* remember one's father's ghost, especially after the revelation of such a crime? What is at stake in being asked to remember, at this point?

In her discussion of ghosts, Alice Rayner suggests: 'Ghosts animate our connections to the dead, producing a visible, material, and affective relationship to the abstract terms of time and repetition, sameness and difference, absence and presence' (Rayner, 2006a: xiii). The ghost's words acknowledge that death is bound up with forgetting and the distortion of memory. They hint at a projection forward to a time when grief wanes. Saying 'Remember me' is a bulwark against the living subject's inevitable recovery from grief, a request not to be forgotten even though forgetting is intrinsic to the survival of the living. The phrase exposes the complexity of the relationship of the dead to memory, to active remembering, to the acuteness of grief. The living cannot sustain such blows; structurally, grief must evolve, but the act of forgetting is bound up with feelings of guilt. 'Remember me' is a bafflingly superfluous injunction, exposing language's ambiguity. 'Remember me' indeed embodies the very instability of words that grief generates, where simple terms are shaken by the powerful disruptions of an overdetermined past and an unknowable, deregulated future. The more one dwells on the phrase, issued by a ghost, the less sense it makes.

Grief, one might suggest, is equally evasive: it slips and slides in protean and elusive ways. The impact of grief leaves us in a state of linguistic chaos, where simple things become complex, the singular becomes plural (the living replaced by multiple dead ghosts, memory-selves). In the wake of grief, tenses lose coherence, words undo themselves or contradict their surface meanings. Does 'remember me' in fact mean 'write about me', 'recreate me as a character in a play', 'perform and re-embody me as theatre'? The very redundancy of the phrase throws Hamlet and the reader into interpretive confusion.

The phrase 'remember me' has an afterlife in other contexts. It reappears in Nahum Tate's lyrics to 'Dido's Lament' in Act 3 of Henry Purcell's opera *Dido and Aeneas* (c.1688), based on Book 4 of the *Aeneid*. The lyrics are:

> When I am laid in earth
> May my wrongs create
> No trouble in my breast
> Remember me, remember me
> But ah! forget my fate.
> Remember me
> But ah! forget my fate.[1]

The voice in 'Dido's Lament', like King Hamlet's ghost, calls on its auditor to 'remember me', and the statement is as troubling as the one in *Hamlet*. If the ghost in *Hamlet* has asked to be remembered by a son who is all too saturated in memory, Dido is asking to be remembered before she has died, as if her words are the emanations of a ghost post-death. These lyrics embody grief's contradictions more generally. Tate's lyrics contrast with the source text when they have Dido request her wrongs create 'no trouble in thy breast', to be remembered but her fate (abandoned by Aeneas, her death by suicide) forgotten – clearly the spectacle of suicide and self-immolation is a memorable death.

Both King Hamlet and Dido make complex calls on the living. The dead trouble the future with their contradictory demands. Like King Hamlet's ghost, Dido's lament, in the voice of the not yet ghost soprano, singing in the present from a post-death future, confuses temporalities. If Hamlet's ghost embodies a past crime, a present haunting and a future act of revenge, as well as being a spectral critique of disrupted intergenerational kin relations – 'a little more than kin and less than kind' (1.2.65; Shakespeare, 2016b: 1770) are Hamlet's first words in the play – Purcell's opera rewrites the source text to turn Dido into a figure of elegy even before she has actually died, asking to be simultaneously remembered and forgotten.[2]

A fiction, a dream of passion

Hamlet as a play is full of scenes driven by grief, exposing its effects, patterns and contradictions, especially when private grief becomes a public concern, or when grief threatens power structures with chaos or shaming. One of the most powerful of these occurs in Hamlet's second soliloquy: 'O, what a rogue and peasant slave am I' (2.2.468–524; Shakespeare, 2016b: 1799–800). The speech shows us at least three different Hamlets: Hamlet as theatre theorist, reflecting on the performance he has just seen; as thinking, feeling subject, working through his complex emotions and relative inability to give them expression; and as theatre director concocting a performance to expose the crime and pinpoint the guilty. It both reflects on and demonstrates the dynamics of grief, especially as they are structured by theatre as art form and performance as mode of expression.

The relationship between real and performed grief preoccupies Hamlet in the early part of the speech, before the impact of the injunctions of the dead result in the self-criticism and desire for vengeance that follow. Most intriguingly, the link between grief and theatre-making is embodied in Hamlet's plan to write a piece of theatre that will expose Claudius's culpability. Theatre and mourning, the dynamics of grief staged through a compulsion to write and direct, offer fascinating insights into grief's complexity and its relation to creativity, whereby grief is linked to the impulse to construct versions of the traumatic real in a serial repetition and *mise en abîme*.

Not only has Claudius managed to hide his guilt, but he has chastised Hamlet for the inappropriateness of the latter's grief: 'to persever/In obstinate condolement is a course/ Of impious stubbornness – "tis unmanly grief"' (1.2.92–4; Shakespeare, 2016b: 1771). Instead, Claudius has played the role of the rational statesman. Hamlet needs another ploy, a more subtle way to expose Claudius's lies, and theatre seems to offer that. The fictionality of performance is better equipped to lead Claudius to reveal his criminality than other investigative or probative strategies.

Grief's critics in the play figure it as unmanly, excessive, chaotic and emotional. In Claudius's words:

> It shows a will most incorrect to heaven,
> A heart unfortified, a mind impatient,
> An understanding simple and unschooled. (1.2.95–7;
>   Shakespeare, 2016b: 1771)

Claudius recognises the danger of Hamlet's grief when he exaggerates its severity, calling it 'a fault to heaven/A fault against the dead, a fault to nature,/To reason most absurd' (1.2.101–3; Shakespeare, 2016b: 1771), displacing the attributes of his own capital crime onto Hamlet's apparently disproportionate reaction.

There is a notable homology here between grief and theatre. Grief displays many of the characteristics of theatre, as seen from the negative perspective of what Jonas Barish has termed the 'antitheatrical prejudice': it is excessive, effeminate and a source of chaos and unreason.[3] It becomes a kind of unruly act which involves a failure to exercise control, to be masculine and rational enough to give the right performance as dictated by patriarchal norms.

'This player here'

Lines 3–9 of the soliloquy contain Hamlet's analysis of the First Player's ability to convey emotion in performance:

> Now I am alone.
> O, what a rogue and peasant slave am I!
> Is it not monstrous that this player here,
> But in a fiction, in a dream of passion,
> Could force his soul so to his whole conceit
> That from her working all his visage wanned
> Tears in his eyes, distraction in's aspect,
> A broken voice, and his whole function suiting
> With forms to his conceit? ... (2.2.468–76; Shakespeare, 2016b: 1799)

The soliloquy is not only signalled by a temporal marker 'now' in '[n]ow I am alone', but also by a locational one, the deictic 'here': 'Is it not monstrous that this player *here* ...?' (line 470; my italics). At the outset, the text anchors us in time and space as it launches us into Hamlet's philosophical thoughts. The word 'here' indicates the live moment of performance, bringing the ghostly scripturality of the speech back into the present moment and space. 'Here', then, is a pivotal term, a kind of switch or relay point, capturing the tensions between the phenomenal, material art of theatre and the conceptuality of the literary. Paradoxically, as the word situates us in space, perhaps accompanied by the actor's gesture, there is no one there. The word 'here' points to an empty space: to the ephemerality of the body in performance, to the conjurations of theatrical language and the vanishing spectre of theatre.

Hamlet's ensuing lines contrast the idea of 'a fiction' with the real or genuine; 'a fiction' is something fabricated, and it is 'monstrous' that the player can manufacture convincing signs of grief when Hamlet cannot, despite having real grief to motivate him. The phrases 'in a fiction, in a dream of passion' are juxtaposed to appear analogous, the second amplifying the first to incorporate the deregulated imagination ('dream') and powerful emotion ('passion').[4]

The soliloquy continues:

> ... And all for nothing.
> For Hecuba!

> What's Hecuba to him, or he to Hecuba,
> That he should weep for her? What would he do
> Had he the motive and the cue for passion
> That I have? (2.2.476–481; Shakespeare, 2016b: 1799)

Tanya Pollard has demonstrated how crucial the figure of Hecuba has been in expressions of grief, especially female grief, since Greek tragedy, saying that '[a]s an epitome of female grief, Hecuba offers a synecdoche for her genre' (Pollard, 2012: 1065). The chiasmus ('Hecuba to him, or he to Hecuba') captures Hamlet's obsession but also his disorientation as the looping syntax threatens to collapse into incoherence. 'Nothing' and 'Hecuba' seem to be substitutable in the phrase and it sounds jarring to call Hecuba, or her story, 'nothing', given the pathos of her suffering. 'What's Hecuba to him', Hamlet asks, not 'who' – she is more of a narrative figure or a character from tragedy, a fictional construction. Hamlet's grief leads him both to recognise and to question the poetics of fiction and the expressive power of performance. Yet the loss of his father disrupts the conceptual distinctions between the real, the fictional and the theatrical, blurring boundaries between genuinely experienced and skilfully manufactured emotions of loss. Thus, the eloquent description of fiction as a 'dream of passion' is double-edged, referring also to its imaginary or invented quality, in contrast to the very vivid, physical grief Hamlet is experiencing and which he cannot adequately express.

The speech as a whole grapples with the question of how theatre can be both material and magic, both Caliban and Ariel, impacting on the real, but as ephemeral as dreams and shadows. Hamlet goes further, though, to theorise theatre's power to expose guilt and crime and to be a vehicle for justice. His reanimation of the scene of the crime is a utopian act of corrective justice, reversing the events of the real, which allow a murderer to prevail, and exposing a criminal's guilt.

Reanimating the crime

From theorising emotions, the soliloquy goes on to explore the constraints the dead impose on the living. Grief is crucial to the contradictions in Hamlet's subjectivity, the confessional interiority associated with what Stephen Greenblatt calls:

> … an epochal shift not only in Shakespeare's own career but in Western drama; it is as if the play were giving birth to a whole new kind of literary subjectivity. This subjectivity – the sense of being inside a character's psyche and following its twists and turns – is to a large extent an effect of language. (Greenblatt, 2016: 1753)

Hamlet's voice now starts to speak outside the constraints of the revenge ethic and instead becomes conspiratorial and vulnerable. Grief interrogates aspects of our identity and being; it requires us to act.

The speech moves on to explore the relationship between theatre, guilt and the exposure of a crime. As Gillian Woods suggests, '[t]heatrical performances may be mere pretence, but they produce a real impact on those who view them. And Hamlet was not alone in believing that the tragic performance of crime could compel criminal spectators to admit their guilt' (Woods, 2016: 4).

> I have heard that guilty creatures sitting at a play
> Have by the very cunning of the scene
> Been struck so to the soul that presently
> They have proclaimed their malefactions;
> For murder, though it have no tongue, will speak
> With most miraculous organ. I'll have these players
> Play something like the murder of my father
> Before mine uncle. I'll observe his looks,
> I'll tent him to the quick. If a but blench,
> I know my course. (2.2.507–17; Shakespeare, 2016b: 1800)

Theatre offers Hamlet a mechanism for exposing Claudius's guilt, disguised in his earlier speeches by the glib formality of his rhetoric. Rhetoric and words are unreliable, whereas the performance, 'the very cunning of the scene', can operate more directly so that Claudius's body exposes his guilt physically: 'I'll observe his looks.'

The final section of the soliloquy shows theatre's power to conjure up convincing phantoms:

> The spirit that I have seen
> May be the devil, and the devil hath power
> T'assume a pleasing shape; yea, and perhaps,

> Out of my weakness and my melancholy –
> As he is very potent with such spirits –
> Abuses me to damn me. (2.2.517–22; Shakespeare, 2016b: 1800)

Hamlet's reflections on the potential malevolence of the ghost are also thoughts about the reanimatory power of theatre, its seductive power to assume 'a pleasing shape'. As a character, Hamlet loves theatre, and even though he has lost all his mirth as a result of his mourning, the presence of the Players still gives him, in Rosencrantz's words, 'a kind of joy' (3.1.18; Shakespeare, 2016b: 1801), though since we know he is *performing* madness as part of his grieving and revenge, we cannot be sure if this is genuine or not. Metatheatricality deconstructs the very possibility of a clear distinction between the genuine and the fake, positing instead a new modern subject for whom the real and the performative are mutually constitutive.

As we reach the end of the speech, Hamlet turns to theatre as the vehicle of veracity, with the ringing endorsement of the rhyming couplet 'The play's the thing/Wherein I'll catch the conscience of the King' (2.2.523–4; Shakespeare 2016b: 1800). Theatre has the power to reveal guilt, not through language but through the mimetic embodiment, the reanimation, of crime, affect, emotion, guilt and memory. It is ironic that Hamlet, wordsmith, theatre theorist and philosopher of human consciousness, should leave the scene with a clumsy, galloping iambic line, preceded by four monosyllables: 'the play's the thing', with the stress falling on 'play' and 'thing'. What does 'thing' mean? Is 'thing' all Hamlet can come up with after all his eloquent theorising?

Hurrying to its end, the syllabic stresses in each word seem to fall neatly into the pattern of the iambic pentameter, apart from one word, 'conscience': 'Wherein/I'll catch/the con/science of/ the King'. The word 'conscience' is here haunted by an internal break, a mini-caesura overridden by the way the word 'king' lands at the end of the line, emphatically rhyming with 'thing'. 'King' and 'thing' echo one another, so that 'plays' and 'kings' are contaminated with 'thingness', with its disturbing sense of monstrosity (not human, but a thing) and conceptual confusion (how can a 'play' be a 'thing'?). While Hamlet's plan to trap Claudius seems decisive, running away with language towards the thudding rhyming couplet – a linguistic euphoria captured in the RSC film of the 2008 Gregory Doran production as David Tennant runs off-screen having delivered the lines – that ghostly caesura in 'conscience' bespeaks a hesitation, the pulse of Hamlet's own guilty con/science asserting itself within the word.

Catherine Belsey tells us that the word 'conscience' in *Hamlet* refers 'consistently to the faculty which distinguishes good and evil' (Belsey, 1979: 127). As she points out, called to revenge by the King's ghost, Hamlet's willingness to avenge the murder is 'immediate, intuitive, and passionate' (Belsey, 1979: 142). The ghostly caesura in 'conscience' is the presence of the body in the word, the breath animating the verbal, the reanimation of reflective subjectivity intervening to interrupt the rhythm of the revenge ethic. It is also a disruption of the sensory pleasures of the text (decisive rhythms, single-syllable rhymes) and the seduction of the theatrical (the centrality of 'the play'). Theatre carries us away with seductive rhymes; plays, things and kings are thrown together with compelling force. Yet the unvoiced conscience of the word 'conscience' catches the moment of doubt even in the midst of poetry's own phonic conviction at the level of rhyme and rhythm.

The multiple reanimations in this soliloquy show how *Hamlet* is simultaneously a reflection on death and grief and on the theatricality of mourning. Hamlet, the 'mad' prince, is also a figure for the 'madness' of performance, its disruptive theatricality, its pleasure in the fictional, even as the real threatens to annihilate the characters. He is a character who represents the power of any play to create alternative (theatrical/fictional) worlds in which death might be allowed reparatory expression and mourning. The play-within-the-play, the 'Mousetrap', allows Hamlet to reanimate a brave (utopian) new world where justice prevails, where murderers are exposed, their 'malefactions' (2.2.511; Shakespeare, 2016b: 1800) proclaimed, unlike in Hamlet's real world, where people like Claudius are too good at acting to be caught in the act.

But this comes at a cost. To reanimate the crime, to reimagine the outcome, to create an alternative utopian world, might also entail a failure to act on grief or to mourn appropriately. After the creativity of playmaking comes the need for revenge, when theatre ends.

Ghost, grief

Of all the emotions, we might expect grief (our reaction to an irreversible and singular loss) to be the most authentic. *Hamlet* challenges any clear distinction between fabricated and real grief. It also questions the very form grief takes – ghost or guilty conscience; grief as relational or grief as narcissistic – in the 'closet scene' between Gertrude and Hamlet (Act 3, Scene 4). In the scene, the ghost of King Hamlet only appears to his son and not to Gertrude.

For Hamlet, the ghost is a figure calling for revenge (according to a pre-modern system of justice), whereas for Gertrude, the invisible ghost is a figment of her son's disordered imagination or a symptom of his overwhelming grief. In its earlier appearances, Francisco, Marcellus and Horatio have seen the ghost before Hamlet does, so its existence, within the world of the play, is not in doubt. Hamlet turns Horatio's observation that the ghost is 'wondrous strange' (1.5.166; Shakespeare, 2016b: 1784) into a critique of a limiting rationalism: 'There are more things in heaven and earth, Horatio,/ Than are dreamt of in your philosophy' (1.5.168–9; Shakespeare, 2016b: 1784). However, in the closet scene, the most painful disavowal of the presence of the ghost, the ghost-father, comes from Gertrude, a figure of antagonism but also of much more complicated love than the idealised father figure. It is easier, it seems, to idealise an absent father than to love a flesh-and-blood mother. Even the ghost tells him to doubt his mind: 'Conceit in weakest bodies strongest works' (3.4.113; Shakespeare, 2016b: 1819).

When Hamlet asks his mother: 'Do you see nothing there?/ ... Nor did you nothing hear?' (3.4.131/133; Shakespeare, 2016b: 1819), the questions sound like those of a young child conjuring monsters in the dark. In response, after the ghost leaves, Gertrude replies: 'This is the very coinage of your brain./This bodiless creation ecstasy/Is very cunning in' (3.4.138–40; Shakespeare, 2016b: 1819). These lines bear closer scrutiny. 'Coinage' here refers to something invented, the mind stamping out an invisible character like the production of a coin. Indeed, the word 'character' itself is linked etymologically to ideas of stamping and engraving and is used in this sense earlier in the play when Polonius encourages his son Laertes by saying: 'these few precepts in thy memory/Look thou character' (1.3.57–8; Shakespeare 2016b: 1776). 'This bodiless creation' refers to the idea of a hallucination but is also the perfect description of a ghost, since creation is both a 'fabrication' and something invented for the first time. 'Ecstasy' has a ghostly echo of reanimation, since it implies a doubleness, a standing outside oneself, while 'cunning in' means 'adept at' but with a subtext of deceit. Thus, Gertrude's words oscillate between the positive and the negative, the creation which is both a paranoid hallucination and a powerful imaginary being.

Gertrude's lines can also be interpreted in relation to theorising theatre more generally, signifying its power to create imaginary, fictional beings, an act close to madness, a process of inventing 'bodiless creations' which are both the product of 'cunning' but also of the unconscious. Theatre becomes an alternative to rational modes of thinking, from another magical realm than the one which 'our' philosophy can conceive of. This ecstasy of bodiless creation is also synonymous with the reanimations of grief discussed in this book as a whole, that conjuring of memory and affect central to remembering and forgetting.

Reanimation as memory: Yorick

Hamlet provides numerous encounters with grief, including the sudden irruption of a sense of loss transporting the grieving subject to their past. In the graveyard scene, Shakespeare combines gothic images of death, such as the skull or the open grave, alongside sequences of poetic elegy. The cemetery grounds death in its material substantiality, while memory revives and repoeticises what has been silenced, as Hamlet remembers laughter or living bodies touching and playing in images of childhood intimacy.

There is an emphasis on song in this scene, a relationship between grief, songs and reanimation which I will discuss further in Chapters 6 and 7. When Hamlet sees the gravedigger, he asks, 'Has this fellow no feeling of his business? 'A sings in gravemaking.' (5.1.59–60; Shakespeare, 2016b: 1838). Presented with Yorick's skull, he recollects Yorick's 'songs', as well as how he used to ride on the jester's shoulders and kiss his lips. The encounter with mortality is refracted through his childhood self as the memory of the laughing, singing Yorick is brought back to life via this embodied *memento mori* of the skull, a constant icon of mortality and death in Renaissance visual art and theatre. Yorick's songs recall the line that Gertrude uses in relation to Ophelia's death, that 'she chanted snatches of old lauds [hymns]' (4.4.176; Shakespeare, 2016b: 1836), reinforcing the link between music, elegy and mortality in the play.

The scene will reanimate not only Yorick, twenty-three-years dead, but also Ophelia, whom Hamlet will embrace in the grave, though we might have expected her drowned body to be hidden or buried by now. Ophelia keeps being reanimated in this play in unexpected ways. Looking again at Gertrude's account of Ophelia's death, the language is heavy with references to vegetal matter and organic metaphors. Gertrude recounts Ophelia's last moments in detail, becoming an omniscient narrative voice as she recollects the trees, landscape and water during the final seconds of the young woman's life. It is an extraordinary shift away from any kind of plausible realism, operating instead as an *ekphrasis* of suicide, a rich metaphorology through plants and flowers to itemise with preternatural observation the moment of death, bringing the drowned Ophelia back to minutely observed life for the duration of the speech, only to verbalise her movement towards death as she slips into the water:

> There on the pendant boughs her crownet weeds
> Clamb'ring to hang, an envious sliver broke,
> When down her weedy trophies and herself
> Fell in the weeping brook. Her clothes spread wide …
> (4.4.171–4; Shakespeare, 2016b: 1836)

As well as the references to songs, 'snatches of old lauds' (4.4.176; Shakespeare, 2016b: 1836) and 'melodious lay' (4.4.181; Shakespeare, 2016b: 1836), the specificity here takes Gertrude outside her character's enmeshment in the kin relations of the text and gives her the role of elegist and chronicler, painter and poet, secret observer and omniscient narrator.

Hamlet on grief

Like her father Polonius, Ophelia is at risk of not having a proper burial/funeral, and this is what infuriates her brother Laertes and amplifies his grief. Improper burials, inadequate or incomplete mourning, the wrong type of grief – abbreviated or excessive, feminising or fabricated, performed or unperformable, theatricalised or non-verbal – *Hamlet* as a play explores the many factors shaping grief and mourning. It exposes the complex layers behind this emotion, the mixture of fantasy and theatricality, and the relationship between private and public modes of bereavement. Furthermore, it dramatises the difficulty of accepting loss and working out how to survive it – the knowledge that coping is both painful and necessary.

Hamlet is conscious of the eloquence that grief produces, for example, when he hears Laertes' response to his sister Ophelia's death. Laertes embraces Ophelia's dead body and speaks in elevated terms, leading Hamlet to ask himself:

> HAMLET [*coming forward*] What is he whose grief
> Bears such an emphasis, whose phrase of sorrow
> Conjures the wand'ring stars and makes them stand
> Like wonder-wounded hearers? … (5.1.233–6; Shakespeare, 2016b: 1842)

Grief has given Laertes magical eloquence in a way that makes it hard for Hamlet to recognise him. The compound adjective 'wonder-wounded' (5.1.236) captures the paradox of grief in the play: the conjunction of traumatic loss and poetic eloquence.

In the graveyard, Hamlet remembers the liveliness of the jester and contrasts it with the putrefaction and the death-odour of the corpse and skull. As William Kerrigan suggests:

> The imagination of Yorick alive becomes 'now,' in the presence of Yorick's skull, an abhorrence. That is why Hamlet stresses the affectionate character of his memory of the jester: he is alive to the contrast, his disgust as sharp as his memories are tender. At the thought that he has kissed the lips without any apprehension of the skull beneath, his 'gorge rises.' (Kerrigan, 1994: 135)

Yet where Kerrigan reads the graveyard scene as Hamlet's encounter with the materiality of death, in fact the scene is as much about the joyous memories of the past as it is about lurid fantasies of bodily decay. The images of his youthful games and jests with Yorick make the direct handling of the skull, this 'thing', object, vestige, all the more shocking. But though the scene presents us with what

Kerrigan calls Hamlet's 'death-tracing imagination' (Kerrigan, 1994: 136), it also shows us the living Yorick in Hamlet's memory, his animation and 'infinite jest'. It is this direct encounter with the quintessential icon and embodiment of death, the skull, which most powerfully reanimates the figure of Yorick in the prince's memory.

While the prince's animation and verbal wit contrast with the iconic horror of the skull in the graveyard scene, elsewhere in the play Hamlet's immersion in grief seems to leave its mark on his body. In his essay on grief in *Hamlet*, Arthur Kirsch notes the idea that Hamlet as a character seems 'poised between the living and the dead' (Kirsch, 1981: 27) and that as the play progresses he is 'described in images that suggest the ghost's countenance' (Kirsch, 1981: 27). While the theatricality of the meetings with his father's ghost, or the macabre quality of his handling of Yorick's skull, create vivid moments in performance, as the play continues Hamlet seems to be transforming into a living ghost, embodying the impact of grief and the new understanding of mortality on the living. Kirsch sums up the complexity of grief in the play in his essay's final words:

> The ghost draws upon the emotional taproot of the revenge play genre and dilates the natural sorrow and anger of Hamlet's multiple griefs until they include all human frailty in their protest and sympathy and touch upon the deepest synapses of grief in our own lives, not only for those who have died, but for those, like ourselves, who are still alive. (Kirsch, 1981: 35)

For Kirsch, the play show grief's self-reflexive quality. The experience of grief highlights human vulnerability as well as the grieving subject's own sense of mortality. Grief multiplies, evoking the transience of living and the future griefs caused or experienced by those 'who are still alive'.

Reanimating *Hamlet* in performance

The term 'revival' was first used to describe a new production of an older literary or theatrical work in the seventeenth century, the OED citing uses of the word in this sense by George Chapman in 1611, J. Wilson in 1664 and Samuel Johnson in 1779. *Hamlet*, like any play, is reanimated by new productions but the phenomenon of live performance has a special meaning in a play about the return of the dead in the form of ghost, memory and guilty conscience, conducted via encounters across the range of human experience from the supernatural to the all-too-real material decay of the graveyard. New revivals of *Hamlet* add to the play's critical economy of ghosts and haunting in line with Marvin Carlson's suggestion that all theatre is 'a cultural activity deeply involved with memory and haunted by repetition' (Carlson, 2003: 11). In *Hamlet* in performance, words are re-embodied, language is vocalised, characters are animated from the page to live performance, and themes of reanimation in the form of ghosts, memories and theatrical characters are actualised and enacted.

Watching Richard Burton deliver his version of the speech 'O what a rogue and peasant slave am I?' in the 1964 Broadway production, directed by John Gielgud, knowing Burton died in 1984, Gielgud in 2000, the performance feels haunted by theatrical ghosts, cinematic figures speaking from beyond the grave, preserved on film, permanent in the way the human body and live performance can never be. When I read the speech, I think of the way Burton says 'Hecuba' as if the word is sticking in his mouth, the name a poison to be expelled. David Tennant's 2008 performance of the speech haunts the text in a different way: his interpretation is more physically choreographed and camera conscious. He starts sitting with his back to a wall, his legs crooked in front of him, mentally reconstructing the events that have just happened by indicating 'this player here'. Tennant's delivery puts such emphasis on the line 'a fiction, a dream of passion' that those words dominate the rest of the speech and by falling to the ground at 'O, vengeance', he gives those words a choreographed violence that remains with the text long after the viewing of his performance.

Maxine Peake's 2014 performance as Hamlet brings a gender emphasis to the play, in line with a series of female performers to play the role in a tradition comprehensively documented in Tony Howard's book *Women as Hamlet* (2007). Female Hamlets prompt questions such as '[i]s Hamlet a "universal" figure whose dilemma everyone shares, male or female? Is Hamlet a "feminine" character whose words invite a woman's voice?' (Howard, 2007: 9). In particular, Howard focuses on the way Hamlet's 'unmanly grief' resonates with the performance of the role by a woman (Howard, 2007: 17–20). Peake's voice remains as a trace in one's auditory memory of the play, bleeding into the words on the page during the reading process. What remains from the production, how does it haunt the play? Peake as Hamlet has an extended sequence pulling up masking tape from the floor as the 'O, what a rogue and peasant slave am I?' speech ends. This creates a ripping, tearing sound that marks the conclusion of the scene – it feels like something violent is about to be revealed, as if the play's layers of metatheatricality are being visualised in front of our eyes as the outline of the performance space in spot-tape is removed before the next scene begins.

What remains in one's sense memory from Andrew Scott's 2017 performance, directed by Robert Icke, is the actor's gesturality, his body caught between allowing the poetry of the text to articulate itself and the need to re-enact language physically. Scott's Hamlet is thinking things through at the same time as physically reeling from the impact of grief and betrayal. In 'O, what a rogue and peasant slave am I', his frontal delivery is poised between interiority and externality, suddenly shifting to address the audience directly as he asks, 'Am I a coward?'. His somatic choreography is unpredictable, disjunctive, cerebral and volatile all at once. The least ghost-like or spectral performance, Scott reanimates the play as one in which language pulses through the body and brain of the actor.

In addition to the voices, gestures, choreographies and soundscapes that productions bring to the text, directorial choices or changes also serve to reanimate it. In the 2017 Andrew Scott production, Icke moved *Hamlet*'s 'To be or not to be' speech from its familiar position in Act 3, Scene 1 to Act 2, thus changing the rhythm of the play established by the sequence of soliloquies. An act like this reanimates the text by disrupting its fixity, displacing and reordering the familiar version of the text. Similarly, a choice around actor doubling in Icke's production raises and embodies critical questions about grief, acting and performance. By doubling the role of King Hamlet's ghost with that of First Player, Icke links together different modes of grief (the King as source of grief for Hamlet, the player as performer of Hecuba's grief), as well as highlighting the way theatre's make-do pragmatism can generate unpredictable and striking connections (the actor visibly doubles, detracting from the realist illusion, but creates new embodied, conceptual links between characters).

Hamnet – fiction, 'a dream of passion'

New productions of the play bring voices and bodies into this text's verbal world. The haunted text shimmers with the ghosts of past *Hamlets*, performances of ephemerality and transience that mesh with the scenes of revenance and elegies of mourning in the text itself.

This last section on *Hamlet*'s reanimations examines the way in which a recent novel, *Hamnet* by Maggie O'Farrell, deals with death, grief and mourning, and in its turn can be said to reanimate *Hamlet* the play text. Reanimations are often motivated by the desire to transform, and *Hamnet* enacts numerous transformations of the *Hamlet* story, blurring generic boundaries between fiction, theatre and biography. *Hamnet* focuses on a mother's bereavement, revitalising Shakespeare's play via an imaginary reconstruction of the playwright's family. Instead of a dead father and a grieving son, it focuses on a female protagonist, the death of a child and the subsequent grieving process.

The novel's central character is Agnes, the Anne Hathaway of literary fame, wife of Shakespeare, mother of Susanna and younger twins Hamnet and Judith. O'Farrell traces the relationship between Agnes and William Shakespeare, from their courtship, through their marriage, children, Shakespeare's absence from Stratford when he moves to London, the death of their son Hamnet at age eleven, and the writing and performance of *Hamlet* at the Globe in 1600–1.

O'Farrell puts Agnes at the heart of the novel, a decision reinforced by not mentioning William Shakespeare's name in the text at any point. Shakespeare becomes a spectral presence as Agnes copes with motherhood. O'Farrell's Agnes is an extraordinary character, gifted with psychic powers and preternatural knowledge of medicine and nature, reclaiming the dismissed roles of sorcerer and enchantress. She is part Cassandra, part Circe, spell-binding, sexual, erotic and wilful. Joanna Briscoe in her review of the novel calls Agnes 'a witchy woman of the forest, a quasi-mythical creature who has a way with potions and curses' (Briscoe, 2020). The power of her emotions and her independent spirit dominate the text as she leaves to give birth to her first child in the woods, withdrawing like an animal to a space of privacy, or dealing with the birth of her twins, their illness and the subsequent death of her eleven-year-old son Hamnet.

The book reanimates and reframes *Hamlet* by putting women's experiences at its core, in particular communicating Agnes's sexuality, her pregnancies, the lineaments of her mourning and her preternatural knowledge. In each of these areas, O'Farrell uses the fictional form to open new perspectives on what we know of Shakespeare's life and family or the events prior to the composition of *Hamlet*, particularly from a female perspective and in the context of maternal grief. The novel depicts her as a threat to gendered social norms through her refusal of a certain kind of femininity and domesticity. In the process, *Hamnet* encourages us to think about how *Hamlet* prioritises the male point of view and how it filters female subjectivity through male perspectives. The novel becomes the explicit meditation on grief and mourning which the play refracts through self-reflexivity and metatheatre. Reading *Hamnet* prompts us to compare the strategies of fiction writing and theatre, to look at their different rhythms and mappings of interiority. *Hamnet* reanimates Shakespeare's play by decentring it, positioning its expressions of grief within a wider gender framework and offering a fictional theorisation of the play's encoding and theatricalisation of grief. The act of fiction-writing gestures towards areas of women's experience and viewpoints not adequately represented or voiced in the play or in the literary historical record that surrounds it.

The link between *Hamlet* and the death of Shakespeare's son is articulated most clearly at the end of the novel. While we learn of Agnes's acute grief at the young boy's death, the character William Shakespeare in O'Farrell's novel absents himself, unable to mourn or deal with his wife's grief. It is only much later, as Agnes suspects him of having affairs with other women while he is away in London, that he confesses his sense of loss. This occurs when Agnes discovers he has written a play, *Hamlet*, four years after Hamnet's death.

O'Farrell's earlier book, her memoir *I Am, I Am, I Am* (2017), also deals with the subject of death, or more accurately with near-misses, what O'Farrell in the book calls 'brushes with death'. *I Am,*

I Am, I Am is haunted by lives not lived, those who have died – most shockingly, a young woman who is murdered in the first section, 'Neck 1990', a death intimately bound up with O'Farrell's own survival. Ghost selves, possible extinctions, roads not taken all haunt the book. These include a powerful exploration of the social silence around miscarriages where O'Farrell quotes Hilary Mantel's 2003 memoir *Giving Up the Ghost* in relation to unborn children: '… they become ghosts in our lives … The unborn, whether they're named or not, whether or not they're acknowledged, have a way of insisting: a way of making their presence felt' (Mantel in O'Farrell, 2017: 105). O'Farrell adds her own words to this, observing: 'If asked, I could reel off exactly, instantly and without hesitation, what age all my miscarried children would be, had they lived' (O'Farrell, 2017: 105). The image of the ghost ('they became ghosts in our lives') evokes the loss of the child and memory of miscarriage, a trauma that is also about a loss of duration, a failed maturation that is replaced by the painful memory of miscarriage instead. For Mantel and O'Farrell, memory is a form of reanimation, but perhaps 'memory' is not quite the right term for what is a kind of permanent presence in consciousness, a ghost-presence, as O'Farrell suggests – something constant and living, if spectral. Writing, too, is part of this reanimatory process. For O'Farrell, discussing her own miscarriages, explicitly challenges the fact that 'miscarriage is still a taboo subject, one women will rarely broach, share or discuss' (O'Farrell, 2017: 106).

In *Hamnet*, O'Farrell uses fiction to theorise grief. The child's death, burial and spectral return, in and as memory, are subject to moving sequences in which the everyday choreography of absence and other manifestations of grief are given powerful expression. When Agnes nudges one of her dead son's boots to realign it with its pair, it operates as a delicate acknowledgement of absence and the forgetting of grief, a metaphor for the twins now separated and Agnes' unconscious desire to reunite them:

> It is hard to know what to do with his clothes. For weeks, Agnes cannot move them from the chair where he left them before taking to bed. A month or so after burial she lifts the breeches, then puts them down. She fingers the collar of his shirt. She nudges the toe of his boot so that the pair are lined up, side by side. (O'Farrell, 2020: 288)

Like Hamlet's grief in Shakespeare's play, Agnes's grief does not conform to the time's prevailing gender norms of mourning, according to Mary, her mother-in-law, who finds it disproportionate:

> Mary, Susanna knows, is of the opinion that grief is all very well in moderation, but there comes a time when it is necessary to make an effort. She is of the opinion that some people make too much of things. That life goes on. (O'Farrell, 2020: 306)

Susanna, Agnes' daughter, registers her grandmother Mary's impatience with Agnes's excessive mourning. The refusal to mourn in the prescribed way, to mourn *properly*, that is, discreetly and passively, is part of Agnes's wider rejection of restrictive gender norms in the novel.

In the book's finale, Agnes travels to London with her brother to see her husband's new play, *Hamlet*, at the Globe. We learn about the Globe's interior, its 'stage jutting out into the gathering crowd, and above them all, a ceiling of sky, a circle containing fast-moving clouds, the shapes of birds, darting from one edge to the next' (O'Farrell, 2020: 358). As Agnes recognises her husband playing the King's ghost, the third-person narrative voice merges with Agnes' subjective perspective, and Shakespeare's performance is understood as a form of reanimation of his dead child:

> Hamlet, here on this stage, is two people, the young man, alive, and the father, dead. He is both alive and dead. Her husband has brought him back to life, in the only way he can. As the ghost talks, she sees that her husband, in writing this, in taking the role of the ghost, has changed places with his son. He has taken his son's death and made it his own; he has put himself in death's clutches, resurrecting the boy in his place. (O'Farrell, 2020: 366)

In this scene, the novel theorises the act of playwriting and its relation to mourning, presenting it as a kind of encoded grief, a displacement and inversion, much like the dream-text of Freudian psychoanalysis. Reanimation is figured as Shakespeare's way of working through mourning 'in the only way he can' (O'Farrell, 2020: 366). Shakespeare's performance of the father's ghost is a creative transformation of his own experience of grief.

Even further, in O'Farrell's novel, writing the play, staging and acting in it, become the ways in which Shakespeare's bereavement finds expression. Playwriting itself becomes a form of mourning.

In the novel, *Hamlet* is not a play *about* mourning; instead, it is the very act of mourning itself, a coming to terms with grief. The novel thus brings out something latent in the play text itself: that Shakespeare's multiple reanimations in this work of theatre can be seen as the playwright's way of working through grief, bringing the dead back to life in an act of creative reanimation in response to the irreversible loss of a young son. In her novel, O'Farrell explores this act of indirect grieving through the play's myriad reanimations, while at the same time she notes her interest in reanimating not only Shakespeare and Agnes, but also the dead child of the novel's title, as she says in an interview, 'I wanted to give this lost, and forgotten and overlooked boy, a voice and a presence' (O'Farrell, 2021). Again, the link here to motherhood, and the desire to provide space for maternal grief, becomes part of O'Farrell's own critical explanation of the novel's genesis and wider relationship with the play.

Conclusion

This chapter has explored the range of reanimations in *Hamlet*, from ghosts to (meta)theatrical revivals of the dead and a disinterred skull that triggers childhood memories. It suggests that theatre is doubly reanimated through performance. O'Farrell's *Hamnet* takes the play and revives it to restore a missing female figure and a dead child to the heart of Shakespeare's story. As this chapter has suggested, *Hamlet* is criss-crossed by a series of textual, performative and intertextual reanimations relating to death, grief and mourning.

In the interview quoted above, O'Farrell observes that '[w]hat interests me about grief and loss is that it is, for me anyway, the other side of love' (O'Farrell, 2021). For O'Farrell, grief is a consequence of love, almost a corollary of it. Calling it 'the other side of love' acknowledges its difference from but symbiotic relationship with love. It is one of the contentions of this book that reanimations are often acts of reparation, expressions of love for the living that can only be articulated to the dead, or via the reanimated dead. Grief, in this analysis, acts like a melancholy form of love, one predicated on loss and absence. Literature and theatre do not and cannot counter death; instead, they mediate our grief, mime the processes of encounter and separation, creating elegies for loss and metatheatres of mourning.

Notes

1 Tate's ethereal elegy is significantly different to the feeling of violence at the end of Book 4 in the *Aeneid*, where Dido famously says 'exoriare, aliquis nostris ex ossibus ultor/qui face Dardanios ferroque sequare colonos' ['Arise from my ashes, unknown avenger, to harass the Trojan settlers with fire and sword'] (4, 625–6), invoking a future agent of revenge for her abandonment. Virgil's Dido is powerful in death, not Tate's doleful figure.
2 In performance, the aria gives us further insight into the dynamics of grief, its repetitions operating as the return and remodelling of the same (words, affects, regrets). The phrase 'remember me' is repeated six times in 'Dido's Lament' and the section composed of the single phrase 'remember me but ah forget my fate' takes up two of the four minutes of Emma Kirkby's 1981 recording of the aria for the Tavener singers (the recitativo and the words 'When I am laid in earth' are the first half, the aria is the second): www.youtube.com/watch?v=H3wAarmPYKU.
3 Jonas Barish uses the phrase to refer to the long history of opposition to theatre from Plato onwards, documented in his 1981 book *The Antitheatrical Prejudice* (Berkeley and Los Angeles, CA: University of California Press).
4 The idea of fiction referring to the imaginary is coupled in the sixteenth and seventeenth centuries with now obsolete uses of the term that were strongly correlated with deception. Not merely an imaginary narrative, or the opposite of fact, but feigning, counterfeiting, dissimulation and pretence (OED).

4

Dead forms, living characters

We came to fixate on the objects of our childhood domestic theatre, mummy's green suitcase on top of the wardrobe, the occasional black and white photo that turned up, the mass cards for the dead whom we never knew or heard about. It wasn't green, in fact, it was checked green and black squares, a kind of tartan effect, and whenever I see one similar, in a fleamarket or bric-a-brac store, it's a portal to the past. Black handle with stitching. Hidden but visible, there was no space to hide things, we wanted to ransack it for clues, but we knew it was meant to be inviolable. We couldn't leave it alone because it promised us knowledge, evidence – it harboured secrets. We wrestled it down one day when they were out, flipped it open with a thwack, carefully unfolding the fragile documents, noting which pocket or lining items were taken from. Old typewritten names, curlicued Irish handwriting, faded polaroids, thin versions of you from the time before us. Maybe if I find out where and when you bought it, who manufactured it, how much it cost, where it came from, it will tell me what I want to know.

This chapter explores the death and reanimation of realism across two plays by Chekhov, *The Seagull* (1896) and *Three Sisters* (1900). Integral to Chekhov's reconfiguration of realism is finding space in the latter play for the representation of death, grief and its aftermath, and the consequent emergence of a poetics of lost time, ephemerality and fragmentation. Across the two plays, death changes from the conceptual to the affective, from being a metaphor for fixed forms of realism to a recurring, unpredictable site of emotion, memory and nostalgia. By incorporating the poetics of grief, Chekhov reanimates realism, undoing a desire to reproduce the real photographically and embracing instead intermittency, incompleteness and temporal flux.

The chapter begins by exploring Chekhov's critique of realism, as an aesthetic, through the powerful metaphorical object of the taxidermic seagull in *The Seagull*. The bird not only challenges mimetic realism but embodies a wider critique of how art (literature and theatre) should engage with the real, advocating for representational modes that do not aim to be comprehensive, exact or totalising. In *Three Sisters*, Chekhov reanimates realism by creating an impressionistic, compositional text which foregrounds the provisional and fragmentary. Grief sets the play in motion and pervades it via allusions to the dead, and metaphorically, via the accumulation of tropes of ephemerality and transience related to time passing. If *The Seagull* uses the taxidermic bird to symbolise the death (and persistent return) of mimetic realism in theatre, *Three Sisters* employs a kaleidoscope of styles and structural devices to signal the loss of the unitary, realist self. The death of the three sisters' father at the start of the play turns grief and its complex temporalities into a mechanism for reanimating a new form of realism, one haunted by past and future deaths, and the sense that literature and theatre can only ever stage fleeting character-ghosts and snapshots of the real.

The Seagull is a play stuffed with ideas, like the eponymous taxidermic bird that re-emerges at the end of the text. It is a work-in-transition, a strategic but productive failure that emerges into theatre's modernity, an amalgam of the literary, the critical and the theoretical. The failed scenes of theatre and the failed transitions from literature to performance in *The Seagull* produce the innovations of *Three Sisters*, a play which embodies and acts out the theoretical and critical breakthroughs of its predecessor. *Three Sisters* puts into practice the techniques that *The Seagull* consciously exposes as a result of its purposely flawed naturalism.

The Seagull is about literature and criticism, writing and performance, theory and intuition. It features fiction writers Trigorin and Konstantin – the latter is also a playwright – and two actresses, Arkadina and Nina. These characters from different generations are caught in complex love triangles and are surrounded by country-estate workers and their family members, as well as people from other professions such as a doctor (Dorn) and teacher (Medvedenko). The play is about the failure to write, to act, to love. It contains scenes of failed theatre and failed texts, theorising these through characters who reflect on why they cannot write fiction or theatre. In some ways, you could view the play itself as a failure: it is verbose, literary and self-conscious, focusing on major aesthetic ideas one moment, and on minor quotidian details the next. The play-within-a-play at its beginning is aborted, its key tragic events take place off stage and its ending is deliberately botched. Indeed, Chekhov himself famously said that it was 'contrary to all the rules of dramatic art' (Borney, 2006: 147).

The seagull itself changes status and meaning a number of times throughout the play. It starts off as a living creature associated with Nina and connoting freedom, and in its subsequent iterations we see it shot and killed as a symbol for doomed love, then mentioned to illustrate the ethics of fiction, and finally as a concrete metaphor for the aesthetics of realism. As a symbolic object, it accrues depth and complexity as the play progresses, as well as metacritically connoting the instability of meaning. We finally encounter the seagull which Konstantin shoots in Act 2 as a taxidermic object in Act 4, stashed away and forgotten.

One of the most prominent things the play fails to represent is death. Between Acts 3 and 4, two years elapse in which one of the central characters, Nina, has a child who dies, yet the play only mentions this in passing.[1] At the end, Konstantin's suicide happens offstage, anticlimactically, replaced by the lie that the overheard gunshot is an exploding medicine bottle. Death is excluded, and grief is impossible in this self-conscious world of art, literature and performance. The only death we see is Konstantin's shooting of the seagull, yet even here the demands of the aesthetic immediately convert it into a symbol, a literary trope and then an artistic object, the taxidermic version of the living animal which resurfaces at the end of the play. In contrast, death and grief are at the heart of *Three Sisters*, and one of the crucial reanimations Chekhov makes across the plays is to find a form of realism which revives theatre's capacity to represent death and to communicate grief and mourning.

Taxidermic naturalism

The famous taxidermic seagull at the end of Chekhov's play is a powerful symbol of frozen Naturalism, lifelike but inert, a copy more like a corpse than a living creation. As Patrice Pavis says, it represents 'the rhetorical figuration of the work of art petrifying [figeant] life' (Pavis, 1999: 26; my translation). It is the embodiment of Nina's critique of a play 'which doesn't have any living characters' (Chekhov, 1993a: 66), an observation she makes about Konstantin's futuristic play-within-a-play at the start of *The Seagull* and, by extension, a criticism of the new avant-garde plays emerging around this time. Notably, Trigorin will echo Nina's words in Act 4 of *The Seagull* when he gives his pointed evaluation of Konstantin's limitations as a writer, in the process exposing his own tendency to plagiarise others' ideas (at this point in the play Trigorin has had and ended an affair with Nina in Moscow):

> TRIGORIN. He's not having much success. He still just can't find his own voice. There's something odd and formless about this work – something verging at times on the nightmarish. Never a single living character. (Chekhov, 1993a: 116)

This criticism applies to naturalistic theatre too, which cannot escape its model in the real, merely reproducing with photographic realism the world 'as it is'. Yet as the fate of the seagull itself suggests, the transition from life to art kills its subject because it removes the animacy of the living thing.

The taxidermic seagull in the play is a warning both to realists about the risks of their aesthetics but also to symbolists, and other experimental playwrights, about the absurdity and pretentiousness of the symbol. Like the stuffed seagull, that kind of meticulous realism feels like it belongs behind glass, an exhibition of concept over lived experience, and like the stuffed seagull it soon becomes moth-eaten and anachronistic, a museum piece or a minor curio that does not even allow us to think about the death of the living creature it is identified with.

According to the OED, the word *taxidermy* comes from the Greek τάξις, meaning 'arranging, arrangement', and δέρμα, meaning 'skin'. The first quotation cited by the OED as employing the term dates from 1820. The OED definition of taxidermy is '[t]he art of preparing and preserving the skins of animals, and stuffing and mounting them so as to present the appearance, attitude, etc. of the living animal'. This last point in the definition is intriguing: the idea that the taxidermic process emulates or gives the appearance or impression 'of the living animal'. Discussing taxidermy in the context of Lewis Carroll's *Alice's Adventures in Wonderland*, Lin Young suggests:

> The taxidermic animal in the museum display ... represents an attempt to construct the animal *from* the object, to reverse the transformation made when the animal was first taken apart, and to create, through the objectified body, an observably 'authentic' animal, reassembled. This desire for authentic preservation, however, is ultimately troubled by the fundamentally objectified nature of taxidermic bodies, as mounted animals necessarily existed simultaneously as both animal *and* object. (Young, 2017: 51; italics in original)

Of course, nothing could be less lifelike than a taxidermic version of a living creature. The object has what one might call a superficial realism, a surface, or 'skin-deep', approximation of the real thing, but by extending our observation of the object we soon come to see it as inadequate. Indeed, the fact that the taxidermic object is the object itself, void of animacy, blocks the very act of representation, which relies on distance and displacement. The taxidermic realism of the stuffed object, seductive at first, alluring in its apparent mimesis of the real, is in fact an obstacle to genuine animation. Here then Nina's elegant critique of Konstantin's avant-garde play has intratextual resonance: the play's absence of living characters, missing any 'living' quality, any animacy, is a critique of static realist techniques as much as it is a critique of avant-garde or conceptual theatre.

In relation to taxidermy, whereas the OED highlights the emulation of the living animal, the creation of a domestic curio or trophy, equally important are the scientific reasons behind taxidermy, particularly during the Victorian era. Naturalism as a movement claimed to operate along scientific lines, explaining why Chekhov makes this taxidermic bird the centrepiece of the play, referencing this increasingly common way of preserving species for scientific examination by killing and displaying them. Taxidermy is, of course, a death-bringing art or science, a failed reanimation, providing knowledge by stilling the animate being it proposes to understand, perhaps even to preserve.

In *The Seagull*, the dead bird makes a brief appearance in stuffed form at the end of the play, when Shamrayev, the steward of the estate, shows it to the writer Trigorin:

SHAMRAYEV. This is the thing I was telling you about earlier ... (*Gets the stuffed seagull out of the cupboard.*) You asked me to have it done.

TRIGORIN (*looks at the seagull*). No recollection! (*After a moment's thought.*) No recollection!

A shot, off right. Everyone jumps. (Chekhov, 1993a: 124)

The bird has been forgotten, displaced, buried in or by the text: it is a lost object. Trigorin looks at it but cannot either recognise or remember it. Importantly, the text specifies that neither looking at it nor reflecting on its existence ('*[a]fter a moment's thought*') helps him remember it. He symbolically erases the object that is central to the events of the play and its metaphorical economy. The writer Trigorin here, a proxy for Chekhov (as indeed all the play's characters are proxies for parts of Chekhov's thinking, aesthetic philosophy and sensibility), cannot remember the dead bird, the living creature, the metaphor, the symbol or the young girl who occasioned his desire and gave him the idea for his short story. Symbolisation and mummification make the seagull an ungrievable object. Art tries to preserve it but creates an inanimate museum piece which is lost and overlooked.

What is the use of this dead bird in Chekhov's play? It is a melancholy, superfluous and abject object. The act of theory, embodied by the forgotten stuffed bird in the play, finds itself without a place or role within the work. Operating as a powerful theoretical trope, the dead taxidermic seagull tells us something about realism's failure to embody grief, loss and mourning, but the play itself, as if subsuming its own auto-critique in order to remain animate, loses the bird so that the play can remain 'living'. In the end, the seagull's movements through degrees of symbolicity in the play culminate in a critique that magically vanishes, a source of amnesia for the characters, not even a remnant or *memento mori*. The very eponymous bird of the title, the most powerful symbol in Chekhov's theatre, ends up stored in a cupboard, lost, brought out and not remembered.

Like the seagull, Chekhov's play consciously operates as both the failed art object and the possibility of its reanimation. Its theorisation and critique of theatre and literature provide instructions for what to avoid: 'recitation', as well as including ingredients that are needed for a play to work: 'living characters' and 'love' (reminding us, as Maggie O'Farrell (2021) notes, that grief is a form of love). It is Nina who makes these statements about Konstantin's failed experimental play in Act 1: 'It doesn't have much action, your play – it's just a kind of recitation. And I think a play absolutely has to have love in it' (Chekhov, 1993a: 66). The play provides a critique of the grand themes of tragedy by situating Nina's family tragedy offstage (a lost lover, a dead child) and it shows us that theatre might be most compelling when it jettisons dramatic framings and instead shows us life happening in front of us. This might involve moving away from reduplicatory realism to focus instead on affect, the fleeting and fragmentary, emotions hinted or gestured at, rather than the photographic copy of the real.

The Seagull makes its critique of the failure of theatre more explicit in the melancholy object of the ruined theatre presented to us in Act 4. Medvedenko, pragmatic and prosaic schoolteacher that he is, is almost inspired to poetry as he describes Konstantin's ruined stage in the grounds of the estate:

> MEDVEDENKO. The garden's quite dark. They should tell someone to knock down that theatre. It's as hideous as bare bones, and the curtain slaps in the wind. When I was going past yesterday evening I could have sworn there was someone crying in there. (Chekhov, 1993a: 106)

By incorporating symbolic objects that function as a critique of its own failed aesthetics and representational strategies, Chekhov's play opens up fascinating perspectives on metatheatre and self-reflexivity in performance. Does art survive the incorporation of its own critique, or does it simply lose track of or abandon those mummified static nodes of failed representation in the text?

Reanimation, translation, performability

Even a play about literature and theatre, about the act of writing, has to think about performability, about what works onstage for live audiences. One of Chekhov's recent translators, playwright Martin Crimp, has explained the tension between performability and language: 'all writers have very, very strong emotional connections to the word, to any word, to every word that they select' (Royal Court, 2008). He notes that when he was much younger, he was 'obsessed by language, *only* by the words' (my italics). He goes on to explain how this attitude gradually changed: 'when you start out as a writer, of plays, you don't often look; you're too busy listening, you don't look: now I think I'm someone who listens *and* looks' (Royal Court, 2008; my italics). This act of looking as well as listening is central to the way thinking about the practicalities of performance reanimates the 'literary' or word-centred theatre text.

In his book *Theatre and the Visual*, Dominic Johnson contextualises this obsession with words when he notes how, often, 'the privileged status of written texts – and the attendant experience of listening to words – functions at the expense of a theory of visual perception in theatre' (Johnson, 2012: 3). Crimp responds to this not simply by acknowledging his own 'emotional connection' with words, thereby relativising it, but also by recognising that words in plays are meant to be seen, voiced, pitched and spaced. As a writer, he is traversed by two contradictory impulses: to see the text as language and in verbal terms, linguistically self-referential as fictional and poetic texts are, and simultaneously as referring outside itself to its future embodiment as live theatre, where the material aspects of performance change the status of words entirely from conceptual, cognitive and written, reanimating them so that they become enacted, embodied and ephemeral.

One example of Crimp's attention to the visual in his 2006 translation of the play (commissioned for Katie Mitchell's National Theatre production) occurs at the end of Act 2. The young writer Konstantin has just shot the seagull and lays it at Nina's feet. Konstantin exits when he sees his older rival Trigorin, 'entering like Hamlet, even down to the book' (Chekhov, 1993a: 86). Trigorin proceeds to have a long exchange with Nina about his painful obsession with writing. In Frayn's translation, Trigorin, implausibly, only notices the dead seagull towards the end of the act, after he has been talking to Nina for several minutes, and it prompts him to jot down in a book:

> An idea for a short story. A girl like you, living beside a lake since she was a child. She loves the lake the way a seagull might – she's as happy and free as a seagull. But one day by chance a man comes

along and sees her. And quite idly he destroys her, like this seagull. (Chekhov, 1993a: 91)

Chekhov places Trigorin's observation of the seagull at the end of the act to create a moment of literary, theatrical and critical convergence, showing how Trigorin will 'endeavour to recast Nina as a character in fiction' (Senelick, 1985: 86). Crimp, operating under the visual logic of live theatre, rather than literary concerns about the ethics of writing, has Trigorin noticing the dead seagull as soon as he enters. That is to say, the practical requirements of staging take priority over literary or philosophical ideas about fiction and ethics.

Crimp is producing a text for performance, not simply one to be read. Echoing Crimp's words about the visual dimension of theatre, Mitchell has said that for a director, '[l]earning to hold the whole picture of what the audience will see in your head as you read the text is critical' (Mitchell, 2009: 4). Frayn's translation, following Chekhov, positions the moment of fictional genesis at the end of the act, creating a set of contradictory aesthetic tensions around beginnings and endings. For Crimp, the seagull is visible as soon as Trigorin enters. The scene no longer ends on the emergence of a writing idea evoking questions of ethics and aesthetics because for Crimp the play is no longer being conceptualised as a literary text.

Showing, telling and staging the uses of literature

It is not simply that thinking visually, the act of looking, reanimates the 'literary' play for performance. Something is gained by prioritising performability, but something can also be lost, in particular the compelling *mise en abîme*, the self-referentiality, the layering of levels of meaning that a literary mode allows in a play. The transition from one medium to the other, requiring translators or directors to make decisions about the role of literary textuality onstage, further reanimates the work by highlighting its dual status: as text to be read and script to be embodied in live performance.

At a key point in his version of the play, Crimp prioritises theatrical clarity over literary criticism by removing any reference to a medallion Nina gives Trigorin near the end of Act 3. In his programme essay for the 2006 Mitchell/Crimp production, Dan

Rebellato notes how writing is often under attack in Naturalist theatre, singling out the importance of Nina's medallion:

> These plays are terrified by writing. For Trigorin, writing is parasitic on life; a short inscription on a medallion leads ultimately to Nina's and Konstantin's downfall; letters going astray threaten ruin in *The Father* and *A Doll's House*; writing is a sign of wasted life in Georg Tesman's empty scholarship and the uncut pages of Hjalmar Ekdal's books. Konstantin and Hedda Gabler destroy writing. (Rebellato, 2006: np)

At first, the medallion seems to be a simple love token and Nina tells Trigorin, 'I've had your initials engraved on it … and on this side the title of your book, *Days and Nights*' (Chekhov, 1993a: 93). It's a conventional enough leaving gift, until Trigorin looks at it and sees that it contains a specific page and line reference to his book. Mitchell herself notes the significance of the medallion in *The Director's Craft*, pointing out that 'Chekhov was given an inscribed medallion by an actress' (Mitchell, 2009: 46). So the decision by Crimp and Mitchell to omit it from the text and production is strange. Instead of the medallion, Crimp's version has Nina giving Trigorin a copy of his actual book, which she wants him to write in. The scene is framed recognisably as an author's book signing. In Frayn's translation, Nina's engraving on the medallion reads: 'if ever you have need of my life, then come and take it' (Chekhov, 1993a: 100). In this sense, the medallion does indeed have 'thematic centrality and referential polyvalence' (Golomb, 2000: 697) in the play, simultaneously representing Nina's status as a passionate reader or critic (she has read Trigorin's work and applied a line from it to her own life) and as the ego-less object of fiction (she is willing to be used for literary purposes). The engraving activates theoretical ideas about the purposes of literature, about selective reading practices, about how texts are reinscribed and mobilised. Given that the engraved line is actually from one of Chekhov's own short stories, the medallion also merges the fictional and the real in complex ways.

In Crimp's version, most of the above intertextual resonances are lost:

> NINA. Listen … You're leaving and I may never see you again … (*Produces a book.*) It's one of yours – *When Day Turns to Night* – I want you to write in it for me.

> TRIGORIN. Of course. I'd love to. What shall I put?
> NINA. (*Stopping him opening the book*) Not now please. Later. When you've looked in it.
> TRIGORIN. Oh? (*Slight pause.*) Alright. Later then. Think of me sometimes.
>
>> ... (*He starts to leaf through the book.*) ... *Trigorin has stopped at a particular page of the book, and is engrossed by it.* (Chekhov, 2006: 34–5)

Crimp gives priority to the physical gesture rather than the inscription and its multiple intertextual displacements. The visual, corporeal elements of performance supersede the textual labyrinth that Frayn's version leads us into. Instead of asking us to think about textual mobility and resignification, Crimp focuses more directly on the moment of symbolic exchange between Nina and Trigorin, where the challenge of conveying how lines from literature are eroticised or reframed is given over to the actors rather than to the engraved words on the medallion.

Overall, Crimp and Mitchell are trying to find new ways to perform Chekhov's ideas about the role of writing and literature that balance the temporal and visual limitations on live theatre against the possibility of over-long speeches and moments that resonate when reading the text, but that are lost or insignificant in performance. The medallion is too small, the inscribed line is too coded. A theoretically charged gift that opens up new perspectives on the role of literature becomes in performance an over-detailed, inscrutable moment of distraction from the main events that determine the characters' relationships.

Mitchell's 2006 production of *The Seagull*, using Crimp's translation, refused to create the taxidermic realism the play warns against, while at the same time offering a reanimation of the text for twenty-first-century audiences. It was heavily criticised, with Michael Billington suggesting that 'mise en scène [was] being substituted for meaning' (Billington, 2006). The production emphasised the role of the senses, the visual and the audible, in performance. It disrupted transmission, vibrated with tension, rather than being a cold museum-like translation onto the stage of a classic theatre text. This vibrational quality interfered with the clarity of words, no longer conceptualising the text as a kind of disembodied abstraction, but as material to be vocalised and mediated by bodies, voices, technologies and acoustics. Building on Crimp's ideas of performability and the role of the visual, the production reanimated the text by shifting it from something read and imagined to something viewed, heard and felt, taking place in time and space rather than in the cerebral realm of literary reading.

The production was at times shadowy, inaudible and hard to follow. Scenes blurred into one another, endings overlapping, and action was at times displaced to corners of the stage rather than occupying the centre. The text was being simultaneously animated and obstructed, filtered through the material medium of bodies, objects and technologies. Simon Stephens' words on *The Cherry Orchard* resonate here: 'Playwriting, for me, is not a literary or a linguistic pursuit and plays are not literary artefacts. I think of them instead as being starting points for a night in the theatre' (Stephens, 2014).

Mitchell tells us in her guide to theatre directing, *The Director's Craft*, which uses *The Seagull* as its main case study, that the production was based on meticulous research, a quest for precision and detailed characterisation, yet in practice it consistently disrupted its framing realism, shrouding the stage in penumbral darkness, rendering dialogue indistinct or technologically mediated. As Billington points out, Konstantin's play, 'with Nina whispering her words into a microphone, [was] virtually inaudible' (Billington, 2006). Key set pieces were hurried along by the rushed dynamics of the performance, as if not only the historical period depicted onstage, but any certainty about how to stage and perform Chekhov, were sliding into doubt. Mitchell's production was unfixed and unstable, pushing towards dissolution. It ended up as a kind of productive failure, refusing to illustrate the text realistically, embodying instead scepticism about what to substitute for museum-like realism.

Blotting your copy

Mitchell's production contravened any clear transmission of Crimp's text, bringing a kind of messy, blotched quality to the play. The stage looked dilapidated and decayed, embodying tension and anxiety. Susannah Clapp said it felt like 'the stage is having a nervous breakdown': 'Like the characters, you're never entirely able to relax, to feel at home. Mitchell is the high priestess of fluttering neurosis and ill-suppressed hysteria, which she habitually loves to suggest through restless body language' (Clapp, 2006). The characters in this world were strung out, tired, caught in habits of thinking and loving that exhausted them. Snatched moments of intimacy were overheard by, rather than delivered to, the audience as dialogue trailed off or scenes bled into one another.

Mitchell both captured Chekhov's play's own multi-faceted internal contradictions and refused to resolve those into an illustrative realism. While Crimp's version may have streamlined the original, Mitchell's direction frayed the edges, blurred the focus, troubled any clarity of perception and representation. What was breaking down was the primacy of the text in performance and the idea that language makes sense in theatre principally in terms of its content, that is, that meaning, to refer back to Billington's confusing criticism, is separable from mise-en-scene. Not only did Mitchell's production reinforce the point that language is subject to interference in live theatre (the microphone moment), but it also foregrounded the difficulty of transmission, where words are lost, shadows abound, and hybrid stylistic modes and wilful anachronisms are suggestive of resistance to single or definitive directorial methods. Returning to Chekhov's text again, we see how he licences such a performed critique with characters like Nina who say 'your play is so difficult to do' (Chekhov, 1993a: 66) or complain, Nina again, that they don't understand the meaning of symbols (Chekhov, 1993a: 85), or, indeed, when one of the most powerful visual metaphors in the text is a theatre in ruins.

Three Sisters, reanimating realism

Three Sisters can be said to have assimilated *The Seagull*'s critiques of mimetic realism. It has fulfilled Konstantin's wish when he says that '[w]hat we need are new artistic forms' (Chekhov 1993a: 63), and developed ways to address the problems of representation *The Seagull* stages. *Three Sisters* features older sister Olga, who is a schoolteacher in her late twenties, middle sister Masha, a trained pianist, and youngest sister Irina, who will work in a post office and then qualify as a teacher. The play takes place over about four years (see Turner, 1986: 64–5), charting the sisters' growing frustration, their thwarted desire to return to Moscow and the fluctuating rhythms of their lives, especially in relation to love, work and boredom.

In *Three Sisters*, the text operates more compositionally than it does in *The Seagull*, like a score in which different elements are choreographed to capture rhythms and patterns. As J. L. Styan suggests, '[i]n lieu of a "plot", Chekhov substitutes a pattern; for a focus, he offers a family, even a community, no longer a central character to whom things happen' (Styan, 2008: 150). For Chekhov, embarking on *Three Sisters* felt like entering a textual labyrinth: 'I'm not writing a play but some kind of maze. Lots of characters – it may be that I shall lose my way and give up writing' (Chekhov, 14 August 1900, in Loehlin, 2012: 136). One of the most disorienting parts of this maze is the redefinition of drama so it focuses not on the event but on the 'non-event'. *Three Sisters* flows with micro-events that shift the play as a form away from structured plotting to create a sense of impressionistic contingency instead. As James Loehlin suggests:

> The randomness of [the] dialogue creates the texture of lived reality, where much of social life consists of incomplete conversations, overheard phrases, and half-understood smalltalk. Yet these interactions reveal a complex network of relations among the characters and hint at simmering resentments and desires. (Loehlin, 2012: 138)

The shift from realism to impressionism is a keynote in Krasner's characterisation of the play:

> What we have is what Clement Greenberg describes in Impressionistic painting as 'the "decentralized," "polyphonic," all-over picture which, with a surface knit together of a multiplicity of identical or similar elements, repeats itself without strong variation from one end of the canvas to the other and dispenses, apparently, with beginning, middle, and ending'. (Krasner, 2012: 117)

A close examination of the opening scene of *Three Sisters* demonstrates how Chekhov reanimates the realism critiqued in *The Seagull*. As Loehlin notes, '[t]he play's distinguishing characteristics, its mixture of surface realism, thematic depth, and an impressionistic interplay of words and images, are evident in the opening scene' (Loehlin, 2012: 136). It is not that *Three Sisters* rejects realist techniques, but that these merge kaleidoscopically with motifs, monologues, tableaux, shifts in perspective and polyphonic forms of textuality.

The two-year gap between Acts 3 and 4 of *The Seagull* finds a parallel in Olga's opening words of the play: 'It's exactly a year since Father died' (Chekhov, 1993b: 193). In *Three Sisters*, the time rupture occurs before the play starts, and we are caught in the backdraft of memory, hence the sense of melancholy as the play begins. Olga's ensuing monologue shifts between the past and present, expressing elegiac memories of grief. Words are only one part of this play's aural landscape as offstage voices, whistling and other noises, sounds and music mingle; pauses and silences, laughter, the sounds of nature are all quickly established as expressive systems within the world of the play before the famous refrain is uttered for the first time: 'To go to Moscow ... Yes, to Moscow' (Chekhov, 1993b: 193–4).

In fewer than two pages, Olga's words oscillate between now and then, a year ago, and eleven years ago, when her father left Moscow with his daughters. We are in a blizzard of temporalities, lived, remembered and imagined, a hazy insubstantiality evoked by mentioning weather systems of snow, rain and sleet. As Sarah Wyman says: 'Aside from clocks and season migrations, time functions thematically in additional, abstracted ways' (Wyman, 2017: 196). Olga conjures up a world saturated by time, contrasting with the hurried, 'theatrical' time occasioned by the bustle around Konstantin's avant-garde play at the start of *The Seagull*. *Three Sisters* opens instead with a symphonic elegy on time and memory.

This shift from linear to multi-directional time is a key element of *Three Sisters*. As William Babula says, the play conveys 'an intense consciousness that time is swiftly passing by. It is a feeling shared by the characters on the stage and the audience in their seats' (Babula, 1975: 365). More than this, time, memory and the traces of the past resonate through the present, as Babula notes: 'the play is full of verbal reminders of the passage of time' (Babula, 1975: 365). It is not merely that time is passing, but that it will not stop impinging on the characters' lives, especially via the memory of their father. That grief is displaced onto the sisters' complex metaphorical grief for the living versions of themselves that will not exist because they will never go to Moscow. Olga's opening speech conveys different aesthetic expectations to the metatheatrical opening of *The Seagull*, which prepares us for a play that will critique theatre and literature. In contrast, Olga interweaves the quotidian and the impressionistic so that 'vestiges of plot dissolve and recombine' (Wyman, 2017: 194). This combinatory technique changes photographic realism into a fragmentary, fluid text of shifting flows and rhythms. The paradigm shift is enormous, despite the surface resemblance between the two texts.

A number of the techniques used in *The Seagull* are extended in *Three Sisters*. Though there are moments of interruption in *The Seagull*, this is much more prevalent from the start in *Three Sisters*. Chekhov highlights this humorously in Act 1 when Olga is reminiscing about her father and Moscow, expressing her upbeat mood: 'I woke up this morning, I saw the light flooding in, I saw the spring, and I felt such a great surge of joy' (Chekhov, 1993b: 194). The next lines occur between two characters engaged in their own separate discussion:

CHEBUTYKIN. Stuff and nonsense, sir!
TUSENBACH. Utter rubbish, of course. (Chekhov, 1993b: 194)

These lines serve several functions at once. They interact with Olga's nostalgic speech to signal the play's polyphony. Voices overlap, originating from different points in space. At the same time, they act as an ironic commentary on Olga's words, to criticise or deflate their elevated and possibly sentimental tone. They show us the contingency of meaning since two separate sites of dialogue are linked here to create a new accidental conjunction unperceived by any of the characters. A third function is to evoke the metatheatrical, drawing attention to the compositional strategy of the playwright. Overall, in this exchange, meaning is rendered provisional, the relationship between the two dialogues a possibility. It exemplifies how *Three Sisters* unfixes and mobilises language to create potential resonances, rather than adopting an aesthetics of precise emulation or fixed reproduction of the real.

It is notable in the opening scene how much the dialogue is counterpointed with such disruptions, unlike standard realist dialogue of question and answer, statement and reply, and turn-taking.

This new acoustic polyphony marks both the death of the stylised narratives of existing realism and tells us that this new play will foreground the poetic, the multi-temporal and impressionistic, creating meaning through patterns and potential intersections rather than the parcelled-out structures of plot-driven teleological realism.

Several further elements play a role in reconfiguring realism in *Three Sisters*. The first is the role of quotations. Cynthia Marsh suggests that:

> In scripted theatrical performance, a quotation is at least doubly performed, as it were. The actress performs the character that performs the quotation. There are other shadings present here: the human being becomes the actress who performs the character who performs the quotation; or even more complex: the human being becomes the actress who performs the character who may be performing a particular persona who performs the quotation. (Marsh, 2006: 452)

For Marsh, quotations amplify the role of performance, self-consciously alluding to textual borrowings or intertextual networks. *The Seagull* uses words from *Hamlet* when Arkadina and Konstantin quote an exchange between Gertrude and Hamlet around sexual jealousy. The quotation illustrates their own relationship in the play, since Arkadina's lover Trigorin, a successful young writer, is an obvious rival, and source of sexual and literary envy, for Konstantin. In contrast, the most prominent quotation in *Three Sisters* is Masha's recurring poetic lines, 'On a far sea shore an oak tree grows …', which appear at several points throughout the play to express an unconscious thought or memory. Masha first uses it in Act 1:

> On a far sea shore an oak tree grows
> And from it hangs a golden chain;
> A talking cat forever goes
> Around that chain and round again. (Chekhov, 1993b: 198)

As Styan points out, these are:

> evocative and haunting childhood lines from Pushkin's mock-heroic romance *Ruslan and Lyudmila* (1820). These [Masha] will repeat like a theme in music from time to time. They tell us of her varying states of mind by the tone of voice she uses and the almost imperceptible humming that goes with them. (Styan, 2008: 167)

The quotation is like an ear-worm taking Masha back to childhood, and it repeats itself, a connective skein across the text, charting emotional undercurrents or unexpressed thoughts. Language's indicative or gestural quality is foregrounded in these incomplete iterations, its fragmentation, even its trace, detectable in the form of Masha's sub-vocalised humming.

In addition to the polyphonic soundscape discussed earlier, Chekhov gives his characters linguistic tics and idiosyncracies that show us language's different functions, and the elastic way in which it can be used to communicate. Solyony mocks the philosophising of Tusenbach with the phrase 'Cheep cheep cheep' (Chekhov, 1993b: 204–5), as if Tusenbach's words are so much noise. Elsewhere, instead of meaningful phrases, Chekhov has the medical officer Chebutykin speak or sing the non-words 'Ta-ra-ra boom-de-ay/Ta-ra-ra boom-de-ay...' (Chekhov, 1993b: 262). This opening of a spectrum of expressive functions pluralises language and attunes us to the whole field of linguistic communication, the fragmented, incomplete or inexpressible, the sense that words can be a substitute for, rather than a carrier of, meaning. Here, sounds, sonority, rhythm and volume give the play its atmospheric tonality, able to capture impulses, sensations and pangs of grief, thwarted desire and impossible love, through indirection or other minimal linguistic means. Erika Fischer-Lichte points out Chekhov's attitude to language when she notes:

> Chekhov was filled with a deep scepticism about language ... Chekhov also expressed himself thus [in a 1902 letter]: 'Above all, speech, as beautiful and deep as it may be, only has an effect on the indifferent, and often it cannot satisfy those who are happy or unhappy: that is why the highest form of expression of happiness or unhappiness is mostly silence: those who are in love understand each other better when they are silent ...'. (Fischer-Lichte, 2002: 261)

It is noticeable how many pauses there are in *Three Sisters* too.

The most heart-rending example of non-verbal communication in *Three Sisters* occurs between Vershinin, the battery commander with a wife and two daughters, and middle sister Masha, married to the stolid schoolteacher Kulygin. Vershinin and Masha are in love with one another. When they are alone, Vershinin is effusive: note in the following sequence that Masha's mood is tinged by the memory of grief, and that she is evasive, focusing on the light and space, whereas Vershinin expresses his desire through repetition and hyperbole:

> MASHA. What a noise the stove's making. The wind was moaning in the chimney just before Father died. That same sound exactly.
> VERSHININ. Are you superstitious?
> MASHA. Yes.
> VERSHININ. Strange. *(Kisses her hand.)* You magnificent, magical woman. Magnificent, magical. It's dark in here, but I can see the shining in your eyes.
> MASHA. *(Sits on another chair)* There's more light here.
> VERSHININ. I'm in love, I'm in love, I'm in love … In love with your eyes, with the way you move. I dream about it … Magnificent, magical woman! (Chekhov, 1993b: 222–3)

In Act 3, Masha declares to her sisters her love for Vershinin, but just preceding this Chekhov has them communicate with each other using the notes from music, an exchange reprised with variations several times later:

> VERSHININ. Oh God, but I want to live! *(Begins to hum Prince Gremin's aria from 'Eugene Onegin', Act III, Scene I – 'To love must young and old surrender'.)*
> MASHA. Trum-tum-tum…
> VERSHININ. Tum-tum…
> MASHA. Tra-ra-ra?
> VERSHININ. Tra-ta-ta. *(Laughs.)* (Chekhov, 1993b: 250)

At this point, Chekhov is giving the characters quotations again as proxies for their own expressions of emotion, but in this case words give way to notes of music, and the acme of the two characters' intimacy and desire is not conveyed by language, but by mutually remembering a musical sequence. Like a motif, the verbalised notes return later in Act 3. These powerful motifs of latent desire once again create an 'unfixing' effect on language in the play, putting the words of the text in motion, vibrating in a way later captured by the sound of the broken cello string of *The Cherry Orchard*. The penultimate speech of the play will have Chebutykin *'singing quietly'* to himself 'Ta-ra…ra…boom-de-ay…Ta-ra-ra boom-de-ay' (Chekhov,

1993b: 282) as words dissolve into phonic traces and vanish as the play concludes.

In *Three Sisters*, words are compositional tools among others. The term 'Moscow' becomes a point of cohesion projected forward to give shape to the errant text. 'Moscow' tenses the strings, making taut the loose connections, functioning as a nodal or pivotal point for the lines rippling out of the text. Likewise, the play's ending, its tableau where '*[t]he three sisters stand huddled against each other*' (Chekhov, 1993b: 281), has the characters no longer content to keep to their realist frames, but instead becoming a composite image, a polyphonic icon-text, a visual version of a musical chord, a sculpture where fingers and limbs are interchangeable, a schematic of feminine bodies.

Furthermore, *The Seagull* and *Three Sisters* offer us different tropes for their own form. *The Seagull* gives us a taxidermic object to signal redundant hyper-realism and satirise art that reproduces a dead copy of the real, while *Three Sisters* suggests a very different figuration of birds in flight as a metaphor for its new, revitalised form:

> TUSENBACH. The birds that fly south in the autumn – the cranes, for example – on and on they fly, and whatever lofty or petty thoughts they have fermenting inside their heads, on they will continue to fly. On and forever on, whatever philosophers they may have among them. (Chekhov, 1993b: 227)

The birds at large in *Three Sisters* do not have a clear explanation; we cannot know their thoughts; they operate independently of human consciousness and aesthetic regulation. There is something autonomous about them, and the mere evocation of them is beautiful. They resist symbolisation, being mobile and transitory instead. Chekhov has progressed to a new aesthetics of the quotidian, a poetics of perception, interweaving the significant and the aleatory, finding a place for flow and interruption within the tightly organised form of the text.

Replacing the theatre in ruins of *The Seagull*, Krasner picks up on the use of the photograph as self-reflexive metaphor in *Three Sisters*. While photographic realism might be the very mode of aesthetics rejected in *The Seagull*, *Three Sisters* employs the photographic as a de-realising trope, interrupting linear realism with a tableauesque stilling of the action and a compression of time. As Krasner says:

> The characters in The Three Sisters [sic] exist in stasis, as if they are posing for a photograph. The first act of The Three Sisters, in fact, appears to be constructed like a photograph. At the end of the first act a photographer takes a family portrait with the invited guests. The temporal progression of the first act is the process of a photograph that is moving into focus, but also, in Roland Barthes' words, moving towards the 'imperious signs' of 'future death'. (Krasner, 2012: 128)

The photograph at the end of Act 1 is cognate with Konstantin's avant-garde theatre set from Acts 1 and 4 of *The Seagull*, but it has gone through a metamorphosis. The derelict theatre, like the stuffed bird, is a purposely crude symbol. In contrast, note the multi-focal quality of the following sequence:

FEDOTIK.	Hold on a moment! (*Takes a photograph.*) One! Just half a moment more … (*Takes another photograph.*) Two! Now we're all set!
	They take the basket and go into the main room, where they are given a noisy reception.
RODE (*loudly, to* IRINA):	The best wishes to you, all the very best! Enchanting weather, simply magnificent. I've been out walking all morning with some of the boys from the school. I take them for gymnastics. If I have my way, the entire high school will be for the high jump!
FEDOTIK (*to* IRINA):	You can move, it's all right! (*Taking a photograph.*) You're looking very pretty today. (*Takes a top out of his pocket.*) Oh, and I've got a top for you … It makes the most amazing sound …
IRINA.	Oh, how lovely!
MASHA.	On a far seashore an oak tree grows,

    And from it hangs a golden chain …
    And from it hangs a golden chain … (*Pathetically*)

What am I saying that for? I've had those lines on my brain all day … (Chekhov, 1993b: 214–5)

The photograph here is a point of convergence in the play, calling on the characters to pose. It picks up on the empty picture frame that Irina's brother Andrey has given her for her nameday earlier in Act 1, and anticipates the quick valedictory photograph that Fedotik will take in Act 4 as the army are leaving town. The Act 1 photograph stabilises the action into a tableau that anticipates the more complex tableau-merging at the end of the play as the three sisters dissolve into a painterly image of intertwinement, aesthetic figuration, and memory-body. This photographic moment decorporealises the human bodies gathered in the present time and space of realism, overlaying the scene with an elegiac trace of the event-as-already-captured and consigned to photographic memorialisation. The taking of the photograph foregrounds the way technologies of the visual mediate our memories of the past, perhaps even replacing them. The photograph acts like an optical reordering of the text's linear sequentiality, jamming time, ripping a second out of the temporal flux.

In contrast to the excess melancholy of Konstantin's dilapidated theatre, this photograph is a quickly consumed visual moment, shimmering through the text rather than sitting on top of it. It is too ephemeral to be fixed, yet at the same time it leaves a memory-trace of the bodies as posed, composed and decomposed through the act of writing, undoing their coherence rather than delimiting it in the realist tradition. In the quotation, Fedotik gives Irina permission to operate outside realism's photographic stillness, 'You can move, it's all right!' (Chekhov, 1993b: 215), making us conscious of the artificiality of the act of recording – Irina has been trying not to move.

The end of the quotation gestures towards realism's undoing, if by realism we understand plot-driven, structured forms of time-ordered mimesis. The spinning top takes our attention away from the human characters and substitutes a child's toy, revolving, tipping and making a distracting noise, rather than offering complex philosophising, theorising or aesthetic analysis. The toy is a superfluous object, transporting Irina to the past, acting as a memory trigger, a time-travelling device that takes us spinning back into childhood emotions and impressions, once again doing what the play does throughout in weaving plural temporalities together almost symphonically.

The scene ends with Masha's repetition of the 'oak tree' quotation, now a repetition-within-a-repetition, a signifier of habit. The quotation generates self-reflection on Masha's part as she expresses her uncertainty about meaning, a lack of clarity about why she is singing or reciting these words. The words operate as a memory-text, interrupting the scene, creating space for the contingent, the inexplicable, the evocatory function of language, especially quotations, melodies or proverbs, which stand in for the emotion they are associated with. In this context, the words are no longer simply a quotation but also an act of self-quotation, surging up as emotions, memories and melodies resurface without fixed or deducible meaning, or whose meaning is not self-contained but relational, part of the multi-layered visual, verbal, aural and acoustic-spatial text around it.

Impressionism and the polyphonic in *Three Sisters* shift the play away from rigid realism to engage other modes in which the visual and the vocal operate compositionally. As Krasner explains about the opening of *Three Sisters*: 'Nothing comes into focus until the end of the act' (Krasner, 2012: 128). Like a camera with an adjustable lens, the loss of focus brings a kind of blurring that reorganises perception, abstracting the visual and in the process enlivening the other senses, especially the auditory.

Conclusion

In *The Seagull*, the dead object is turned into an abstraction, an absurd item, a theory for a failed aesthetic, and ends up hidden, superfluous and forgotten. Meanwhile, the actual death of a child, and a mother's likely grief, takes place between the acts, outside the play's representational economy. Thus, the play stages the difficulties of conceptualising new forms while also trying to compose them. In *Three Sisters*, symbols are mobile and transitory: birds in flight replace the densely coded body of the taxidermic seagull. The itinerary of the theatre stage from the site of miscued, avantgarde experiment to symbolist dereliction is replaced by the photographic scene which folds the transience of the moment into the fixed photographic image, incorporating this instantaneity as a metonymy for the work as a whole, consequently seen as ephemeral and contingent, a snapshot of the real that is immediately restored to vibrant motion.

Finding space for grief in *Three Sisters* moves the text away from the taxidermic, mimetic realism which *The Seagull* symbolically exposes as rigid and inadequate, killing its object, purporting to display it and capture its beauty, but in fact hiding it (away). In *Three Sisters*, grief pervades the play, complicating the sense of time, reconfiguring the treatment of memory, and operating in literal and metaphorical terms. By starting the play in the wake of death, *Three Sisters* creates a poetics of grief as memories surge up unexpectedly, or dissolve into fragments, the concrete and the solid ceding position to the half-remembered or forgotten. In this way, grief reanimates Chekhov's realist aesthetics by predicating a newly revived realism on absence, on the gaps and fissures in memory, and on the unpredictable mechanisms by which the dead are reanimated by the living as part of the grieving process.

Note

1 In Act 4, Konstantin tells Dr Dorn that Nina 'had a child. The child died' (Chekhov, 1993a: 112). This brevity is partly explained by the exchange between the characters just beforehand: 'DORN. I heard [Nina] was leading some strange sort of life. What's it all about?/ KONSTANTIN. It's a long story, Doctor./DORN. In a nutshell' (Chekhov, 1993a: 111).

5

Burying the living and the dead

That was part of the problem. Roots, or lack of them. We lived in a vacuum of secrecy and shame, airlocked and hermetic, a tiny little world apart from everyone and everything around us, estranged from ourselves, our parents alien, especially our father, always called daddy, whose Irish accent never made the journey from Ireland towards the Britain he'd been working in since the early 1950s.

We had to translate what my dad said to our schoolfriends, my brother doing bilingual translation for his school buddy, translating from English to English, much to our bemusement: how can it be that you cannot understand what this man is saying to you? YOU are the problem, he is speaking in lucid, direct, concrete terms, and all you hear is a rhythmical incomprehensibility punctuated by 'fecking' this and 'Jaysus' that. Bet you didn't even know 'Jaysus' died for your sins.

Because we occupied no space at all, no cultural space, we were interstitial, we belonged nowhere. The omerta about the past, about Ireland, distilled a kind of grief about exile that translated for us into endless diffuse shame and guilt and querulous non-belonging.

In this chapter, living characters are buried, the dead speak to us, while exhausted forms and dead avant-gardes are revivified by comedy, anarchy and excess. In *Krapp's Last Tape* and *The Walworth Farce*, theatre grapples with memory: the tape recorder in *Krapp's Last Tape* is a substitute for the volatility of memory, while the repeated farce replaces the memory of a crime with a pantomimical version of the real. Enda Walsh's reanimations of Beckett acknowledge the power of Beckett's legacy but act as an exposure and critique of some of its omissions. Walsh's work shunts Beckett's trapped characters into the contemporary postmodern world where racism, identity, gender and trauma all operate in unpredictable ways; where comic excess and the grotesque are found alongside the themes of loss, grief, and myths of national identity.

The chapter looks at coffins, burials, urns and trash cans, cartoon and grotesque deaths, and themes of stasis and hyperactivity to explore the burial of the living and the return of the dead. We go from the existential coffin of language and the metaphorical burials in Beckett's plays to the fake, pantomimic and cardboard theatrical coffin of Walsh's postmodernist metatheatre. The chapter first looks at the stalling of grief in Beckett's *Krapp's Last Tape*, a play about linguistic crisis and the failure of words to go on. It then explores the vivid stage metaphors exposing us to living death and burial alive in Beckett's subsequent plays, in particular *Happy Days*. Finally, we turn to Enda Walsh's *The Walworth Farce* as a postmodern reanimation of Beckett's themes, turning bleakness into farce, and Beckettian visual austerity into rehearsable chaos.

The end of the avant-garde

In 1999, Simon McBurney said: 'there is no such thing as an avant-garde anymore. It ended in the 1950's and 60's. Once you've arrived at Beckett's play "Breath," in which only one breath is heard, how far avant can you push the garde?' (McBurney, 1999). Written in the period just before 1969, and performed that year in New York and Glasgow, *Breath* is a work of theatrical minimalism, composed of two identical cries (the 'vagitus' or first cry of the newborn baby) and lighting synchronised with the inhaling and exhaling of breath. It also features a 'stage littered with miscellaneous rubbish' (Beckett, 1990: 371). The elements of the piece act like minor interruptions of silence and darkness, and the theatre is reduced, beyond the theatre in ruins at the end of Chekhov's *The Seagull*, to a pile of rubbish, superfluous, abject, toxic: theatre as waste or excess.

The issue McBurney raises is how post-avant-garde work can revive, or survive, techniques that have had a profound impact on the DNA of theatre, taking an experimental trajectory to its logical conclusion. From McBurney's perspective, Beckett's *Breath* forces writers and theatre artists to ask whether it is possible to reanimate theatre in the context of Beckett's late work whose most powerful symbols were a dark or shadowy stage, buried or mechanised bodies, and a voice stuttering semi-coherently in the void.

Beckett's 'black ball'

Beckett's third play, *Krapp's Last Tape* (1958), featuring an old man listening to self-created tape recordings from his past, is well known for its experiments with repetition, its deconstruction of character and its continual self-interruption. It is at the same time a text which revolves around a maternal death. This is a play about containment: the character Krapp is trapped by the light and darkness division of the stage space; his memories are contained within a tape recorder, and his grief is contained within a black rubber ball.

Krapp at one point is rewinding one of his old tapes to listen to his past reaction to his mother's death, an event from which he was physically and emotionally excluded. If the voice on the tape sounds inexpressive, its recorded reproduction by the machine signals one further remove from any affective connection with his mother's death and the grief one might expect him to feel. Playing the tape is not a way of remembering grief but of escaping it. Even syntax cannot unfold expressively, but instead is interrupted by the observation of a banal object: 'Mother at rest at last, the black ball' (Beckett, 1990: 220).

The voice on the tape is switched off, turned back on again, and continues:

> I was there when – [KRAPP *switches off, broods, switches on again.*] – the blind went down, one of those dirty brown roller affairs, throwing a ball for a little white dog as chance would have it. ... A small, old, black, hard, solid rubber ball. (Beckett, 1990: 220)

All of the speaker's inadequate grieving is translated onto the description of the ball, whose sequence of adjectives is extended, illogical, arhythmical, as if the unexpressed grief is wreaking havoc on the tacit harmonies of euphonic language, so that Krapp's 'mother-tongue' fluency is lost. The adjectives preceding 'ball' can only be said with focus and concentration, their plosives colliding against one another.

It is evident from different manuscript variants compiled by Dirk Van Hulle and Vincent Neyt for the Beckett Digital Manuscript Project that Beckett nuanced and refined the sequence of adjectives qualifying this ball of non-grief on numerous occasions. There are eight versions of the line that finally appears in the 1959 Faber version of the text in its ninth version as: 'A small, old, black, hard, solid rubber ball.' In earlier versions, Beckett had an 'old tennis ball', 'sodden', 'not punctured' or 'unpunctured', which becomes a 'small, old, black, solid rubber ball' in version 5 and in the typescript of version 6, the word 'hard' is added by hand after 'black', which becomes the published Faber version. In French, the typescript, *Lettres Modernes* and Minuit versions all use the translation by Beckett: 'Une petite balle de caoutchouc, vieille, noire, pleine, dure.' In the French version, the pile-up of adjectives is not quite as artificially extended, nor is there the collision of plosives or the sense of accumulative details found in the English version.

The ball is the opposite of an animate object: it is pure solid substance, rubber in a way that is both like and unlike the dead human body. In French, the sequence of four adjectives, with the word 'vieille' an irregular feminine, perhaps raises more awareness of the gendered link to the dead mother, while in English there is a kind of reduction to the neutral, to the state of object, to this inexplicable thing that only the dog understands and can use.[1] The 'black ball' is a form of evasion, and at the same time operates as an extreme focalisation of grief, whereby the absence of expression speaks more powerfully of the unarticulated emotion. The absurdity of this object becomes the focal point at the moment of (Krapp's recollection of) his mother's death, thus *a contrario* capturing the acuity of pain and loss. To notice the blind going down, its nondescript colour, its roller mechanism, at such a moment, in the absence and void of grief, testifies to a mind searching for stimuli in the post-mortem blankness.

The 'black ball' becomes a substitute for a chasm of grief, or rather holds the place for a grief not felt or not yet conceived; grief displaced, or in abeyance. It occupies the place where grief should be. The adjectival precision with which Krapp describes the ball operates meta-syntactically to communicate the shape of a loss. The ball might be understood as a small punctuation mark in the real, a black hole in language; after a chaotic disordering of adjectival sequence, it is all that remains of the emotion of grief.

With the black ball, Beckett's reanimation of the lost object, the mother not grieved for, is displaced onto the nondescript item. The ball's non-expressivity is central to its signifying function. It operates both as a small dense ball of matter and as a gap in language and the fabric of memory, not-held, not retained, simply marking a scar in the text, a tear in the spool. As an object, it is also banal, undoing its own metaphoricity, a meaningless 'thing' to be carrying the weight of such grief, or indeed of its absence. This deflection of metaphoricity finds its corollary in Krapp's own indifference to what happened to the ball: as Krapp says, 'I might have kept it' (Beckett, 1990: 220), the ambiguity of the phrase (potentially meaning 'it is possible that I kept it' or 'perhaps I should have kept it') signalling a featureless indifference or indecision. The ball is the nodal point of vectors of grief and *anhedonia* generated by the capacity of language to waste its efforts on this stupid object, powerful as an expression of the inadequacy of poetic figuration, its solid irresolvable ball of knotted redundancy.

Beckett's ball, then, is the arbitrary host of the scene of failed affect, reanimating all the more powerfully the omphalic knot of meaning that ends up being its own self-explanation, a kind of limit-object where words battle against the headwind of affectless observation, capturing through negation the powerful requirements to grieve in certain ways, to feel certain emotions, to feel love when one might only feel a void.

As the recorded voice of Krapp says near the end of this sequence, the dog takes the ball 'gently, gently' (Beckett, 1990: 220). The repetition of 'gently' signifies the intrusion of the speaking voice addressing the dog, the indication of a vocality, corporeality and liveness that have been deadened and nullified by time and the mechanical reproduction on the tape, bound up with the effects of grief as the words are directed to the dog but seem also to reflect back onto the speaker, as if he is telling himself how to respond to this complex emotion. 'Gently, gently' is the spectral presence of the voice (perhaps even of the maternal voice) and its tenderness at the moment of most acute loss.

Burying the living

Krapp's Last Tape was already restricting its central character to a confined space and challenging the expressive capacity of language. The tape recorder divorces language from consciousness and emotion, while the 'black ball' turns grief into an absurd, small object, or rather turns the banal object into a black hole of evasive, involuted affect.

This tendency for language to operate in the context of increasing restriction is a recurrent feature in Beckett's post-*Krapp* theatre. The plays written after *Krapp's Last Tape* regularly include restricted, semi-buried or incarcerated bodies. It is hard not to view Beckett's post-*Krapp* work as an engagement with living death and the terrors of the grave, as characters are buried or their bodies are disposed of or are disappearing so that only their voice remains, like an animate memory in the dark.

As we progress through Beckett's plays chronologically, characters follow a trajectory from minimal life to life on the brink of extinction. Vladimir and Estragon in *Waiting for Godot* (1952) play with the idea of suicide, but their quibbling pedantry and understated need for one another prevent them from enacting their plan until Estragon concludes 'Don't let's do anything. It's safer' (Beckett, 1990: 19). Hamm in *Endgame* (1957) is blind and starts and ends the play stationary in a wheelchair. Moving through the body of theatre work, characters become increasingly cloistered, confined and trapped: Nagg and Nell in *Endgame* are in ashbins; Winnie is buried up to her waist in Act 1 and then up to her neck in Act 2 of *Happy Days* (1961). The forms of burial become increasingly drastic as the body is subjected to more definitive immersion or erasure. In *Play* (1963), three characters are trapped in large urns so that only their heads are visible. Beckett's stage direction, '*the neck held fast in the urn's mouth*' (Beckett, 1990: 307), conveys an image of strangulation, decapitation and ingurgitation (by the urn) all at once. In *Not I* (1972), Mouth is detached from the body and isolated in black space, becoming an organ/orifice, losing specificity to become buccal, vaginal and anal simultaneously as it spits, pisses and shits out its neurotic fragments.

In later works, the body becomes derealised, ghost-like, almost post-mortem, with characters in *Footfalls* (1976), *Rockaby* (1980) and *Quad* (1982) moving in patterns or engaging in obsessive rituals of loss or grief; they are almost like flickering, traumatised memory-bodies, ghosting the stage, theatrically caught in a repeated combination of language, movement and oscillation. They even stop being characters, functioning instead as mere speakers of language. Bodies in motion seem designed to go through all the possible permutations in order to use up potential variations. Fulfilling an obligation to keep moving in the knowledge of impending annihilation, they are deferring the stillness that makes the final stage direction of *Waiting for Godot* so heart-stopping: '[*They do not move*]' (Beckett, 1990: 88).

Anna McMullan notes that 'Beckett's distorted and dismembered bodies have become part of the global cultural imaginary of the 21st century' (McMullan, 2010: 1). Nowhere is this more powerful than in *Happy Days* (1961), Beckett's sixth play, begun in August–October 1960 and completed in May 1961. Writing to Alan Schneider, who directed its first production in New York in 1961, Beckett said: 'It's a much more difficult job I've given you here than any so far – all poised on a razor-edge and no breathers anywhere' (Craig *et al.*, 2014: 421–2). The play revolves around a central character, Winnie, a woman in her fifties, who is trapped in a mound up to her waist in Act 1, for no explicable reason, and then from the start of Act 2 is buried up to her neck. She feels alone most of the time, despite the presence of her partner Willie buried behind her in a hole.

Describing a painting by Jack Yeats in 1937 – painting and music were crucial influences – Beckett speaks about its depiction of 'two irreducible singlenesses & the impassable immensity between [them]' (Fehsenfeld and Overbeek, 2009: xciv), an apt description of Winnie's experience in the play. We follow her as she is abruptly awoken in the morning by a loud ringing noise, evoking associations with prison cells or school bells rather than morning alarms. So it begins, almost like clockwork: Winnie's stream of words cataloguing the items in her bag as she removes them one by one, peering myopically at the printed words on her toothbrush, digressing into reflections on language and meaning, recalling half-forgotten quotations from her schooldays and shifting into memories of early sexual encounters or traumatic events from childhood, voiced out loud in the hope that 'something of this is being heard' (Beckett, 1990: 145).

As happens in *Waiting for Godot*, Act 2 contains minor changes which have a major impact. As Winnie's body is buried further, with only her head remaining visible, the sense of this being a metaphor for ageing and immobility becomes terrifyingly apparent. Winnie remains alive and sentient as her body is mysteriously encased in a kind of burial mound, encoffining her as she survives first via her daily minor routines with objects, and later on via the fragments of words and phrases, stub-ends of texts, half-remembered quotations and scraps of memory from her past.

McMullan argues that *Happy Days* 'draws attention to the limits of the visible, what is hidden, withheld, unseeable, or unreadable from the audience's perspective' (McMullan, 2010: 55). As Winnie's body disappears, her words become more elliptical. Winnie is waiting for reanimation, the moment when she can renew or author herself, when she can sing her song that signifies 'I', but that moment of self-expression is shrouded in anxiety. She constantly addresses herself in the third person, lamenting how 'words fail' (Beckett, 1990: 147). Typical of Beckett, Winnie moves between tenses, the present constantly sucked into the past, or projected forward in the future perfect. *Happy Days* is a play of failed reciprocity in which words find no auditor, leaving Winnie asking at the end: 'what's it mean? What's it meant to mean?' without the possibility of an answer (Beckett, 1990: 156).

Rhythms and repetitions, meanings and graves

The great achievement of Beckett's work is the suspension of the very question 'what does it mean?'. What is buried in Beckett's play along with Winnie is theatre's need to search for definitive meaning. In a letter written in October 1961, soon after he completed *Happy Days*, Beckett notes, 'I know creatures are supposed to have no secrets from their authors, but I'm afraid mine for me have little else' (Craig *et al.*, 2014: 436). Instead of trying to explain or interpret Winnie, Beckett wants us to listen – in a way that Willie never really does – to the rhythms, repetitions and interruptions of her dialogue, and to really see her, to observe her stasis and vulnerability, hence the immobilisation of her body. As early as 1930, talking about Proust, Beckett famously notes the challenge for the writer to find 'the expression that there is nothing to express, nothing with which to express, nothing from which to express, no power to express, no desire to express, together with the obligation to express' (Beckett, 1987: 103). Winnie's words do not express meaning but enact its convoluted, slow implosion; instead of articulating thoughts and ideas, they become disarticulated as Beckett's syntax registers the tensions and torsions of failing expression.

In the plays after *Happy Days*, the distortion of the body goes from physical to metaphorical: heads float, mouths utter words in darkness, voices echo through the texts incorporeally. A number of Beckett's later characters are presented to us as if they are buried alive, literally or figuratively. Those not trapped in ashbins, urns or mounds are caught within the limits of the text or the geometries of the stage space, never able to stop 'revolving it all', as May's mother in *Footfalls* says (Beckett, 1990: 400). They exist in twilight, in shadow, in intermediary, transitional, purgatorial spaces, both derealised and spectral. 'To revolve', with its ghostly merging of resolve and solve, also refers to the circularity of inconclusivity, the revolving door of memory, from which there is no escape until the end of the text or the exhaustion of the space.

In Beckett, characters are trapped by physical containers, but also by darkness, solitude and the limits of language. His work operates a kind of coffin-aesthetic: the linguistic system as a coffin, space as a casket, the body a fleshy sarcophagus, eating time, heavy with age, while language unspools mechanically and disjointedly. Consciousness animates the coffin-flesh, the 'cerceuil' of French, etymologically from 'sarcophagus' (literally 'flesh-eating'), echoing 'cercle' – circle – circulating memory and perception. The Beckett text is the coffin-space of language, the play, the stage and the body operating as *mises en abîme* of these confinements, proleptic of the grave, an idea most trenchantly expressed by Pozzo in *Waiting for Godot*: 'They give birth astride of a grave, the light gleams an instant, then it's night once more' (Beckett, 1990: 83).

Theatre after Beckett

Given the challenges of developing avant-garde theatre after Beckett, Walsh's adoption of Beckettian techniques and themes in conjunction with theatrical playfulness and exaggeration is all the more notable. Walsh's plays reanimate Beckettian tropes and images by drawing on excess, chaos and the grotesque as antidotes to Beckett's aesthetics of diminution and minimalism. Both playwrights deal with ideas of entrapment, confinement, repetition and rehearsal, depicting characters using up space and exhausting permutations. Both authors deal with trauma and guilt by exploring how the present is haunted by the past and endeavour to represent those traumatic events and memories in language that circles, hedges and gestures at meaning without ever being able to express it fully.

Similarly, both writers can be read as challenging theatre as medium and form. Beckett's work is subtractive, removing elements of theatre in order to explore alternative modes of expression such as linguistic patterning, verbal and physical repetition and deviation, or little events of syntactical disruption. Walsh tests theatre's limits through accumulation and acceleration, creating verbally rich texts of linguistic excess that expand and distort neat realist frameworks. Both playwrights push theatre to the brink of collapse, setting challenges for the actor which border on the unsustainable. Look, for example, at Billie Whitelaw's account of the frustrations of rehearsing *Happy Days* directed by Beckett (Knowlson, 1997: 658). Watching *The Walworth Farce* at the Edinburgh Festival in 2007, the sense that the whole wig-swapping, costume-changing play-within-a-play could break down any minute because of the actors' exhaustion or potential confusion as they switched between characters was never far away.

In plays like *The New Electric Ballroom* and *The Walworth Farce*, Walsh engages with Beckett's legacy by opening it up to messiness, chaos, a self-consciously amateurish aesthetics and linguistic over-production. Walsh turns the patterned rigour of plays like *Krapp's Last Tape*, *Play* and *Not I* into the playful, pantomimic and farcical tragi-comedy of his own work. In an interview with Michael Billington, Walsh says:

> Beckett's not a conscious influence ... but he taught us all two great things. One is that he helped free drama from any obligation to be sociological: the other is that he showed us the power of real time. (Billington, 2014)

Earlier in the same interview, however, Billington claims that Beckett's 'influence on Walsh is palpable' (Billington, 2014). Ideas of repetition, entrapment and circularity characterise both authors' work, with Walsh's plays reinjecting theatre's anarchy and provisionality into the ordered world of Beckett's texts. At the same time, Walsh's work also reflects on national and cultural identity, the 'sociological', dealing as it does with questions of race, gender, ideology, migration and collective trauma.

In a discussion of Walsh's *Ballyturk*, Michelle C. Paull notes that the play 'suggests human feeling is numbed and quashed *by surfeit not by absence* as in a Beckett play' (Paull, 2015: 184; my italics). This contrast between 'surfeit' and 'absence' is central to the distinction between Walsh and Beckett. The very excess of a play like *The Walworth Farce* is predicated on the idea of a Beckettian avant-garde at the point of exhaustion, against which subsequent theatre reacts with chaotic energy. Walsh's plays operate in opposition to Beckett's pursuit of austere formal rigour. In *The Walworth Farce*, Walsh raises issues of race, class, and nationalism. His reanimations of Beckett's oeuvre exploit Beckett's innovations and compositional strategies but create space for the 'sociological', the explicit political, social and cultural observations missing from Beckett's stripped-back works.

Walsh's reanimations

In *The New Electric Ballroom* (2004) and *The Walworth Farce* (2006), Walsh maps his status as a post-Beckett writer who is explicitly diasporic, thinking about migration, myths of nationhood and national identity. He asks important questions about Irish self-mythologising, both in terms of historical narratives and cultural representation. *The New Electric Ballroom* is reminiscent of Beckett in its staging of three main characters caught in a cycle of traumatic repetition. Whereas Beckett's oeuvre tends towards the vanishing of the body and language to create a space that is distilled into abstractions, Walsh's characters remain psychologically realistic as they engage in frenetic rehearsals of traumatic memory and adolescent sexuality, tinged with nostalgia and a strong sense of time and cultural location.

Walsh's work is evocative of the past and critical of its repressiveness. This conflict marks the writing of a number of Walsh's

Irish or Anglo-Irish contemporaries such as Marina Carr, Martin McDonagh and Conor McPherson, all of whom work through contradictions between tradition and modernity, between a mythical, romanticised view of Ireland and the harsher, more violent reality of the present. As Lionel Pilkington puts it:

> One major idea of Irish plays from the 1980s to the present is that Ireland has to choose between two modes of expression: between a bizarre, backward-looking and almost exclusively rural premodernity often portrayed as gothic grotesquery and an identity based on speed, sexual attractiveness and an amazing, acrobatic, ability to compromise and adjust. (Pilkington, 2010: 67)

The difference in Walsh's work is that the 'gothic grotesquery' and 'gratuitous violence' are cartoonish, consciously and self-reflexively non-mimetic; the opposite of the real, not an exaggeration of it. In *The New Electric Ballroom*, the intrusion of a rock star, an ersatz Irish version of Elvis Presley or Jerry Lee Lewis, disrupts the rural lives of the three sisters (note the echo of Chekhov) from an Irish coastal fishing village. Without the austerity of a Beckett text, *The New Electric Ballroom* brings colourful, chaotic images to the usual chiaroscuro of Beckett's palette. The play's absurdism is overintensified, discordantly vivid, its brash reds and pinks signalling the transition from a Beckettian monochrome.

The theatrical coffin

Walsh's *The Walworth Farce* is a play concerned with a death, a coffin and a burial. So far, so Beckettian. But *The Walworth Farce* is like Beckett's *Endgame* on speed, with a more comprehensive metatheatricality and greater emphasis on performance about to spin out of control. It recalls Joe Orton's work in plays like *Loot* (1964) and *What the Butler Saw* (1967), with sequences involving money hidden in a coffin and cross-dressing gender-bending.

The play revolves around a tyrannical Irish patriarch, Dinny, who forces his two grown-up sons to perform the same farcical version of a family narrative every day of their lives. It is set in the kitchen, living room and bedroom of a cramped fifteenth-floor council flat in a tower block on the Walworth Road in Southwark,

South London. Dinny and his sons, Blake and Sean, play younger versions of themselves in the farce, while also performing multiple different characters, for which the actors have to swap wigs, props and costumes with increasing speed. Their farce is an invented slapstick version of the violent crime committed by Dinny that led to them leaving Ireland when the boys were small. Whereas in *The New Electric Ballroom* we see several iterations by a different character of a traumatic event, in *The Walworth Farce*, the characters are trapped in the repeated farcical performance from the outset. As the play progresses, the structure starts to unravel and, as Walsh says, 'when that breaks down – that's when the play really begins to speak' (McMillan, 2007).

The play invests in anarchic comedy, with Dinny pretending to be a brain surgeon, featuring tall tales and shaggy-dog stories about flying animals and people setting fire to nuns. On the surface, the text seems to be all play-acting and pretence, like children's games with a manic edge, full of 'Irish eccentricities galore' (Nightingale, 2007). But when Dinny notices a mistake with one of the props for that day's performance, an error with the items of food that his son Sean has to buy every morning from the local Tesco (where he speaks to a young Black female cashier named Hayley, against his father's orders), the audience suddenly realises that the farce, as well as being highly comical, is also oppressive, tyrannical and controlling. Dinny stops the performance of the farce, ominously pointing out the problem: 'The story doesn't work if we don't have the facts' (Walsh, 2007: 13).

Given the obviously cartoonish nature of their rehearsed performance, we have to read this line's wider implications: that it is the fierce adherence to the details of this manufactured narrative, no matter how absurd, which allows Dinny to escape from the truth of his crime. Yet even this is too literal: the obsessive rehearsals are not simply a way of processing his crime psychologically, but instead are a grotesque version of the past, one with no correlation with the truth, whose very form is a comical and sceptical commentary on the desire for escapist narratives that mythologise and idealise home, nation and self.

A '*coffin-shaped cardboard box*' (Walsh, 2007: 5; italics in original) prominently occupies one of the junk-filled rooms in the flat. The cardboard box is both a prop in the metatheatrical performance the family is locked into, in which it stands in as a coffin, and also operates as a symbol of the comical death at the heart of the metatheatrical performance around which the re-enacted farce revolves. It is a fake coffin which contains not a corpse, not the dead maternal body, but a stash of money (in this case, fake money in the form of Monopoly banknotes). The cardboard box coffin in the play signifies a false demise, a theatrical, farcical death, the very possibility of genuine grief dispelled by the Monopoly money notes that scatter across the stage. As Tanya Dean says, the 'obviously fake coffin serves as a visual clue that this squalid council flat doubles as a performance site' (Dean, 2015: 120).

For Walsh, the coffin-aesthetic of Beckett's textual entrapment gives way to an amateurish interest in theatre's ad hoc, make-do provisionality, its non-serious masquerade and playful fabrications. As Dean says:

> Watching the characters interact with the cardboard coffin – a prop *qua* prop, a theatrical signifier for a real artefact – makes it clear that Dinny and his sons are engaged in some kind of bizarre performance, and destabilizes the audience's notions of what is 'real' onstage. (Dean, 2015: 121)

The cardboard coffin tells us Walsh is substituting a purposefully amateur version of the tropes of loss, grief, incarceration and entombment found in Beckett, reanimating Beckett's avant-garde, but with a fake coffin made of cardboard, not of language; it gives us instead a missing body, language spilling out of the coffin like notes and a missing gravity (this coffin will not weigh much if you have to be a pallbearer) – a missing seriousness, a text without a corpse. That missing weight of grief will be redirected to become a self-reflexive meditation on contemporary theatre as 'post-tragic', no longer capable of the certainties of tragedy, only able to communicate powerful emotion by showing us the gap between representation and its referent. In this framework, the pain of grief or migration is conveyed through the pathos of its representational failure.

In *The Walworth Farce*, the shabby scenographic aesthetics, the visual chaos of objects, props, furniture and junk, stage these very limitations, creating a provisional space which foregrounds a kind of half-finished quality that acts as a critique of former aesthetic and representational certainties. The aesthetics of the shabby inverts and de-solemnises events, inserting the anarchies of comedy into the ostensible space of familial and diasporic tragedy. The amateur aesthetics result from acknowledging the avant-garde's critique of the older super-genres (tragedy and comedy), while at the same time throwing theatre and its inadequate representations back together again after the Beckettian avant-garde has dismantled it. The genres of tragedy, farce, diasporic narrative and domestic crime drama all overlap, with searing monologues of Irish identity, migration and displacement sitting alongside high slapstick, pratfalls, and absurdist, surrealist, cartoonish and hyperbolical speeches.

In a 2007 interview, Walsh explains what attracted him to farce as a genre:

> In *The Walworth Farce* I decided to experiment with the idea of writing farce – because in a way it's a form that's all about structure. It's certainly not about full characterisation. It's more about mathematics and movements. (Walsh in McMillan, 2007)

In *The Walworth Farce*, Walsh takes his exploration a step further in a text haunted by Marx's famous words: 'Hegel observes somewhere that all great incidents and individuals of world history occur, as it were, twice. He forgot to add: the first time as tragedy, the second as farce' (Marx, 1907: 5). Structurally a farce, with speeded up repetitions and near-misses, identity confusion and comical misunderstandings, the play creates cardboard coffin elegies for the real that can only flimsily duplicate their powerful precursors. The play's pathos comes from the tonal disjunction between the subtext of psychic pain, loss and grief, and the jocular exaggeration of its theatricality and amateurish performance aesthetics.

In *The Walworth Farce*, the characters' lives are constrained, as they often are in Beckett's work too, by the inability to escape trauma. They are trapped, as O'Brien suggests, 'within metatheatrical reenactments of traumatic memories and imagined pasts' (O'Brien, 2011: 648). The play is about migration and mythmaking, about lies and the power of narrative. It is also about Walsh's own role as a writer grappling with post-avant-garde quandaries about the status of language and a negotiation with form. *The Walworth Farce* uses form to express what Walsh's texts cannot, coming, as they do, after Beckett: loss, absence and inadequacy. His use of the genre of farce allows him to critique reactionary notions of Irish identity while undercutting the definitiveness of that critique through physical comedy. His plays acknowledge the power of consoling narratives of nationhood and identity while exposing their corrosiveness. Form, the tragedy as farce, for Walsh, is critique without condemnation.

In a 2008 interview, Walsh describes his work as follows:

> I don't like seeing everyday life on stage: it's boring. I like my plays to exist in an abstract, expressionistic world: the audience has to learn its rules, and then connect with these characters who are, on the surface, dreadful monsters. (Costa, 2008)

Once Walsh's characters are set in motion, they adhere to the logics of narrative (the account of a traumatic memory) or dramatic form (the rules of the farce), so that they function as a critique of notions of authentic expression or individualised thinking. By composing characters who fail – the failure to move on from a traumatic sexual betrayal in *The New Electric Ballroom*; the failure to turn migration and grief into tragedy and diasporic, postcolonial narrative in *The Walworth Farce* – Walsh engages in a double deconstruction both of national myths and of Ireland's theatrical/literary legacy.

The decision to write a farce can be seen as a way for Walsh to explore his characters' autonomy: 'I always feel as if I'm completely observing where these characters are going to go or what they're going to do' (Walsh, 2009). In *The Walworth Farce*, that autonomy mutates into a kind of de-psychologised automatism. Characters resemble puppets, in line with Eric Bentley's view of farce as 'a theatre in which, though the marionettes are men, the men are supermarionettes. It is the theatre of the surrealist body' (Bentley, 1965: 252). As in Beckett's *Krapp's Last Tape*, a tape recorder prompts the action by playing Irish songs, 'An Irish Lullaby' and 'A Nation Once Again', accentuating the sense that the script being rehearsed is pre-recorded and fixed. The increasing speed and mechanisation of the action are central to the play's comedy. Like Feydeau's farces, which convey 'the Bergsonian view that as man begins to resemble a machine so he becomes less human and increasingly an object of laughter' (Booth, 1988: 147), Walsh's play seems to be spinning out of control, a characteristic of the genre itself, as Booth suggests: 'the speeding up of stage action is an old and familiar technique in farce' (Booth 1988: 148).

For Charlotte McIvor, '[u]ltimately, *The Walworth Farce* captures multiple narratives of transnational Irish histories pinpointing themes of immigration, emigration, race and home' (McIvor, 2010: 463). The play deals with a violent crime, the erasure of history and the dark side of myths of migration and nation. Instead of depicting Dinny's murder of his brother and his brother's wife, it shows us a character who is using performance to hide or, more precisely, to theatrically displace the truth.

In doing so, Walsh's play fits into a long line of theatrical predecessors, as Benedict Nightingale says: 'From Synge through O'Casey to Martin McDonagh and beyond, Irish dramatists have regularly arraigned their characters for escaping from the harshness of reality into dream, fantasy, illusion, pretence' (Nightingale, 2007). Walsh takes from Synge's *The Playboy of the Western World* a concern with crime, fathers and sons, and the tendency towards escapist self-aggrandisement. From a play like Tom Murphy's *Bailegangaire*, revolving around an elderly grandmother in a country-cottage kitchen, telling the same incomplete story again and again, he takes his concern with storytelling as a habit of mind or obsessive act, and his interest in juxtaposing the past and the present, old Ireland and the modernity of the new. The difference between Walsh and his predecessors is the way he uses a deliberately amateurish aesthetic, cartoonish characters, comic hyperbole and all the resources of the visual and physical elements of the stage to foreground the artificiality of the action and the pathos of the characters' hyper-investment in their own illusions.

As with *The New Electric Ballroom*, the play is most powerful when dealing with the transmission of guilt and trauma across generations. Dinny's crime implicates his sons and can only be sustained with their forced collusion. At a key point, the story breaks down when Sean asks, 'Is any of this story real?' (Walsh, 2007: 29). This prompts Dinny to begin a monologue about his experiences as an Irish migrant to London: 'I run the same race a million Irishmen ran. But pockets full of new money and Paddy's keys in my hands with Walworth Road a final destination, a sure thing, a happy ever after. I run' (Walsh, 2007: 30). But, crucially, at the end of the monologue, Dinny asks Blake to continue his speech, once again showing how the father's own narratives are handed down to his sons: 'I stand there looking at the green scabby grass of the roundabout and my knackered shoes. Fuck. (*A Pause.*) And then what happened, Blake? What then, tell me? *BLAKE continues, detached*' (Walsh, 2007: 31). That ostensibly confessional narrative is reframed by the line 'And then what happened, Blake?' as coercive and restrictive. Equally, the play asks us to compare the speech to the exaggeration of the rest of Dinny's tales from Ireland, leading us to question whether these apparently more authentic words about migration may not in fact be just as fantastical and illusory as the overt farce itself, with its flying horses and cardboard coffins. As Blake says, there was a time when his father's myths of Ireland convinced him, but no longer: '… all them pictures have stopped. I say his words and all I can see is the word. A lot of words piled on top of other words. There's no sense to my day 'cause the sense isn't important anymore. No pictures. No dreams. Words only' (Walsh, 2007: 22).

In a review of the Traverse Theatre production of the play at the 2007 Edinburgh Fringe, Lyn Gardner noted that:

> It is not an easy play to watch in any sense, especially as the bodies pile up and the wigs and moustaches are swapped with lightning speed. But its two-hour duration repays the effort and you leave shattered, not only by its Greek tragedy ending but also by its depiction of theatre as an imprisoning lie rather than a force for good. (Gardner, 2007)

Gardner's response to the play as an 'imprisoning lie' is echoed in other reflections on the work: 'What does it mean to suggest … that performance might augment and reproduce, rather than rehearse in order to assuage, the traumas of the past?' (Solga, 2011: 89). For all its comedy, *The Walworth Farce* offers a profound critique of Dinny's mythmaking, his refusal to confront his guilt and his rehearsal of Irish narratives of diaspora in the name of repression and domination.

It is the tension between the play's comic excess and its probing critique of such myths which makes it so effective. In his discussion of farce, Eric Bentley argues that farce 'characteristically promotes and exploits the widest possible contrasts between tone and content, surface and substance' (Bentley, 1965: 243). This is fundamental to the success of *The Walworth Farce*: on the surface, it is a caricatural rehearsal of an outlandishly grotesque version of events, resolutely comedic in its treatment of death, grief and exile. Underneath, it shows us characters confined at multiple levels: emigrants imprisoned both physically and psychologically, trapped by guilt, whose construction of the utopian space of Ireland, home and nation, is comically absurd. We also detect the desire to escape into fiction, a theatricalised version of the past and of home, which the play depicts as grotesque while at the same time exposing the powerful compulsion to repeat those narratives. It is precisely the gap between surface and substance which leads the audience to read the play in terms of what it cannot express: failed tragedy, or its status as post-tragedy; its desire to construct narratives but anxiety about doing so; its rejection of psychological realism and its substitution of a kind of marionette-character without the capacity for authentic or direct expression.

Reanimating Beckett

As mentioned above, Walsh has said that Beckett's work 'helped free drama from any obligation to be sociological' (Billington, 2014), yet his own reanimations of Beckett's texts are deeply imbued with political critique. *The Walworth Farce* acutely exposes the exclusionary ideology of family, home and nation in a shocking gesture at the end of the play when the young Black cashier, Hayley, accidentally drawn into the re-enactment of the farce when she tries to deliver the right bag of food to Sean, has her face suddenly and without her permission daubed white by Dinny, using his tub of moisturiser, so she can play the role of his wife Maureen in the farce. In one complex gesture, Walsh captures the repressive and reactionary cultural and identity politics behind some of the romantic myths his play has turned into comic farce up until this point. If the farce form has disarmed the audience, then this moment suddenly challenges the whole system of representation, the interplay of genres, within which Walsh is operating.

At this point, the play confronts the make-do aesthetic of this amateurish rehearsal with its own potential irresponsibility by introducing a moment of casually racist symbolic violence. In one single gesture, Walsh demolishes his own substitution of farce for tragedy by bringing the mechanisms of racial violence and gendered oppression into the hyper-theatricalised world of these comic grotesques. If the genre of tragedy is no longer a possibility, then farce is only ever a partial comic expression of its disappearance, and one whose own recourse to the critique value of theatricality is suddenly subverted by its collision with the material reality of racism, sexism and the symbolic violence of theatrical representation.

This is the corollary of Dinny's tyrannical mythmaking: a narcissistic self-obsession with his own identity, his own myths, to the exclusion of others, leading him to erase Hayley's blackness so that she can become a performer in his whitewashing of his crimes. The play ends with the younger son Sean being given the chance to escape from the scene of the farce as his father and brother lie dead. Instead, he daubs his own face brown with shoe polish in a feeble shouldering of a theatrical guilt that mirrors and inverts his father's earlier imposition of white supremacy onto Hayley's skin. Sean will remain trapped in the world of the play, the chaotic flat, now in the guise and role of Hayley. The farce is over, creating a new form of post-tragedy in which the comic genre which allowed the characters to confront and rehearse the crimes of the past is no longer possible.

Conclusion

Beckett's plays sublimate and displace traumatic experiences, capturing affect, loss and grief in the interplay between words and silence, in gaps which resonate with the unsaid. In contrast, Walsh's reanimations of Beckett bring these experiences to the surface, purposely undoing the rigour of Beckett's visions to create a kind of structured disorder, or slow unravelling into excessive theatricality. *The Walworth Farce's* ramshackle, amateurish farcical quality, its low-fi, provisional, make-do visuals and aesthetic, its stage interiors saturated with logos and insignias, brand names and outdated furniture all operate as antidotes to the way words jab away at meaning in Beckett's later plays. Walsh brings the material body, objects and things back into the restricted space of Beckett's texts, reanimating the avant-garde through the injection of messy theatricality and anarchic performance.

In *The Walworth Farce*, music plays a key role in triggering each iteration of the farce as the playing of the Irish folk song 'A Nation Once Again' by the Dubliners on an old-fashioned tape recorder signals the beginning of the characters' daily performance. The next two chapters revolve around songs in the context of grief. In different media, they are linked to memory, and the reanimations of the dead are examined as part of the grieving process in which songs and music evoke bereavement and loss. This includes versions of one of my key examples of reanimation in this book, the ballad 'Finnegan's Wake', which will allow me to revisit the themes, sites and reanimating griefs of this project and to bring it to a close.

Note

1 A critical reader says, 'I'm not sure I agree that the rubber ball is the *opposite* of an animate object or that *only* the dog understands its purpose. Though a ball remains lifeless it is nonetheless set in motion (animated) by the logic of the game, and the game is shared between the dog and the person who throws it.'

6

Musical afterlives

I was thinking about Joyce's story in relation to a conference paper I was writing in 2011 about death and dying, and I wanted to include a discussion of the folk song 'Finnegan's Wake'. 'The Dead' emerged as an immediate reference point as the revival of the memory of a dead man found its parallel in the comic resurrection of Tim Finnegan in the ballad. Added to this was Joyce's fascination with the song more generally. The crossing between literature and theatre had marked my own intellectual trajectory, but so too had the difference between those two cultural forms, the Irish folk songs I had listened to growing up and the novels and short stories I had started reading at school, their educational prestige and literary status in tension with the oral and folk traditions of my pre- and extra-school identity, which was often conducted in solitude. Alongside these memories of past displacements, as I prepared my conference talk, was the act of working through my grief at the death of my father, its vestiges of guilt, regret and failed expression. Re-reading 'The Dead', focusing this time on the construction of the scene of grief in the text, linking that metaphorical reanimation in Gretta's mind to the comical physical reanimation of the protagonist in 'Finnegan's Wake', not only revived my memory of grief, it revived the grief itself, refracted through literature and music. Perhaps these events taught me how to grieve differently, or made me ponder the reappearance of grief through encounters with cultural forms, in particular repeat encounters from before or after the period of bereavement. Bound up with the charged affect of those cultural reanimations are other pulses of dissonant emotion: my work with cultural texts, stories and songs in odd disalignment with my father's work as a stonemason or in construction, configured in the impossible contradictions at the heart of 'Finnegan's Wake', and the unsettling memory-spectre of Michael Furey in 'The Dead', a queer intrusive ghost dissolving Gabriel Conroy's worldview.

This chapter looks at the relationship between grief, music, performance and memory, examining the way songs reanimate grief, and how death and grief create intertextual connections across and between texts in different media. I discuss the short story 'The Dead' by James Joyce from his short story collection *Dubliners* (1914), the folk song 'The Lass of Aughrim' (1819/1844) and the novel *Beautiful World, Where Are You* (2021) by Sally Rooney. The chapter looks at the link between song and individual and cultural memory, examining how the role of grief shifts from the ballad into Joyce's modernist short story and then Rooney's novel about female knowledge, friendship and Ireland's cultural legacies.

In 'The Dead', Joyce uses the epiphanic moment of hearing, grief and the memory of loss to expose the illusions of bourgeois marriage and to precipitate the end of a certain version of realism. The story explores epistemological questions about intersubjectivity and aesthetic questions about the gender ideology of literary realism. Joyce's story invokes the idea of female subjectivity as alterity and difference, before using a complex textual metaphor to suggest that fiction needs to find new forms of representation. The key epiphany in the story is a reanimation as memory, where a song opens up a secret chronology of desire and grief for a dead young man. The chapter goes on to explore the lyrics and narrative function of the folk song 'The Lass of Aughrim' in 'The Dead' to think about gender relations and the transmission of cultural memory, noting how it operates as elegy, mnemonic, epiphany and narrative device all at once. The final part of the chapter links Joyce's story to Sally Rooney's novel, in which the song 'The Lass of Aughrim' appears at a crucial point towards the end. Rooney's text gives us female characters who are philosophers, thinkers and intellectuals, exchanging long emails to explore ontological questions about being and identity. If 'The Dead' challenges male constructions of female subjectivity, Rooney engages with a contemporary Dublin in which shifting, unstable gender relations, sexual identities and social formations mean that old folk ballads like 'The Lass of Aughrim' no longer have the evocative, connotative power they once did.

The song is given a talismanic quality in Joyce, opening into multiple pasts, channelling inexpressible grief, and creating complex fictional intersections of voice, musical performance, memory and desire. Rooney's novel exemplifies the failure to make these elegant syntheses in the contemporary moment, where frames of references are dispersed and fragmented, where cultural legacies are diluted, and where surface and depth, historical resonance and contemporary acoustic pleasure are reorganised. While 'The Lass of Aughrim' reanimates the past and grief in 'The Dead', in Rooney's *Beautiful World, Where Are You*, the song crystallises a loss of cultural moorings but also the possibility of a new negotiation with Ireland's past, freed from some of its repressive social structures and ideologies.

'The Dead' and the epiphanic moment of memory

'The Dead' appears at the end of Joyce's collection of short stories, *Dubliners*. It famously revolves around the annual dance at the Dublin home of the late-middle-aged sisters Misses Morkan, at which their nephew, Gabriel Conroy, a man in his thirties, will deliver a speech. Joyce's story culminates when Gabriel hears his wife, Gretta, talking for the first time about the grief she still feels many years after the death of a young man she used to love. As Kevin Whelan explains:

> [Gabriel's] comfortable middle-class journalistic world has disintegrated with his devastating realization that the passionate love of his wife Gretta was the young Galway man, Michael Furey, who had literally died for love of her. Gretta's buried passion had been resurrected by the singing of 'The Lass of Aughrim'—a folk song which summoned the deep, oral, Irish-language, Jacobite, Gaelic past of the west of Ireland. This song was a favourite of [Joyce's wife] Nora Barnacle and her mother. (Whelan, 2002: 69)

The 'Lass of Aughrim', which Gretta overhears just as she and Gabriel are preparing to leave the dance, makes her weep and reminds her of her loss, as she says: 'I am thinking about a person long ago who used to sing that song' (Joyce, 2006: 190). As Harry White suggests, the song releases 'soft detonations of feeling' (White, 2005: 114) but with very different effect for Gabriel and Gretta.

Gretta's words lead Gabriel not only to learn something new about his wife's past, but to realise that the very foundation of his marriage is a sham. Revealing the unknowability of a crucial aspect of Gretta's life, a powerful unspoken first love and first grief, the hearing of the song 'The Lass of Aughrim' rips open Gabriel's understanding of intimacy and gender relations. This event ripples out to cover wider questions of intersubjective relations, as well as troubling issues for Gabriel around female sexuality, especially around virginity, childbirth and paternity. A young dead lover haunts Joyce's story, but the text is haunted even more subliminally by a lost or absent child, an anxiety stirred up by the lyrics of the very song which resurrects Gretta's past.

The narrative of 'The Dead' is mostly filtered through Gabriel's perspective. Towards the end, with Gretta listening to the impromptu rendition of 'The Lass of Aughrim' by the tenor Bartell D'Arcy, we see Gabriel framing Gretta visually, imagining her thoughts and motives, feeling sexually and emotionally rejected by her. He not so much objectifies as aestheticises her:

> He stood still in the gloom of the hall, trying to catch the air that the voice was singing and gazing up at his wife. There was grace and mystery in her attitude as if she were a symbol of something. He asked himself what is a woman standing on the stairs in the shadow, listening to distant music, a symbol of. (Joyce, 2006: 182)

Note the perspective here, with Gretta viewed from below, almost as if she were a painting hung on a wall in a museum. As Julie Henigan says, 'Gabriel translates the scene into an emotionally deficient, but ultimately safe, aesthetic abstraction' (Henigan, 2007: 146), while Eric Bulson picks up on the sense of 'grace and mystery in her attitude' by calling the image 'idealized' (Bulson, 2012: 46). Rather than an abstraction, Gabriel's thinking is shown to be derivative and over-intellectualised, his perception mediated by visual arts, paintings of the feminine as object of the male gaze, hung on the wall in male-dominated institutions. As Vincent J. Cheng notes: 'Gabriel engages here, as the Western patriarchal tradition has for centuries, in the aesthetic objectification of women as art and symbol, as object rather than subject' (Cheng, 2006: 357).

Instead of connecting with Gretta at this moment of grief and memory, and acknowledging her authentically, Gabriel actively seeks to convert her into a symbol, speculating on what she might represent. He is unable to view Gretta as a grieving subject with emotions and desires pre-dating his knowledge of her. Gabriel is the embodiment of the 'thought-tormented age' (Joyce, 2006: 177) he laments in his speech, erasing Gretta's body and emotions and co-opting them into masculinist categorical frameworks.

Gabriel is humiliated by Gretta's account of her enduring grief: 'While he had been full of memories of their secret life together, full of tenderness and joy and desire, she had been comparing him in her mind to another' (Joyce, 2006: 191). Grief here dislodges Gretta from the mediating male gaze: its affective force is to allow her to escape the frame of his desired portrait, his imposed fantasy representation of her. As with the story as a whole, this scene allegorises a wider transition from representational realism and its restrictive mimesis to fictional modes that challenge the very foundations of such controlling representations (in this case, Gabriel's aesthetic, pictorially mediated representation of his wife in his mind).

The exposure to Gretta's grief makes Gabriel conscious of his own embarrassing performance earlier in the story, when he is making a speech before the gathered company at the invitation of his respectable aunts. Gretta's genuine, decades-long, grief contrasts with the superficial theatricality of his self-conscious role-playing. The figure of the intellectual and journalist, the man of letters, the good nephew, the *paterfamilias* are all exposed as inadequate parts he plays badly. In this connection, the quotation cited earlier continues:

> A shameful consciousness of his own person assailed him. He saw himself as a ludicrous figure, acting as a pennyboy for his aunts, a nervous wellmeaning sentimentalist, orating to vulgarians and idealising his own clownish lusts, the pitiable fatuous fellow he had caught a glimpse of in the mirror. (Joyce, 2006: 191)

Authentic grief reveals the falsity of the theatrical self. Even Gabriel's torrent of internal self-criticism is couched in grandiose terms, the negative adjectives accumulating rhetorically. This will only be the first stage in his epiphany, prompted by the reanimation of Gretta's dead lover as memory, in which her grief is still very much a living emotion.

As a story, 'The Dead' is haunted by echoes of past deaths. Gabriel's awkward dinner speech at the dance remembers the dead in a formulaic way that contrasts with Gretta's private, vivid form of grief memory. Gabriel is eloquent but insincere compared to

Gretta's silent act of listening to music before narrating her loss. Earlier in the story, we have heard about the great singers of the past who have died. As Ellmann notes, '[t]he partygoers prefer dead singers to living ones, the wife prefers a dead lover to a live lover' (Ellmann, 1959: 260). There is even a reference to the opera *Lucrezia Borgia*, which ends with poisoned dinner guests being shown the coffins they will be buried in (Joyce, 2006: 173). Coffins also crop up when we learn about the Trappist monks of Mount Melleray who 'never spoke, got up at two in the morning and slept in their own coffins' (Joyce, 2006: 175) to embrace their mortality, an example of Catholic self-abnegation that completely baffles the one explicitly Protestant character in the story, Mr Browne.

The imminent deaths planned by the coffin-revealing Lucrezia Borgia remind us that along with past deaths, 'The Dead' also imagines future ones, especially in the plangent final pages of the story, in which Gabriel, as a figure, a fictional being, a character or a realist representation, loses substance and solidity. He imagines the death of his Aunt Julia, noticing the signs of ageing that will be confirmed via the subsequent reference to her in Joyce's 1922 *Ulysses* where we learn that Aunt Julia dies within six months of the celebratory dance at the centre of 'The Dead'.[1] Hélène Cixous observes the trajectory of Gabriel's emotions in the story, seeing 'successive paragraphs widen the moment of awareness from shameful egoism to pity, equanimity, solidarity in grief, communion with others far and near, dead or alive' (Cixous, 1972: 615). Just before the 'verbal music' of the story's ending, Gabriel will have reached what Cixous calls 'the luminous stasis, the enchantment of the heart that suspends death for an instant' (Cixous, 1972: 615) .

'The Dead' culminates in Joyce's famous elegy as the snow desubstantiates everything, operating as a complex metaphor of erasure, a slow blanking out of history, the material and the corporeal. We imagine the characters' deaths, the death of the author, the deaths of those we love, all our deaths, as these hypnotic lines undo realist representation and operate as an unloosening of the relation of words to things – a generalised dissolution of pictorialisation, of the visual: '[Gabriel's] soul had approached that region where dwell the vast hosts of the dead. He was conscious of, but could not apprehend, their wayward and flickering existence' (Joyce, 2006: 194). As we read, we are drawn into a slow annihilation of the text, achieved through language – words cede to rhythm and tonality, and the rich material world is suffused with a falling, snow-covering of silence, stillness and whiteness.

In aesthetic terms, Joyce's writing at this point is marking a transition away from realism and its location in the material. The generalised snow is a whiting out of the real and the substitution of another textual modality, a snow-burial of the tangible world and its objects, and the textual facsimiles of literary reduplication. Its symbolic erasure of realism prepares the ground instead for new forms that emulate that very erasure, operating in line with a wider modernist aesthetics of scepticism, repetition and loss of orientation.

'The Lass of Aughrim'

The song that Gretta overhears being sung by the tenor Bartell D'Arcy, 'The Lass of Aughrim', is pivotal to Joyce's story.[2] Vincent J. Cheng calls it 'a stunningly appropriate choice on Joyce's part' because it is 'a song about mastery, domination, and mistreatment (even rape) of a peasant woman by a patriarchal nobleman' (Cheng, 2006: 358). The song is a ballad, a form, according to Sean Williams, that often uses 'a narrative technique called "leaping and lingering" in which the plot moves rapidly forward, then halts for a verse or two of emotional content, or other element before leaping forward again' (Williams, 2009: 188). As well as providing a synopsis of the song and its historical context, Whelan argues that it 'releases the emotional charge in the story' (Whelan, 2002: 83). In the first verse, the narrator, a male figure called Gregory, addresses a young woman, but for some reason is unclear about her identity:

> If you be the lass of Aughrim
> as I suppose you not to be
> Come tell me the last token that
> passed between you and me.

The failed recognition requires her to show the love token she was given at their last meeting. Gregory is asked by the woman to remember their first meeting 'on yon lean hill':

> Oh Gregory don't you remember
> that night on yon lean hill

> when we both met together
> which I'm sorry now to tell.

The scene is one of pathos, with the woman standing in the rain and cold, and as the chorus suggests, a baby 'lies cold within my arms' (whether alive or dead, it is not clear):

> Chorus: The rain falls on my yellow locks
> The dew it wets my skin.
> My babe lies cold within my arms
> oh Gregory let me in.

As the young woman asks, 'O Gregory don't you remember', we wonder whether she is a ghost, a memory or a real figure returning to seek revenge, compensation, love, acknowledgement, or a combination of all of these.

> Oh Gregory don't you remember
> One night on yon lean hill
> When we swapped rings off each other's hands
> Sorely against my will
> ...
> Oh Gregory don't you remember
> That night in my father's hall
> When you had your will of me
> And that was worse than all.

Her consent to sexual intercourse in the first place is questionable ('sorely against my will'; 'that was worse than all'), and the outcome is a baby, abandonment and destitution for the mother and child, hence their appearance at the narrator's door.

When the song appears towards the end of 'The Dead', precipitating Gretta's memory and Gabriel's epiphany, it operates at several levels at once in Joyce's story. It is a mnemonic for Gretta of a former young male lover's devotion and fragility, but also of the link between death and desire. The song acts as a marker of grief as well as allegorising a scene of tragic erotic desire and self-sacrifice. The baby in the chorus is at risk of exposure to the elements, echoing the description of the young lovestruck man, Michael Furey, being fatally drenched by the rain as he waits for Gretta.

For Gabriel, the song leads to jealousy, emotional rejection and self-criticism all at once. It is about a sexual relationship and perhaps stirs up doubts for Gabriel about Gretta's sexual past, even the possibility that she conceived a child with Furey, especially by association with the female protagonist in the song itself. It is also about an emotional betrayal. Bound up with this are the geographical connotations of the song, highlighting contrasts between Dublin and the west of Ireland, ideas of authentic Irish identity and subjection to British colonialism. As a song with the name of a village in Galway, 'Aughrim', in its title, as Henigan puts it, 'this song is a product, not of the cosmopolitan world Gabriel's Dublin friends and relatives aspire to, but of his wife's native West' (Henigan, 2007: 147). The song seems to represent for Gabriel a purer Celtic version of Irishness, more in touch with native traditions of the ballad, than the more English-influenced Dublin attitudes which might deem folk ballads as primitive popular cultural forms.

The ballad is about rape, sex, childbirth, illicit marriage, possible death, all sublimated into the direct lyrics and elegiac melody of the tune. Critics have different views of the relationship between the ballad's content and the themes in the story, but Smyth's summary is reasonable:

> Gabriel's culpability is thus implicit: with his privileged access to metropolitan culture, he is (like Lord Gregory [i.e. the Gregory addressed in 'The Lass of Aughrim']) guilty in some manner and to some degree of the moral exploitation of a simple country girl. His narcissism, materialism and inability to empathise are exposed by her capacity for 'love'; and this was an inference which fitted well with Joyce's impugnation of the central male character, and of the patriarchal culture which that character in some senses embodied. (Smyth, 2009: 37)

Gabriel has intruded on an intimate moment of memory and emotion during which Gretta's grief excludes and exposes him. 'The Lass of Aughrim' not only hints at Gretta's retrospective emotional, if not literal, infidelity, but it goes further than this. What the story also shows is the complexity of song. If the song and the grief are synonymous, or sequential, they are bound to one another, and the ballad within Joyce's story in fact operates as the pivotal moment of self-realisation for Gabriel as a character. 'The Lass of Aughrim', one could say, takes Gabriel out of the narcissism by which he remains a fictional being (the controlling perspectives of the third-person omniscient narrator, familiar in literary realism) and propels him towards a new self-relation connected to death, grief and unknowability. The ballad opens him to mortality and exposes him to the possibility of grief, a grieving for the death of a former self, for the death of an erroneous vision of his wife, of his aestheticising impulse, or his lies about himself, his desire and the world.

Grief strikes unexpectedly, transforms the grieving subject, rendering her opaque and unknown. At the same time, Gretta's grief communicates to Gabriel a sense of his own mortality, an understanding of grief as a genuine affect. Textually, grief is the snow that blankets the self-constructions of realism, an imposition of a moratorium on realism's fictions, and instead Joyce's words ebb towards the rhythmical lyricism of music that the song itself with its contradictory but evocative lyrics embodies. As we shall see, its association with questions of knowledge and gender relations are taken up and explored in Sally Rooney's work.

Beautiful World, Where Are You

The song 'The Lass of Aughrim' appears at a key moment in Sally Rooney's third novel *Beautiful World, Where Are You* (2021) which, like 'The Dead', also deals with self-consciousness, withheld desire and inexpressible parts of the self. The novel is set in contemporary Dublin and on the rural coast of Ireland. It revolves around two pairs of characters who have intricate friendship and sexual relations. Towards the end of the novel, echoes of Joyce's 'The Dead' become more discernible.

Anne Enright has called Rooney's novel's style a 'repudiation of shame' (Enright, 2021) and says of the two female characters that 'Alice and Eileen are best friends, about to turn 30, who are agreed that human civilisation is facing collapse, beauty is dead, art is commodified and the novel irrelevant as a form' (Enright, 2021). Rooney's novel echoes with allusions to Joyce's story but can also be read in terms of writing in Joyce's wake, cognisant of Joyce's lyrical erasure of his story's realist aesthetics with the symbolic snow falling and whiting everything out. Instead of the structuring gender relations in 'The Dead', notwithstanding Joyce's critique of the male, subject/object perspective of the narration, Rooney's writing gives us objectiveless description and a kind of textual rootlessness instead. This is a post-blanket-of-snow world with reconfigured gender relations and sexualities, bristling with distrust and masochistic sexual erotics.

In an explicit intertextual reanimation of 'The Dead', Rooney's novel depicts a party scene in Chapter 27 (of 30) at which Felix, the bisexual lover of writer Alice, sings 'The Lass of Aughrim', surprising Alice, and their friends Eileen and Simon, with the quality of his voice. The novel twice echoes the crucial scene in 'The Dead' in these pages, the first when Felix is singing. Rooney tells us that:

> From across the room Alice watched him. He was standing against the counter, under the ceiling lamp, so that his hair and face and the slim slanting figure of his body were bathed in light, and his eyes were dark, and his mouth also. For some reason, because of the low quality rich quality of his voice, or because of the melancholy lyrics of the song, or perhaps because of some prior association the melody brought to her mind, Alice's eyes filled with tears as she watched him. (Rooney, 2021: 303)

The last phrase echoes the 'generous tears' Joyce ascribes to Gabriel Conroy in the penultimate paragraph of 'The Dead' ('Generous tears filled Gabriel's eyes' (Joyce, 2006: 194)). In Rooney's novel, Felix is a male character singing, the object of the female gaze, rather than the female subject being shown to be emotional at the evoked grief of the overheard song and as the object of the aestheticising male (and authorial) gaze.

Rooney's characters discuss the song Felix has performed. Felix says he chose it because the two women are from 'around there', that is, Aughrim in Galway (this is the same reason for the choice of song by Joyce in relation to Gretta's Galway origin) but he also explains his lack of knowledge about the song:

> Not that I really know what the song is about, to be honest. I thought it was a man singing to a woman, but then in the chorus I think it's a woman singing. Saying her babe lies cold in her arms. It's probably one of those old songs that's got a few different lyrics mixed together. It's a sad one anyway, whatever it's about. (Rooney, 2021: 305)

That mixture is reflected in the longer version of the ballad discussed in Williams (2009: 190) where the young woman seems to be 'a king's daughter' and yet at the same time her handkerchiefs are worth nothing and the ring she offers Lord Gregory as a love token is inferior quality: 'Yours were fine silver, love, and mine was old tin.' Likewise, the young woman is both deeply in love and coerced into sex. At the same time, she is a haunting figure who could be dead and alive, as could her baby.

Felix as a character is a composite of hedonism, self-destructiveness, sexual energy and queer sexuality. He comes from a different social class to the university-educated Alice and Eileen, and is attractive because of his nihilistic charisma. His reading of the song aligns with these traits, sensitive to the song's contradictions, lacking a grounding in its history or context, unsure of its speakers, but aware both of a significant song tradition that mixes different song parts together and at the same time registering an affinity with it because of its emotional tenor and tone. Felix's relationship to the song signifies a more generalised relation to the country's past, a loss of cultural moorings, yet still strongly engaged in its folk, oral and ritual traditions, happy to continue to hand down the heritage of oral songs but now displaced and distanced from them.

At the same time though, Felix's uncertainty about the song is actually intellectually freeing since his supposition about it corresponds with scholarship about cultural transmission and the pragmatic splicing and merging of parts of works from different milieus and tradition. Take, for example, Smyth's characterisation of ballads, which aligns quite closely to Felix's: 'ballads are notoriously protean when considered in historical and geographical terms. The "same" text may exist in multiple forms, with variant melodies and narrative structures dispersed over numerous "versions"' (Smyth, 2009, 33). It turns out then that Felix's characterisation of 'The Lass of Aughrim' is more accurate than it might seem at first.

Rooney's evocation of Joyce's 'The Dead' in *Beautiful World, Where Are You* is an act of homage, foregrounding a kind of apprenticeship in literary language, but also entails a reconception of the premises of Joyce's text, leaching Joyce's story of its epiphanic revelations and expression of powerful grief, and substituting instead a more diffuse postmodernity that has lost touch with foundations around folk identity, the authenticity of the west of Ireland and the transformative power of song.

The final echo of 'The Lass of Aughrim' scene in 'The Dead' relates to the moment when Gabriel looks up at Gretta and the narrative voice calls her a 'symbol of something' (Joyce, 2006: 182). This shifts in Rooney's novel to a scene in the chapter after Felix's performance in which friends Alice and Eileen encounter each other on a staircase in the aftermath of a violent row. The exchange between the two characters vertically connected by a staircase returns:

> When Alice reached the bottom of the staircase a few minutes later, Eileen was coming out onto the landing. By the low light of a lamp in the hallway they saw one another and paused, Eileen at the top of the stairs looking down, Alice looking up, their faces anxious, wary, aggrieved, each like a dim mirror of the other, hanging there pale and suspended as the seconds passed. Then they went to each other, meeting halfway down the stairs, and they embraced, holding one another tightly, their arms clasped hard around each other's bodies, and then Alice was saying: I'm sorry, I'm sorry, and Eileen was saying: Don't apologise, I'm sorry, I don't know why we're fighting. (Rooney, 2021: 324)

By comparison with the scene in 'The Dead', here the two women are separated vertically but the text edges them towards a laterality and mutuality as it progresses. Their vertical arrangement is decomposed through the mirror simile 'each like a dim mirror of the other', the word 'aggrieved' perhaps evoking Joyce's Gretta and her reanimating grief. They meet halfway, both leaving their fixed position to join mid-staircase, in an act of touch, a physical embrace that prioritises a tactile friendship over gendered and sexual differences. Rooney's text switches between the figures via 'they' pronouns and the phrase 'each other', effecting an intertwining very different from the aesthetic and affective chasm between Gabriel and Gretta. Rooney's trademark omission of quotation marks around the characters' dialogue allows the spoken words to merge into the fabric of the scene, their 'I'm sorry' repeating, and aligning the two women even further. The slightly unwieldy syntax, the manoeuvering of personal and reflexive pronouns, captures their sense of reticence and resistance.

Rooney's reworking of Joyce's scene here resituates relationships in queer terms. Friendship and the tentative steps towards mutual acknowledgement replace the polarised gender categories 'The Dead' fictionalises. At the same time, the intertextual allusion to

Joyce's story also acknowledges the genealogy of affective states and their powerful precursor forms of representation, be they fiction, painting, music or song. The reanimation of the scene from Joyce echoes its spatial dynamics but repositions the characters so that they act out coming together rather than being pushed further apart.

Conclusion

This chapter has explored grief's reanimations across different genres and media, producing epiphanies and self-knowledge, as well as exploring the collapse of existing systems (literary realism, gender matrices, cultural knowledges) in their wake. In 'The Dead', the moment of performance, in which Gretta hears a song from her past, even though the singer is out of the frame, is the source for Gabriel's realisation that Gretta is completely inaccessible to him, and for the reader to comprehend the way in which 'The Dead' will allegorise the collapse of realism by exposing its sustaining gender structures, illusions, and epistemologies about intersubjectivity. As this analysis has suggested, a certain form of realism is also 'dead' at the end of Joyce's story, as it merges with the lilting rhythms of Joyce's writing, the revenant snow at the end of the story dissolving the real, seeming to drift and swirl in time to one's breathing or heartbeat.

Beautiful World, Where Are You builds on Whelan's claim that 'The Dead' can be read as 'a series of sophisticated variations on other texts' (Whelan, 2002: 73) by the way Rooney imports 'The Lass of Aughrim' into her novel to invoke and critique her famous predecessor. For Rooney, the song represents an objectless affect, a nexus of connection and historical continuity, a placing of one's writing within a famous tradition and canon, but at the same time a scepticism about what underpins that tradition, especially in terms of gender relations.

As I have shown, the novel alludes to key scenes in Joyce's text to recalibrate them towards female mutuality and exchange rather than male/female hierarchies and subject/object perceptual distinctions. The whiting out of the old forms, the inadequate realism of 'The Dead', is effected by the snow found all over Ireland and the almost camera-eye perspective of the prose as it swoops, pans and zooms into close-up, cutting across the realms of realism to create a different, more cinematic form of viewing. This translates across to Rooney's novel which rebuilds realism in the wake of Joyce's textual deconstruction of its central tenets.

A song about gender violence and female abandonment, male wealth and female poverty, touching on destitution and a child born outside marriage, is appropriated by Joyce to reflect on bourgeois life and the vacuity of its deceptions and literary forms. The song's content is subordinated to its narrative function as a mnemonic, its account of a history of violence against women elided and marginalised (the song is out of the frame, overheard, a male operatic tenor singing about the pain of a young woman).

For Rooney, the folk song becomes a leftover from an old tradition, and we contemplate Felix's words as the only response possible to us from our contemporary vantage point: 'Not that I really know what the song is about, to be honest' (Rooney, 2021: 305).

Notes

1 See Whelan 2002: 95, fn 76, regarding the mention of Aunt Julia's death in *Ulysses* (Joyce, 2000).
2 A beautiful version by tenor Fran O'Rourke can be found at: www.youtube.com/watch?v=5AN9YRPPIWY

7

Mothersongs

'Whatever happened to that old song?' (The Pogues, 'Rainy Night in Soho')

I could have been a David-Bowie-lover, a tender Bowie bender, but we were Bowieless, Bowie-free, Cockneys (yes really) not the true Bow-Bells-born kind, but no Bowie in our council bower. Other musicians from the 1960s and 70s made it through, somehow. Simon and Garfunkel's 'Bridge Over Troubled Water' album cover is part of the iconography of my youth, owned by my mother much missed, Margaret Mary (or was it Mary Margaret), her name written in blue biro on the back cover, the top left corner, the cursive's flourishes and odd sudden capital letters some kind of wormhole into a schoolroom in Wicklow in the 1950s and teachers with straps and some kids walking three miles to school in bare feet and three miles back to the strap at home too.

What filled this gap was another kind of music altogether. The LPs, the vinyl, the records played on the turntable of the grandiosely named 'music centre' starting off with words like 'armoured cars and tanks and guns…'

Being Irish meant being guilty, but I wasn't Irish. They were, mummy and daddy, but their own deracination doubled and propelled mine. But I certainly wasn't English. No way would I ever call myself that, despite sounding like an extra from Oliver! *You become the box you tick, sometimes. So, British, maybe. Not Irish, not English. Maybe, thinking about it, my nationality is Londonish.*

So some of the cultural space that should have been filled by figures like Bowie was supplanted by the rebel songs of the Wolfe Tones, or the more raucous, rowdy, folk ballads and rousing choruses of the band I love most in the world, the Dubliners, singing about illicit sex, prostitution, deportation, famine and genocidal violence, in ballads of searing, keening melancholy, aural and vocal spaces of grief and mourning, channelling the losses of the past and the unthinkable violence of 800 years of colonialism.

I listen to Ronnie Drew from the Dubliners now and I hear a voice hewn from granite, a voice singing about Finnegan's Wake, and the Foggy Dew, and the Parting Glass, and My Auld Alarm Clock, about the IRA, the older-style IRA.

Irish voices were dangerous in my youth. Gerry Adams was dubbed by an actor. As if the voice itself could seduce you into murdering innocent civilians, as if the voice itself would stop him being the monster of the Tory propaganda machine. Voices from the radio.

Harrods. Hyde Park. Canary Wharf.

Maybe there was no space, no bandwidth in my youth, for Bowie and Punk and New Romantics. I could not have come to British music in my youth. It would have been a betrayal. It would have meant to push the deadlock on that diasporic domestic domain off the Cally Road, before Islington got posh.

I'm still not sure if that lyric is from 'Rocket Man' or 'Starman'. But ask me to sing 'The Rocky Road to Dublin' or 'The Galway Races' or 'The Mountains of Mourne' or 'The Homes of Donegal', and I'll give you an account of my childhood in songs, in misheard lyrics, in parties and fights and quarrels, in the songs, reanimated every time their insistent melodies come to mind.

This chapter builds on the ideas of grief, music and performance by looking at a series of Irish folk songs that in literal and metaphorical ways deal with reanimation. The chapter links together 'critical' and 'expressive' forms of writing, to come back to Barthes's terms in *Camera Lucida* (Barthes, 2000: 8), as well as thinking about the phenomenology of memory, the desire to reconstruct the dead through cultural knowledges (in this case Irish folk music), and the relationship between language, song and identity. Part of the discussion revolves around the fragmentary and unfinished, touching on mishearings and the wider role of the acoustic in the grieving process.

This is the most autobiographical chapter of this book since it relates to my early years growing up in London to Irish parents, listening to recordings of Irish folk music, which were at once familiar, strange and lewd: the soundtrack of my childhood. These songs sometimes involve characters literally coming back to life but they also feature songs which, when I hear them, revive the memory of my parents, sometimes one parent in particular, often my mother. The chapter focuses principally on the Irish folk songs 'Finnegan's Wake', 'The Ballad of William Bloat' and 'Navvy Boots On'.

Killishandra, Athenry, Shanagolden, Aughrim, Kilconnell, Kilmore

'Finnegan's Wake': origins

The ballad 'Finnegan's Wake', which provides James Joyce with the title of his 1939 novel, is familiar to me from my childhood years. Joyce famously adapted the title of the ballad so that, in Ellmann's words, 'the apostrophe [was] omitted because it meant both the death of Finnegan and the resurgence of all Finnegans' (Ellmann, 1959: 556). It was a ballad associated with Joyce's childhood – as Ellmann tells us, the party piece of Joyce's brother Stanislaus as the family was growing up in Bray, a town on the east coast of County Wicklow, while James and Stanislaus were young boys in the 1880s (Ellmann, 1959: 26). The version of 'Finnegan's Wake' I listened to on my mother's LP, performed by the Dubliners, is notable because it is a raucous live performance and because of the inimitable lead vocals of Ronnie Drew, whose voice may not be in 'a brogue both rich and sweet' (to quote from the song) but is remarkable for the craggy depth of its baritone.

Joyce features a wake of sorts in the opening story of his 1914 collection, *Dubliners*. 'The Sisters' revolves around the death of Father James Flynn, as recounted by the priest's sister Eliza in a conversation with the young child narrator's aunt:

> He knew then?
>
> He was quite resigned.
>
> He looks quite resigned, said my aunt.
>
> That's what the woman we had in to wash him said. She said he just looked as if he was asleep, he looked that peaceful and resigned. No one would think he'd make such a beautiful corpse.
>
> Yes, indeed, said my aunt. (Joyce, 2006: 9)

The idea of a 'beautiful corpse' is linked to the appearance of a body at rest in death, no longer in pain, free of the travails of mortality.[1] It also alludes to the often uncanny similarity of the living body and the dead corpse: the dead corpse that still looks lifelike, not already a decaying, putrefying object. The idea of a last repose of the flesh before the predations of death is also part of what is meant by a 'lovely' or 'beautiful' corpse.[2]

The association with Joyce, the key figure of Tim Finnegan and the cultural importance of the wake connect the song closely to Ireland in my mind and memory. So it came as a surprise to me when beginning the research for this chapter to discover that the song was originally written in the United States, and was therefore at its very inception marked by a sense of displacement, embodying a version of Irishness that is diasporic, displaced, nostalgic and fantasised. Frank McNally reports how the migration of the song from the US to Ireland was accompanied by a change to its opening line, relocating the address of its eponymous hero Tim Finnegan to Watling Street in Dublin (McNally, 2019). The earlier versions of the lyrics referred to Walker Street, situated on the Lower West Side of Manhattan, in New York, which is where the song may first have been composed, as far as research has been able to determine. McNally points out that recent investigations have traced earlier versions of the song to the 1850s and 1860s.[3] The 1854 published version by John J. Daly in New York has been identified as the earliest extant version and was frequently performed by singers in the decades after the 1850s, in particular in an 1864 version by the Bryant Brothers, a minstrelsy group led by Dan Bryant, who were popular in New York and the surrounding region between the 1860s and 1870s. The song is therefore characterised not only by diasporic reappropriation but also by the context of American minstrelsy and blackface, a racist genre of performance in which white variety performers like Bryant would adopt blackface and perform variety songs and acts.

'Finnegan's Wake' is a ballad about a death-defying resurrection, a wake that goes wrong, a conflict around the dead body and a confrontation between different versions of Irishness. It is a song shaped by a history of Irish emigration and fantasy constructions of Ireland, in this case emigrating from New York, as well as discourses and cultural forms that draw on racist and, in particular, anti-Black discriminatory tropes and stereotypes as a form of variety entertainment. If 'Finnegan's Wake' the ballad was popular with white, Irish-identifying audiences in the 1860s in New York, Boston and other cities with large populations of Irish emigrants on the US's east coast, that history of performance is also bound up with cultural productions or associations of whiteness. This is not to say that 'Finnegan's Wake' is an exclusionary song about and for white people, but that its early popularity takes place in the context of discriminatory cultural production in which Black identity is a source of parodic, dehumanising and appropriative minstrelsy.

As we saw earlier, Enda Walsh's *The Walworth Farce* integrates totemic Irish folk songs into the rehearsal script the characters recite, specifically 'An Irish Lullaby' by James Royce Shannon (1913) (Walsh, 2006: 5) and 'A Nation Once Again' by Thomas Osborne Davis (mid-1840s) (Walsh, 2006: 7). It is a play that culminates with complex scenes about racism, appropriation and performance, and it is interesting to note the parallel here with the popularity of this Irish ballad in a context of nostalgic constructions of white Irishness in the early decades of the ballad's existence on the US East Coast.

The analysis of 'Finnegan's Wake' in this chapter revolves around two different performances of the song, which are, of course, two distinctive *versions* of it. The first is a performance by the Dubliners from 1966. The second, by the Clancy Brothers with Tommy Makem and the Dubliners, dates from the 1970s. The Dubliners' version (1966) was performed live at the Gate Theatre in Dublin on 26 April 1966. This is the exact performance and version of the song which I grew up listening to, so my analysis will use this version as its starting point. Learning the date of the performance, I wonder whether my mother, whose records of the Dubliners I played as a child, attended this concert, since I know she first went to live and work in Dublin in the early 1960s. Perhaps the record she bought and that I played was a record of a particular memory of a performance.

Addressing the live audience before the Dubliners perform the song, the band's lead singer Ronnie Drew, joking, we may infer, about the spectators' largely working-class roots, says on the recording: 'My lord bishop, reverend fathers, reverend mothers, your excellencies, my lord mayor, ladies and gentlemen, and fellow peasants' (Dubliners, 1966), then the song lyrics, which I have transcribed to incorporate minor variations deriving from Drew's live performance, continue as follows:

> Ah Tim Finnegan lived in Walkin Street
> A gentleman Irish, mighty odd
> Well he had a brogue both rich and sweet
> And to rise in the world he carried a hod
> Ah but Tim had a bit of a tippler's way
> With the love of the liquor he was born
> And to send him on his way each day
> He'd a drop of the craythur every morn
>
> **Chorus**
>
> Whack fol the da, will you dance to your partner
> Round the floor with your trotters shake
> Isn't it the truth I told you
> Lots of fun at Finnegan's wake
>
> Ah one mornin' Tim was rather full
> His head felt heavy, which made him shake
> He fell off the ladder and he broke his skull
> Then they carried him home his corpse to wake
> Well they wrapped him up in a nice clean sheet
> And they laid him out upon the bed
> With a bottle of whiskey at his feet
> And a barrel of porter at his head
>
> **Chorus**
>
> Well his friends assembled at the wake
> And Mrs. Finnegan called for lunch
> Well first she brought them tay and cake
> Then pipes, tobacco and brandy punch
> Then the widow Malone began to cry
> 'Such a lovely corpse she did ever see!
> Ah but sure Tim a mornin' why did you die?'
> 'Will you hold your gob!' says Molly McGee
>
> **Chorus**
>
> Ah well Mary Murphy took up the job
> 'Ah Biddy,' says she 'you're wrong I'm sure'
> Oh well Biddy fetched her a belt in the gob
> And left her sprawling on the floor

> Well civil war did then engage
> Woman to woman and man to man
> Shillelagh law was all the rage
> And a row and a ruction soon began
>
> **Chorus**
>
> Ah well Tim Malone he ducked his head
> When the bottle of whiskey flew at him
> He ducked and landing on the bed
> The whiskey scatters over Tim
> Ah bedad he revives and see how he rises
> Tim Finnegan rising in the bed
> Saying 'Twiddle your whiskey around like blazes
> Be the thundering Jaysus, do you think I'm dead?'
>
> **Chorus**
>
> (Dubliners, 1966)

Noteworthy elements of the Dubliners' 1966 live recording include the way a woman's penetrating laugh punctuates the opening introduction by Drew, and the inclusion in the last line of the ballad of the phrase 'by the thundering Jaysus', which sounds like a swear and a curse combined until you listen carefully and, also, that the twist in the tale, the resurrection of Tim Finnegan, leads to loud laughter from the audience, who, of course, all know the ballad and how it ends very well. Yet they laugh again as the song finishes, and their laughter merges with the tin whistle and banjo playing the final iteration of the chorus in Drew's leathery baritone. I am intrigued by this laughter. My mother's laugh had a similar raucous quality to the woman's laughter punctuating Drew's short verbal introduction to the performance.

Modes of mourning

'Finnegan's Wake' mixes traditional ballad storytelling and a chorus exhorting people to dance in unison ('will you dance to your partner'). In the song, narrative and choreographic forms of performance operate side by side. The story takes place over one or two days and records the work accident of the eponymous hero. Why the name 'Tim Finnegan'? The internal rhyme of 'Tim' and 'Finn' gives the name a comical quality, and the association of the name 'Finnegan' with the traditional nursery rhyme 'There was an old man named Michael Finnegan' evokes the act of beginning again, which is of course relevant to the story of the song.[4] 'Finnegan/begin again' is what happens in Joyce's novel *Finnegans Wake* when you reach the end.

In the ballad, we learn that Tim Finnegan is a builder, more specifically a bricklayer (as the lyrics say, 'to rise in the world he carries a hod', a device carried on the shoulder with a handle and a rectangular scoop for transporting a number of bricks at a time). We also hear that he is a habitual drinker ('Tim had a bit of a tippler's way'), and that on this particular morning he has drunk a significant amount ('One morning Tim was rather full'), the impact of which causes him to fall off his ladder and badly injure his head. The rest of the song is an account of the removal of Tim Finnegan's lifeless body, the preparations for his wake and the fight that breaks out as a result of a disagreement between some of Tim Finnegan's friends at the wake.

The cultural practice of the wake is particularly associated with Irish funeral rituals. Kevin Toolis describes the wake as an event 'where the dying ... the living, the bereaved and the dead still openly share the world and remain bound together' (Toolis, 2017). Toolis explores the historical context of wakes as a form of mourning:

> The wake is among the oldest rites of humanity first cited in the great Homeric war poem the Iliad and commonly practised across Europe until the last 200 years .... For our ancestors, a wake, with its weight of obligations between the living and the bodies of the dead, and the dead and living, was a pathway to restore natural order to the world, heal our mortal wound, and communally overcome the death of any one individual. (Toolis, 2017)

The etymology of the word 'wake' indicates that it comes from the Old English 'wacu' and the OED gives definition 3 of 'wake' as:

> 3. The watching (*esp.* by night) of relatives and friends beside the body of a dead person from death to burial, or during a part of that time; the drinking, feasting, and other observances incidental to this. Now chiefly *Anglo-Irish* or with reference to Irish custom. Also applied to similar funeral customs in other times or among non-Christian peoples.

Used in relation to the deceased, the earliest citation in the OED dates from 1412–20 in John Lydgate's *History of Troy* and there are citations of work by poets John Skelton in 1529 and John Dryden in 1700. There are four citations dating from the nineteenth century, which is when the ballad 'Finnegan's Wake' was written, including one that refers to a usage of 'wake' in William Gladstone's translation of Horace's *Odes*: 'New contracts for new marbles thou dost make,/ But thou art near thy wake' (W. E. GLADSTONE tr. Horace *Odes* II. xviii). The next line of Gladstone's translation is: 'Thou build'st afresh, unheeding of the tomb', continuing the idea that death overshadows life but that human beings live, work, suffer, build houses and monuments, even despite the knowledge of the inevitability of death. The Latin text (lines 17–19) shows that Gladstone has translated the Latin 'funus' as 'wake', a word more commonly translated as 'funeral': 'tu secanda Marmora/locas sub ipsum funus et sepulcri/ immemor struis domos'.

Discussing wakes in her book *Sorry for Your Trouble* about how Irish people deal with death, Ann Marie Hourihane explains that the wake has often be seen as a threat by the repressive forces of the Catholic Church in Ireland, a tension which is evident in the song 'Finnegan's Wake'. As Hourihane says:

> There is no strict definition of the Irish wake – it can refer to almost any social interaction associated with a death. But the classic image – open coffin in the middle of the room, mourners mirthfully toasting the dead – has deep roots in Irish culture. The old Irish wakes were carnivals and at times they were talent competitions, they were matchmaking festivals (to put it politely) and they were fights. Catholic Church authorities spent centuries trying to suppress them, threatening those who took part in them with the withholding of sacraments and even excommunication. (Hourihane, 2021: 56)

Narelle McCoy glosses the wake as follows:

> Waking the dead stems from an ancient Irish custom which persisted well into the twentieth century, in which the body of the deceased was laid out in the family home in order for relatives, friends, and neighbours to pay their final respects and for the corpse to be keened, or lamented, so that the spirit might pass safely to the next world. (McCoy, 2012: 616)

The ballad 'Finnegan's Wake' explicitly engages with this hostility by inverting the act of baptism, substituting for pure holy water the corrupting liquid, whiskey (as another Irish folk song has it, 'Whiskey you're the devil'), and giving it the reanimatory power that God alone should have.[5]

As part of an extended performance of 'Finnegan's Wake' that also includes a recitation of some lines from Joyce's novel, the Clancy Brothers' singer Paddy Clancy, in the course of providing some context about the ballad, explains Irish wakes to his concert audience:

> An Irish wake ... starts off very respectably, little old ladies talking very quietly ... talking about the corpse, 'how well he looks', they 'never saw him looking better', which was probably true, the drinking-tea way, and then the men come in later and the heavy stuff comes out, then things begin to degenerate and by nightfall you have a fantastic hooley going. (Clancy Brothers, 1988)

Clancy quotes parts of the Finnegan story from Joyce's novel, joking about the length of the book, and citing Joyce's description of Tim Finnegan in the novel, as follows: 'during might odd years this man of hod, cement and edifices in Toper's Thorp piled buildung supra buildung pon the banks for the livers by the Soangso' (Joyce, 1992: 4). It is noteworthy that while introducing us to Tim Finnegan, Joyce makes reference to 'a waalworth of a skyerscape of most eyeful hoyth entowerly' (Joyce, 1992: 4), linking Finnegan to Walsh's farce-rehearsing inhabitants of the Walworth Road in London.

Different ways to mourn

Elisabeth Bronfen's discussion of the contradictions underpinning the imagery of dead female bodies in art and literature can also be applied to thinking about what repels and fascinates us about the events of the ballad. Bronfen argues that '[i]f symptoms are failed repressions, representations are symptoms that visualise even as they conceal what is too dangerous to articulate openly but too fascinating to repress successfully' (Bronfen, 1992: xi). While the carnivalesque jocularity of events in the song helps it avoid sensations of horror or abjection at the thought of a corpse in its coffin actually still living, about to be buried alive, or suddenly returning in undead form, at the same time the dead body returning to life exerts precisely the form of fascination that is both amplified and defused by comedy. The song's comical quality comes from the idea of excessive consumption of alcohol leading people to do and say outrageous things, and the almost cartoonish violence of the brawl, before the slow-motion resurrection (Drew slows down the delivery of the lyrics, 'Ah bedad he revives and see how he rises/Tim Finnegan rising in the bed'), added to the incredulity of Tim Finnegan's words 'do you think I'm dead?'. Finnegan's devotion to alcohol literally wakes him from the dead, outraged at the sight of whiskey being wasted in conflict rather than being drunk in a celebratory, life-affirming way (the word 'whiskey' comes from the Irish words literally meaning 'water of life').

'Finnegan's Wake' records different ways of grieving as the mourners react to the sight of the corpse. One mode of grief is celebratory, and involves waking the body of the deceased, a carnivalesque intoxication with eating, drinking, smoking, singing and dancing. The other involves a more emotional form of grieving, a self-questioning, melancholic, existential mourning. Just as there is conflict about ways to mourn at the wake, so there is a collision between narrative storytelling and the more choreographic components of the wake (as the chorus says 'will you dance to your partner/Round the floor with your trotters shake'), the latter a self-forgetting which is also a forgetting of the finality of death. The mind grieves; the body sings and dances to forget grief. In the second half of the ballad, a physical fight ('civil war did then engage') breaks out between the mourners, friends of Tim Finnegan, about the most suitable approach to the grieving process. As the lyrics say, the widow Malone responds sentimentally to Tim's death, uttering a kind of lament for his untimely demise, while Molly McGee responds aggressively, asking her to be quiet:

> Then the widow Malone began to cry
> 'Such a lovely corpse she did ever see!
> Ah but sure Tim a mornin' why did you die?'
> 'Will you hold your gob!' says Molly McGee.

Another mourner, Mary Murphy, takes Molly McGee to task, and is punched in the face as a result, triggering the mass brawl:

> Ah well Mary Murphy took up the job
> 'Ah Biddy,' says she 'you're wrong I'm sure'
> Oh well Biddy fetched her a belt in the gob
> And left her sprawling on the floor.

As a result of the escalating fight, a bottle of whiskey scatters over the body, which at that point is laid out in a 'nice clean sheet' on the bed. As this happens, Tim Finnegan is resurrected from the dead and asks them the most extraordinary question, 'be the thundering Jaysus do you think I'm dead?'. This is not a question one expects to hear from the person whose wake one is attending.

Listening to recordings of the song in preparation for a conference paper some years ago, and realising my audience might appreciate closed captions for the lyrics, I sought out a version with subtitles, and heard for the first time a rendition of the song by Tommy Makem and the Clancy Brothers. Both the Dubliners and the Clancy Brothers were part of a revival of Irish traditional music that dated from the 1950s. As Sean Williams says, '[b]oth groups offered an explicitly politicized sensibility, ... in response to the civil rights movement of the United States as well as the heating up of the Troubles in the north' (Williams, 2009: 230).

Comparing the two versions led me to realise that Tim Finnegan's words in the song, his reaction to being revived by the whiskey scattered over him, are sometimes expressed in different languages, Gaelic and English. In the Clancy Brothers' version, Tommy Makem sings, 'D'ainm an diabhal [in the name of the devil], do you think I'm dead?'. When he reproduces the song lyrics in the course of his biography of James Joyce, Ellmann renders this as 'Thanam o'n dhoul' and explains that '[t]he Irish phrase in the last line means "Your souls [sic] from the devil!"' (Ellmann, 1959: 557).

What are we supposed to make of this question? And why am I drawn to it? First of all, it attracts my attention because of a mishearing. Growing up, I heard the Dubliners' version of this song, and the words in the Makem version that are sung in Gaelic, Ronnie Drew in the Dubliners' performance sings in English: '*By the thundering Jaysus* do you think I'm dead?' (my italics). I was (am) the son of Irish emigrant parents, whose Irish accents and vocabulary, first the assumed norm, then became anomalous as we heard them through the sometimes uncomprehending ears of our north London schoolfriends. Listening to this heavily accented, rowdy group of singers, I had thought that the English-language curse '[b]y the thundering Jaysus' was itself Irish Gaelic, projecting the linguistic and cultural difference onto Drew's energetic delivery of Tim Finnegan's bewildered first utterance as he comes back to life.

It thus became doubly intriguing to hear the Clancy Brothers' version with the line delivered in Gaelic, clarifying the fact that the Dubliners, to my ears a quintessential Irish band, had preferred an anglicised one. The layers of displacement, the fact of being distanced from a language, a culture, from one's own parents, from an accent, from something so close and yet 'a foreign body', became notable as I relistened to the song in the process of looking for a version with subtitles so that someone not used to strong Irish accents might be able to follow the lyrics.

The issue of reawakening, revival, resurrection – choosing the right word is difficult – is central to the song. As a result of a conflict between modes of grieving, and the ensuing fight with alcohol-filled projectiles, Tim Finnegan comes back to life. Neither narrative nor choreography, neither fiction nor theatre, revive him; what brings him back from the dead is the uneasy confrontation between these two incommensurable responses to death. Even more directly, his reanimation occurs as a result of a secular inversion of the baptismal sacrament and in response to the waste of the whiskey, the lost opportunity to celebrate a life as well as mourn a death.

On the 1966 recording of the Dubliners' version at the Gate Theatre in Dublin, the audience reacts to the words '[b]y the thundering Jaysus do you think I'm dead?' with a wave of laughter. The same laughter greets the question: 'D'anam don diabhal! Do you think I'm dead?' in the Clancy Brothers' 1970s version. Songs renew and rehearse laughter and grief; they prolong our grief and highlight its melancholy quality, lending poetic form and force to strong emotion, allowing us to laugh again at twists in the narrative with which we have become familiar. The song is a reanimation of emotions in ways few other art forms can replicate.

Listening to the Dubliners singing 'Finnegan's Wake' as a child, especially in Ronnie Drew's hewn-from-granite voice, felt like an encounter with another, inscrutable, foreign side of who I was, or where I came from: a voice and a genre of music from the mythical, displaced country of my parents. The drawl, the unfeasibly deep singing voice, the Irish-accented English-language lyrics, stressed an internal displacement, an inner contradiction in us as the children of parents who had left home behind with haste, regret and a definitiveness that would only be reversed over a decade later, as the shadow of another death loomed.[6]

'Finnegan's Wake' marked out an alienation from our parental song; it was a song imported from an historical past and an alienated space both of loss and regret and of repression and implicit violence. It incarnated a not knowing of the past, of the places of that foreign yet familiar country, an internal self-estrangement and a schism between me and my mother ('s) tongue. As Julia Kristeva has suggested in *Strangers to Ourselves*, identity is never singular and fixed, but instead is a process with internal plurality and contradictions, to the extent that very crucial parts of our subjectivity and memory can also be forms of estrangement or alienation (Kristeva, 1991): the paternal and maternal language and voice suddenly precipitated as foreign, other or destabilising. Jacques Derrida in *Monolingualism of the Other* similarly focuses on the contradictions within the apparently self-identical subject by exploring language and the way even one's mother tongue can be a source of difference and otherness, generating displacement rather than stability and singularity. For Derrida, 'an identity is never given, received, or attained; only the interminable and indefinitely phantasmatic process of identification endures' (Derrida, 1998: 29). While one's mother tongue might seem to be the natural expression of the most authentic and familiar self, Derrida suggests rather that:

> The language called maternal is never purely natural, nor proper, nor inhabitable. *To inhabit*: this is a value that is quite *disconcerting* and equivocal; one never inhabits what one is in the habit of calling inhabiting. There is no possible habitat without the difference of this exile and this nostalgia. (Derrida, 1998: 58; italics in original)

The reason this language is internally schismatic and non-self-identical is because it comes from the other, from the mother, the father, as other: the mother tongue asserts difference as well as similarity: 'It is the monolanguage *of* the other. The *of* signifies not so much property as provenance: language is for the other, coming from the other, *the* coming of the other' (Derrida, 1998: 68; italics in original).

Wakes and comedy

As with the ballad 'Finnegan's Wake', the funeral wake has been a source of comic business in numerous recent theatre and TV forms, especially in the context of Irish plays and TV comedy shows. Examples include Father Jack's false demise in the finale of Season 1 of *Father Ted*, 'Grant Unto Him Eternal Rest', written by Graham Linehan and Arthur Mathews and first broadcast in 1995. In theatre, at the Edinburgh Festival in 2002, Pauline Goldsmith's show *Bright Colours Only* featured Goldsmith as solo performer talking about wakes and funerals on a set constructed to look like her front room, coffin installed, turning the audience into mourners as the casket was carried out of the performance venue (in Edinburgh 2002 this was in the Assembly Rooms) into the streets of Edinburgh, spectators forming a bemused cortège behind the coffin.[7] As explored in Chapter 5, a pantomimic, pretend coffin full of fake money is central to Walsh's *The Walworth Farce* from 2006. Wakes have the potential not only to turn mourning into a form of celebration, but to generate comedy and laughter, revitalising the mourning body, substituting the animation of laughter for the cold litanies of grief or the stilling of the body of the dead. The comic form of the wake might not always raise the dead, as in 'Finnegan's Wake', but it certainly reanimates the living and revives those grieving; their laughter, its physical convulsions, its heightened production of the breath, is the antithesis of the cold objecthood of the corpse.

Nicholas Ridout explores the irruptive laughter known in British theatre slang as 'corpsing' by suggesting that it relates to the sudden death of a fictional character in a drama, or to the discomfort which causes you or your fellow actors to 'die' onstage because of the disruption to the script (Ridout, 2006: 134–5). In 'Finnegan's Wake', it is the revival or reanimation of the corpse, the act of uncorpsing, that generates laughter.

Derry Girls: the '*dead* corpse'

The conjunction of intoxication, comedy, corpses and wakes finds expression in Season 2, Episode 4 of Hat Trick Productions' TV comedy *Derry Girls* (2018–), written and created by Lisa McGee and first broadcast in 2019. In the episode, a wake occurs in which one of the eponymous girls, Michelle, spikes a batch of scones with marijuana, and when these get accidentally distributed among the mourners it causes chaos and comic hilarity. In one scene, the central cast of *Derry Girls*' characters, Michelle (Jamie-Lee O'Donnell), Clare (Nicola Coughlan), Erin (Saoirse-Monica Jackson), Orla (Louisa Harland) and James (Dylan Llewellyn) (who is Michelle's English cousin and an honorary 'Derry Girl'), enter the room of the wake house to see the body of the deceased, Erin's great aunt Bridie. McGee's script captures the different mourning traditions and attitudes to death in Northern Ireland and England, showing the characters' divergent reactions to the dead body, and their varying expectations about how the living interact with the dead.

After Michelle, Clare, Erin, Orla and James enter the room in which Bridie is laid out in her coffin, the dialogue is as follows:

> JAMES. OK, can I just check something? Everybody else can see the dead body, right?
> ERIN. It's just Bridie.
> JAMES. It's Bridie's corpse. It's Bridie's *dead* corpse.
> MICHELLE. It's her wake. What were you expecting?
> ERIN. Haven't you ever seen a dead body before?
> JAMES. Of course not!
> MICHELLE. Christ but the English are weird.
> ORLA. You can touch her if you want.
> JAMES. Why the hell would I want to touch her?
> ORLA. It's nice.
> JAMES. Stop it.
> CLARE. It's just a dead body, James. We're all going to be one some day.
> JAMES. Oh thanks for that, Clare. Yeah, that's helped.
> MICHELLE. It really makes you think, doesn't it…? … (McGee, 2019; my italics)

English-born James is alarmed by his exposure to the dead body. He sees an inanimate object, not the person. The Northern Irish girls' claims of familiarity with and affection for the corpse come from the traditions of open-casket wakes and funerals with which they have been familiar growing up. James, brought up by his Northern Irish emigrant mother in Liverpool, has evidently not been to this kind of event before. The actor Dylan Llewellyn brilliantly conveys James's baffled double take at seeing a dead body for the first time, comically questioning his own senses as the sequence starts. The tautology of the phrase 'dead corpse' reinforces James's confrontation with the reality of death, rather than the corpse of representation in the cinema, or on television, in vampire or zombie movies. This corpse is real and dead, really dead, a pleonastically '*dead* corpse'. Then, as the scene progresses, the girls in turn make claims for the cultural, social and affective importance of this kind of encounter with the dead body.

For Erin, the body is not fundamentally different to the living person, 'it's just Bridie', while Michelle, foul-mouthed, brash, but highly pragmatic, asks James to note that he is attending a cultural ritual where mourning involves proximity and contact with the dead. She then points out the national and cultural differences which turn the exposure to the body into the norm, and by contrast the non-visibility of the dead body is associated with English 'weirdness', something James comically embodies through much of the first two seasons of the show (he is an avid *Dr Who* fan, for example). Clare notes that the presence of the corpse merely reinforces the universal fact of death, that all bodies will make this transition from animate to inanimate, while Orla, the kooky, quirky figure, makes one of the simplest but most moving points when James questions why he would want to touch a dead body, replying 'It's nice.' Behind 'it's nice' is an ethic of care, a different form of relationality with the dead, the lost loved one (though this doesn't necessarily apply to the rather cantankerous Bridie herself, whom we have met earlier in the episode), reinforced in the scene by Orla putting her hands on Bridie's cheeks and forehead (before Erin gently slaps her hand away for being a little too excessive in her caress).

The sequence ends with Michelle's comment that 'it really makes you think, doesn't it?' but this is just a transparent attempt by Michelle to lead the situation towards her ulterior goal, thwarted earlier at the wedding party at which Bridie died, to get the girls high on drugs, in this case disguised in the marijuana-spiked 'space scones' she has baked. Michelle, too, like some of the mourners at 'Finnegan's Wake', wants to celebrate the excesses of the body, to be intoxicated, whether at a wedding or at a funeral, refusing to follow the correctly melancholic form of mourning a wake requires.

The scene captures the alternative modes of mourning familiar from 'Finnegan's Wake', but shows how these are bound up with local/national traditions and conventions, in the process asking us to think about death and to conceptualise the dead body not as something to be hidden away as the guilty antithesis of the living, but instead seeing the wake as an act of respect, a chance for a last encounter, a last touch, a last convivial (etymologically, 'living with') drink, before the closing of the casket and the permanence of the burial. Thinking about the term 'wake' suggests both the Christian possibility of the resurrection of the dead, given comically incongruent literalisation by the reanimation of Tim Finnegan, but also the occasion for a *memento mori* in which the transience of the living is greeted not with melancholic grieving, at least solely, but by animation, laughter and choreography.

Shenballamore, The Rag and Ross Green, The Bluestack Mountains, Barnesmore Gap

Forms of reanimation

This chapter so far has examined a song, 'Finnegan's Wake', that deals with a workplace accident, a subsequent wake, a fight over how to grieve and a resurrection from the dead. The song places narrative and performance, storytelling and choreography, the verbal and the physical alongside one another. Dance and physical performance are a way of forgetting grief, holding it in abeyance, rejecting death by performing corporeal presence, liveness and animation. The conflict about how to mourn in the song suggests that as well as grief for the dead, commemoration should also celebrate the living, and the liveliness of the deceased, the dancing and the singing retaining a dual temporality: being in the present and gesturally recollecting the capacity for merry-making of the deceased. The celebration at the wake is both an act and a re-enactment, a memorial that is about making new memories, an event that creates space for the formation of the future, living with, and without, the dead. This enacted memorial is an embodied acknowledgement of the inextricable contradictions for the living at a wake, confronting death, rejecting its finality via the chaos and corporeality of enacted intoxication and forgetting. Grief will return, the dead will remain but let this wake mime the refusal and rejection of death's permanence: hence, in the song, the reanimation of Tim Finnegan and the repeated laughter that greets this rejection of death's dominion.

Raheen, the Mount of Kilfagel, the Bridge of Aleen, Malin, Bundorna, Portsalon, Killybegs

Mothersongs

The progression from life to death and reanimation also features in the comic song 'The Ballad of William Bloat'. Written around 1926 by Raymond Calvert,[8] the words of the version performed by Tommy Makem, including a brief spoken introduction in the version I am using, are as follows:

> I'm going to sing you a song about a fella that wouldn't know Lourdes if he walked over it barefooted
> In a mean abode on the Shankill Road
> Lived a man named William Bloat;
> And he had a wife, the bane of his life,
> Who always got his goat.
> And one day at dawn, with her nightdress on
> He slit her bloody throat.
>
> With a razor gash he settled her hash
> Ah never was crime so quick
> But the steady drip on the pillowslip
> Of her life's blood made him sick.
> And the pool of gore on the bedroom floor
> Grew clotted and cold and thick.
>
> Ah but he was glad he had done what he had
> As she lay there stiff and still
> Till suddenly awe of the angry law
> Filled his soul with an awful chill.

And to finish the fun so well begun
He decided himself to kill.

Well he took the sheet from his wife's cold feet
And twisted it into a rope
And he hanged himself from the pantry shelf,
'Twas an easy end, let's hope.
With his dying breath, in the jaws of death,
He solemnly cursed the Pope.

But the strangest turn of the whole concern
Is only just beginning.
He went to hell but his wife got well
And she's still alive and sinning.
For the razor blade was British-made
But the rope was Belfast linen.
                      (Calvert, 1926; Makem, 1986)

This was the last song my mother introduced me to before she died in December 2015. 'YouTube' and 'Smartphones' still felt like new technology, when listening to music came at the entry of a search term, not as a result of riffling through old-looking LPs. The possibility of finding a cache of songs on YouTube from her youth was a source of joy for my mother, who did not use a computer. One evening, she asked me to look up 'The Ballad of William Bloat', which I quickly located, priding myself on being the provider of such technical pleasures via YouTube searches.

The version of the song by Tommy Makem starts off with the sectarian prelude making reference to Lourdes (the Marian shrine in France, associated with the Catholic St. Bernadette's visitations by the Virgin Mary in 1858), thus pitting Protestants against Catholics. It smacks of old antagonisms from the Northern Irish 'Troubles' of the 1970s onwards, stories, news reports, stern-sounding voices filtering their way from the TV and radio into our north London council estate flat: reports about IRA bombs, Sinn Féin leader Gerry Adams's voice so dangerous that it had to be dubbed by an actor on the orders of the Thatcher government in the 1980s. On first listening to the song in 2015, I recoiled as it started to play. This was not a suitable song for Ireland of the 2010s, the Ireland about to vote through Equal Marriage (2015) and the Right to Abortion (2018) in ground-breaking referenda.[9]

As 'The Ballad of William Bloat' begins, its first verse exposes the listener to old-fashioned cultural stereotypes of male–female marital antagonism, a wife who is a 'nag' and a husband who uses violence, in this case graphically cutting his wife's throat with a razor blade in an attempt to kill her. On hearing this, I further recoiled from the song, thinking that the ballad form was not enough to justify this sudden pitch into sexist misogyny. The second verse increases the glorification of violence as the effects of the throat-slashing are luridly described; the image of blood coagulating made me feel physically repulsed. Once again, the imagined association of my parents' generation with more schematic gender relations surfaced in my mind, the connection with more reactionary politics, from them, from 'over there', underpinning my reluctance to listen to more of the song. I wanted to turn it off, saying it was too old-fashioned – a handy euphemism – but my mother wanted to continue with the rest of the song. 'No, listen.' I relented.

As this first hearing progressed, with other family members present, the song took an interesting turn as it touched on the issue of guilt, summoning up the image of would-be murderer William Bloat struck by fear of the law and the consequences of his act, leading him to kill himself in a further macabre twist. The broad brushstrokes of the folkloric form, its vivid acts of violence, vengeance and thwarted love, began to become generically categorisable in my mind in ways that offset my initially dismissive political objections. Still, the imagery was gory, the rope made from a bed sheet, like a shroud, the anti-Catholic imprecation, '[w]ith his dying breath, in the jaws of death,/He solemnly cursed the Pope' reiterating the sectarian element of Catholics versus Protestants. The song had started by situating us on the Shankill Road in west Belfast, known for its loyalist affiliations to Britain, a road name that reverberated from my 1980s childhood, and those radio-voices of conflict far away.

But it is the final verse, a scene of revenge, reanimation and the comic payoff of the ballad, which gives the song its significance for me, for my suggestions about the grieving process, and which exemplifies the gradual mutual and self-understandings which grief gives rise to. As the final verse tells us, the murder attempt has been unsuccessful since Bloat died and 'went to hell', whereas his wife, apparently dead, her body, after all, 'lay there stiff and still', comes back to life and gets well, 'still alive and sinning'.

The final couplet provides the punchline, recasting the ballad as a comic song. The lines in this version, 'For the razor blade was British-made/But the rope was Belfast linen', restate the British versus Irish conflict, adding to it by claiming the capital of Northern Ireland, Belfast, part of the UK since 1922, as non-British, that is, Irish, and by casting aspersions on the quality of each nation's industrial products: the razor blade, being British, is implied to be inferior and faulty, since it does not cut in the way a good-quality blade should, and therefore fails to make a deep-enough incision in the wife's throat to bring about her death. By contrast, the linen, made in Belfast, claimed as part of Ireland, is high quality and therefore can be relied upon to operate effectively both as a sheet and as a noose with which William Bloat can hang himself in a way that ensures his death.

Listening to this final new song with my mother in 2015 (though I did not know it was our final song at the time) took me on a trajectory that functions as an allegory of my own relationship growing up with parents from rural Ireland, as I came to terms with my Englishness, Britishness, Anglo-Irishness; my simultaneous inclusion and exclusion from discourses of both national identities. My perception of the song, moving from recoiling at its reactionary gender politics to recognition of its ballad status and the comic allegory it includes, evolved swiftly into a meta-reflection on what the exposure to the song allowed me to learn about myself, my mother, my parents and our relationship. And as I write and reflect now, also what it allowed me to learn about the process of grief and mourning.

The reanimation at the heart of the song is a complex phenomenon. It comes at the cost of the death of one of the song's characters, a murderer whose own demise we are not inclined to mourn because he is a violent, misogynistic bigot and, within the initial terms of the song, worse of all, a Protestant loyalist. The miraculous reanimation of Mrs Bloat gives the song the first of its two lessons to me about my mother and our relationship. For it reverses the reactionary gender politics of the ballad genre to convey, instead, a tale of female survival, a victory over the titular male figure, a kind of glorious overcoming of the Protestant patriarch whose regressive, sectarian politics and authoritarian misogyny are aligned.

Furthermore, the shift in the last two lines recasts the entirety as a comic song rather than a ballad on gendered violence. In the version Makem sings in 1986, the comic bathos of the final couplet recalls but also displaces the Protestant–Catholic sectarianism pervading Makem's introduction and the anti-Pope curse in the lyrics. This alerts us again to the British–Irish conflict, but instead performatively trivialises their rivalry, isolating these everyday goods as the source of competitive pettiness about the quality of one's household products being connected to where they were manufactured.

Of course, the humour of Makem's 1986 performance derives from a much wider set of cultural and religious tensions in evidence in post-1970s Irish–British–Northern Irish politics as a result of the Troubles, the presence of the British army in Northern Ireland, and the increased tensions between Catholics and Protestants in the region, between nationalists and loyalists. But the ballad subverts these conflicts with semi-serious, self-deprecating, borderline-absurd laughter which makes a tale of murder and reanimation an elaborate, grotesque prelude to a little dig about who makes the best razor blades. The song is still about male posturing, petty nationalisms and religious rivalries, but the absurdity of the culmination of the tragedy-themed ballad is an act of comic deflation which critiques the very premises of the adversarial sectarian violence which the song earlier seemed to be replicating and endorsing.

The laughter occasioned by the song's ending, however, merely redirects and reorders the structural gender and religious politics within the song as a whole, rather than dispelling them. As well as the pleasure in female survival and victory over male violence, the ballad both acknowledges and satirises its religious sectarianism, prompting us to think about the medium (song), the pleasure of auditory and the thrill of the gendered twist. The power of the joke lies in the way it releases us from the strangulating fixity of the sectarian and gender conflicts, dissolving them in laughter at the whole sorry parade.

Reflecting on the intellectual allegory of this encounter, thinking back to my mother's life, and illness, to her last weeks and to her death, the possibility of reanimation elicits a painful, melancholy emotion. And her laughter, or should that be her laugh, like the laugh that punctuates Ronnie Drew's introduction to 'Finnegan's Wake' at the Gate Theatre in 1966, was always too loud, too cackling, too animated for this restrained English boy listening to songs sung in an accent unlike my own but like my parents' – the same words when written down, but conveying different geographies and displacements when sung or spoken.

Dingle, Dooneen, Belfast, The Shankill Road, Galway Bay, County Down, Lough Ree

'Navvy Boots On'

While researching this chapter, I came across another song by the Dubliners, 'Navvy Boots On'. Up until that point, I had only ever heard the first two lines. This version was recorded on 8 December 1968 at the Royal Albert Hall, and released in 1969.

Lines from songs, those snagging sung quotations, have a great power of reanimation. The first two lines from this song are deeply associated with my mother. She would often begin singing them around the house, stopping after the second line. I remember growing up hearing the words, the mother tongue, mothersongs, mothermelodies. But as often from the perspective of a child, and perhaps more so with a child of migrant parents, I did not understand the words properly. I couldn't understand what you were saying. What was a 'bonabby'? What was 'the line'? I knew where Newcastle was. But why was my Irish mother singing about working in a city in England famous for its abundant coals?

As with my mother, those lines would come into my mind – a memory of a performance of memory, a chain of displaced memories – and strongly reanimate her, and now, after her death, in an even more complicated way. The lines resonated with the ballad sentiment of diasporic alienation in my recollection of my mother's rendition of them. Other songs fulfilled this role too: Martin Henry/Dominic Behan's 'McAlpine's Fusiliers' (1940s/50s) in the Dubliners' powerful version talking about the labour conditions of Irish navvies working for the major construction companies like Robert McAlpine, Wimpey and John Laing in England, with mention of the Isle of Grain and the Thames in London in the song. Reminiscent of 'Finnegan's Wake', 'McAlpine's Fusiliers' also makes reference to a workplace accident:

> I remember the day that the Bear O'Shea
> Fell into a concrete stairs.
> What the horseface said, when he saw him dead,
> Well it wasn't what the rich call prayers.
> 'I'm a navvy short', was the one retort that reached unto my ears.
> When the going is rough, well you must be tough,
> With McAlpine's Fusiliers.

Similar to these was Percy French's 'The Mountains of Mourne' (1896), a song about living in London but full of nostalgia for the mountains of Mourne in Country Down in Northern Ireland. The song revolves around oppositions between Irish naturalness and London's fakeness and artificiality, using women's bodies to contrast painted beauty with 'the wild rose waiting for me' in County Down.

The Dubliners' version of 'Navvy Boots On' starts with the line 'Oh, I am an auld navvy', so knowing my mother's familiarity with the group's output, I assumed she had misremembered the line since the word 'auld' when she sang it definitely began with a 'b'. Having never heard her progress beyond the first two lines, I was expecting the song to play out in typical ballad form; but instead, it veered into another trope of Irish folk song, the comical courtship of a young man and woman leading to quickly snatched but enjoyable sexual intercourse. The comic element in this particular song derives from the narrator's attachment to his working boots, which provide the refrain 'navvy boots on' at the end of each verse, and reaching its comical climax with the idea that 'the baby will be born with its navvy boots on'.

Revisiting this song, learning the rest of it (and maybe this is our final song together) not only reanimated my mother as singer of quoted fragments of songs, reminding me of Winnie in *Happy Days*, remembering bits of old literary quotations, or Nina in *The Seagull* engraving a line from one of Trigorin's books on a medal for him, but it also reanimated a trajectory familiar from 'The Ballad of William Bloat' away from misplaced knowledge and displaced memory. I thought you were one thing but you are not that thing. I thought your song was a song about longing, nostalgia for home, a lament about manual work (to which you were restricted because you left school at thirteen) in a foreign, colonial country, but in fact it is a bawdy comic song about sexual high jinks. I had misread the words of the song and their relation to my mother's emotions about leaving Ireland, working in England, even misinterpreted the song as coming from a nostalgic genre, when in fact it was about bawdy sexual escapades.

Here are the lyrics of the song in full, adjusted to correspond with Ronnie Drew's live performance in 1968 as part of the Dubliners:

> Oh, I am an auld navvy and I work on the line
> And the last place I worked was Newcastle-on-Tyne
> Well, I'll tell me misfortune it happened in fun
> Oh, it happened one night I'd me navvy boots on
>
> One night after supper I shaved off me beard
> Ah to meet me fair Ellen I was well prepared
> Oh to meet me fair Ellen I then hurried down
> And I met her that night with me navvy boots on
>
> I knocked on her window, my knock it was low
> Oh I knocked on her window, my knock she did know
> She jumped out of bed, saying: Is that you John?
> Ah, bejaypers it's me with me navvy boots on
>
> She came to the door and invited me in
> Saying: draw to the fire, love, and warm your skin
> Well the bedroom was open and the blankets rolled down
> So I jumped into bed with me navvy boots on
>
> And all of that night now we sported and played
> Never thinking of time as it soon passed away
> Then she jumped out of bed, crying: What have I done?
> Ah, the baby will be born with his navvy boots on
>
> I chastised me loved one for talking so wild
> Ah, you foolish young girl, you'll never have a child
> Ah, for all that I've done now 'twas only in fun
> Ah, but I run like hell with me navvy boots on
>
> And very soon after I was summoned to court
> To pay for me sins just like any man ought
> I pay ten bob a week now for all of my fun
> Ah, that I had that night with me navvy boots on
>   (Dubliners, 1969)

The courting of women and sexual derring-do recur in Scottish and Irish folk song. Examples of such songs I learnt growing up include 'Home Boys Home', 'Tibby Dunbar', 'Dundee Weaver', 'Quare Bundle Rye' and others.[10] Listening to 'Navvy Boots On' for the first time, though, it occurred to me that while I may have surmised that the nostalgia for home underpinned its recurrence in my mother's aural hit list, it might in fact have been the later verses of the song, where the scene of the knock at the window, leading to a night of sex, ending with the comical objection that the potential child will be born 'with his navvy boots on', which summed up the appeal of the song: it was fun, raucous, celebratory and sensual. And of course, added to this, another element that may have planted the song in my mother's memory is the last verse which notes the consequences for the young woman, a child for which the narrator is summoned to pay maintenance of 'ten bob a week', and where the last iteration of the phrase 'navvy boots on' is now less comical and hits a more rueful, regretful note.

Thus this song, from which the first two lines are embedded very deeply in my aural memory of my mothersongs, ends with a father denying the possibility of pregnancy, then reluctantly, after legal recourse, agreeing to pay maintenance for his child. The song, then, reverberates with elements of family secrets, of hidden paternity, of sudden departures, and hearing it in full for the first time reanimated for me a whole series of fragments of family stories revolving around my not-known Irish relatives, my mother and grandmother, great-grandmother, greats aunts, a family history of departures and returns from Ireland. These include my own displacement across the Irish Sea, my first crossing of that body of water, to be born in the 'wonderful sight' of London, with parents who did not return 'home' for over a decade after my birth.[11]

Those two opening lines reanimate a whole sequence of events, traumas and buried memories, conflict and loss, grief and its disavowal. They gesture towards hidden identities and names chiselled on gravestones, as the only trace of family lineage, a reminder and remainder of 'all of my fun' that echoes down generations. Even these reanimations, though, are deceitful ghosts or elusive projections. For the plots of folk songs rarely speak of what were undoubtedly the experiences of young women in Ireland in the years when my mother was growing up, the 1950s and 1960s, the period in which Magdalen laundries were in full operation and a country in which divorce would only be legalised by the *Fifteenth Amendment of the Constitution Act 1995* and rape within marriage was only made a crime by the *Criminal Law (Rape) (Amendment) Act 1990*.

The reanimation, again, shows the delusion of the one interpreting the reanimation or experiencing it, its misplaced quality, the claim to knowledge which is actually a form of subjective self-scrutiny and awareness. Sometimes a melody is just a melody, a line or two implant themselves randomly, contingently, surfacing and sinking without explanation. Sometimes the song, like 'The Lass of Aughrim' in 'The Dead', reanimates entire nexuses of loss, grief and regret, resonating with remorse or unfinished mourning. Sometimes the song is our most eloquent way of remembering those we have lost, as my siblings and I felt to be the case as we sang the lines 'For there's home for weary wanderers in/The homes of Donegal' at our mother's funeral. But sometimes the song is just a memory of a comic subversion of all the weight of loss and grief and abandonment associated with the past. Sometimes thinking about the comic sight of a baby born with 'navvy boots on' conjures away all those associations, or even means that you just like singing those words, those lyrics and that melody in the present moment: a singing *with*, which is also a being with, and living with, others.

Yet those songs, or fragments of song, are the expression of the living body, the choreographing of language, rhythm and voice in an utterance in which lyrics become motifs recurring over time, once sent out, now evanescent, only present in ghost-memory form as an aural trace clipped from the flux of the past.

The Homes of Donegal, The Northern Lights of Old Aberdeen, Newcastle-on-Tyne, Dear Old Donegal, The British Army, McAlpine's Fusiliers, Cricklewood, Holyhead, Connacht brogue, Rocky Road to Dublin, Garryowen, My Old Killarney Hat

Notes

1 Joyce's phrase 'a beautiful corpse' recalls the line from the ballad 'Finnegan's Wake': 'such a lovely corpse she did ever see'. For further discussion of the ballad, see below.

2 The concept of the beautiful body in death is often gendered and applied to the female body in particular, as Elisabeth Bronfen has demonstrated in her study of the dead female body in art and literature (Bronfen, 1992).
3 McNally reports that Joyce scholar Peter Chrisp called the discovery of the origin of the ballad a 'great piece of detective work' which he attributes to researcher Brendan Ward, who published his findings in a pair of detailed blogposts (see Ward, 2018).
4 The rhyme makes an early appearance in *The Hackney Scout Song Book* (1921) under the title 'Michael Finnagen' [sic] with an accompanying note: '*Note. – Composed, on the model of an ancient fragment, by Scouts of 12th Hackney Troop, while on hike, Easter, 1921*' (italics in original). Interestingly, in this version, Finnagen gets drunk, sings, climbs a tree and hurts his leg ('barked his shinagen') and then dies: 'Then he died, and had to begin agen/Poor old Michael Finnagen, begin agen' (1921: 95).
5 'Whiskey, You're the Devil' (author unknown), sung by Liam Clancy, the Clancy Brothers, the Pogues and Bella Hardy, among others.
6 People from Ireland often refer to travelling back to the country as 'going home', even if they are not visiting family members or their family residence.
7 See Goldsmith's website at: https://brightcoloursonly.org/about-the-show and Lyn Gardner's review at: www.theguardian.com/stage/2002/aug/10/theatre.artsfeatures
8 Further information about the song can be found at http://clydesburn.blogspot.com/2020/05/the-ballad-of-william-bloat-by-raymond.html
9 To change the constitution of Ireland, first in operation on 29 December 1937, and to add an amendment or revoke a limb, Ireland is required to have a national referendum. Both heterosexual marriage and the right to life of the foetus were protected under the terms of the constitution. My mother's (and father's) home county, Co. Wicklow, voted 68.37% in the Equal Marriage referendum and 74.26% in the Abortion Referendum, compared to national averages of 62.07% and 66.40%, respectively.
10 These were all songs sung by the Dubliners, among others.
11 The phrase 'wonderful sight' is taken from the opening line of 'The Mountains of Mourne', 'O Mary, this London's a wonderful sight, the people here working by day and by night' (Percy French, 1902).

Conclusion: impossible reanimations

> *For it still feels unreal to think that I was one of a group of us in almost ritualistic rhythm shovelling the earth into the grave onto her coffin, next to, on top of my father's (you two never did have enough room). I remember the green plastic shovel we gave to her three-year-old grandson, so he wouldn't feel left out, so he could help with filling the grave. Those lines from 'Navvy Boots On', along with others, 'the northern lights of old Aberdeen/Are home sweet home to me' from the song of that title; 'I just stepped in to see you all/I'll only stay a while' from 'The Homes of Donegal', reanimate you-her-you in gusts of melody, painful fragments of song, torn out of the fabric of the morning shower, the bus ride, during periods of waiting where your performance of lyrics from your own memory unzip time – my voice ventriloquising yours, echoing your intonation, copying your version, searching for its own melody, between accents, decades, welding together 'before' and 'after', multiple temporalities caught in words ribboning away.*

Writing this book has taught me many things about grief and mourning. It has helped me work through a sense of bereavement, and to explore how theatre, literature and music help us cope with potentially overpowering emotions of loss. Reanimations echo and articulate our grief, as well as our anxieties around death, those of loved ones and our own death, sometimes by giving them poetic expression, sometimes by amplifying them through performance. They can also be a way of acting out counter-narratives or alternative histories, the 'joyous shot at how things ought to be', as Philip Larkin puts it in 'Home Is So Sad' (Larkin, 1988: 88), a poem that reverberates with proleptic grief.

I have learnt many things about grief's shifting emotional trajectory. Reading and thinking about reanimations, about tropes of death and dying, of reviving and resurrecting, recreating or reimagining, have led me to reflect on the urgent need we have to find creative forms to express our response to death. Grief allows you to embrace the fragmentary, to become conscious of returning to dictionaries for definitions or to classic texts for foundations, only to find them elusive or shifting. Grief prompts you to read transversally, across texts and media, to find intertextual echoes or connecting threads, propelled by one's search for expressions or examinations of the emotions of loss and bereavement. Our grief and mourning find many outlets, sometimes transformed by, or into, laughter. Grief is unpredictable and reanimations of the dead draw attention to the challenges death poses for expression and, further, the ingenuity needed to capture conjunctions of chaos, guilt, responsibility, relief, laughter and many others that might converge on the grieving subject. Researching and writing this book has helped me see that no two griefs are the same.

Many works discussed in this book explore anxieties around the transition between animacy and inanimacy, whether through acts of fantasised resurrection, in the form of ghosts and spectres, or the destabilising memory of a dead lover or partner bound up with grief, sexual shame, rejection and self-interrogation. Grief troubles categories and blurs boundaries, subjecting the real to the irruptive force of fantasy, memory and desire. Grief reframes and recalibrates subjectivity, issuing in a changed experience of time, a collapse or folding inwards of multiple temporalities and selves; allied to those grieved for, the incorporation of the other into the self, or the self-as-seen-by-the-other into the mind of the grieving subject. There is an element of narcissism in the process of grief, a self-reflection, as writers like Kennicott suggest, where the death of a loved one manifests our thinking and projections of the details and terms of our own death (Kennicott, 2020: 10). Their death becomes a measure, a template, for our own.

Grief and mourning, I have understood, are intimately bound up with questions of performance, whether manifested in the linguistic playfulness of poetry, the intertextual echoes of fiction or the complex embodiments of theatre. Grief has protocols and expectations attached to it, and there are mandates around grief, dictating its form and duration, that can be difficult to negotiate. A number of the works under discussion demonstrate what happens when subjects/characters engage in improper forms of grief and, as a result, show the power of grief to disrupt and challenge social norms and power structures. Grief is gendered and is often seen as feminine or effeminate. Electra's mourning turns her into an obdurate reminder of a crime, an obstacle to power, while Hamlet's grief is criticised as excessive, inappropriate to his masculine status. Mourning that departs from male-controlled norms is deemed excessive and destructive in *Hamlet*, just as it is for Agnes in O'Farrell's *Hamnet*.

Death, grief and mourning, this book has taught me, are subject to multiple reanimations, resignifications and re-embodiments. Literature and theatre reanimate the dead as a form of memorial, as a way of processing loss or to communicate across grief's self-constructed walls of silence. They reanimate the dead because to talk of them outside the pages and spaces of artistic representation is often too painful. In reanimations, it is sometimes the need to displace the real of death which leads to creative forms, substituting instead magic returns to life or sudden shifts from objecthood to animacy. The difficulty of talking directly about the dead in the aftermath of loss leads to the poetic condensations, replacements and displacements of literature and theatre.

Songs and music operate even more tangentially, as shown in the section on 'Finnegan's Wake', the ballad a kind of comical, distantiated performance of the emotions of death and mourning. Grief is a time of crisis which requires that the loved one be remembered (as Hamlet's father says, 'remember me') but, at the same time, for the living, the speaking subject in the wake of grief, verb tenses need to change, the living body has become frozen at a point in time, like a photograph, apparently unable to change, to age, to be animate.

Writing this book has helped me see that we remember and reanimate the dead in countless ways that are not only about the thematics of death as found in literature, theatre and song, but through how we use, remember and redeploy these texts. It is about not merely what these works say but their role in our memory, our inner cultural museum of artworks, objects, films and concerts, experiences of watching, reading and listening, sometimes alone, sometimes with others – the private and the public. Moments of grief arrest us suddenly: a lyric, a melody, a movement, a line of poetry, a re-reading of a book, a memory of a choreographed image or performance sequence evoke grief like a *coup de théâtre*, making this grief a reanimating force. Our memory of the art work's affective moment, its *punctum*, to use Barthes' term from *Camera Lucida* (Barthes, 2000: 43), situates us in a dual temporality, one in which we are pitched back to our previous selves, creating a split between the 'before' and 'after' of grief. Grief folds us in on ourselves, concertinas time into odd contortions and sequences. Grief de-sequences, turns us into interrupted beings, exposes our vulnerabilities.

Maggie O'Farrell says in an interview about *Hamnet* that 'grief is love pulled inside out on itself' (O'Farrell, 2021). Overlaying the duality of love and mourning is the way in which mourning is often a realisation of love's saturation, after the fact. Who knew we would mourn so much and for so long, endlessly, perhaps? That love would only genuinely express itself or reveal itself through mourning, or as a consequence of mourning, manifested via mourning as its co-production? Or that grief would pull us 'inside out'?

Protean reanimations

This book makes the case for reanimation as a term that helps us think about the dynamics and temporality of reading fiction, viewing theatre and listening to songs in the wake of loss, suggesting that grief generates acts of re-reading and re-membering. Grief can be seen as a form of rewriting, a kind of charged reconceptualisation and reconfiguration of our memory-texts of literature, theatre and music, redirecting, destructuring and remaking new connections and echoes across works.

At the same time, figurations of death, grief and mourning have helped me think through the entangled emotions that converge around loss, the complex social components of this most private of affects, the way the authentic is overlaid with the aesthetic and the performed. These textual mediations of our loss are about the living as much as the dying; they are about memorialising without forgetting, while acknowledging the need and inevitability of forgetting. Death and loss have been thematics in many of the texts, but have also operated as metaphors for forms, for transitions between one mode of aesthetics to another, for the phenomenon of intertextuality. Grief opens up new ways of reading, across texts and media, showing that works are not self-identical but are coloured by, misremembered by, our reading selves across different temporalities.

Reanimations are powerful because they are contradictory, achieving in art what is impossible in life, blurring boundaries, showing how grief is never pure, shaped by the cultural forms and expressive desires of prolepsis, memory, silence and exhaustion: a singular affect, uniquely private and individual, but one of the few universals, propelling art into magic and utopian zones to explore the impossible and revive the dead in endless iterations.

Bibliography

Alexander, Rachel K. (2022) 'Memory and Mortality in Homer's Odyssey' in Erin A. Dolgoy, Kimberly Hurd Hale and Bruce Peabody (eds), *Political Theory on Death and Dying*. London: Routledge, Chapter 1.
Babula, William (1975) 'Three Sisters, Time, and the Audience', *Modern Drama*, 18, 4, 365–9.
Baez, Joan (1975) 'Diamonds and Rust', A&M.
Bal, Mieke (2009) 'Working with Concepts', *European Journal of English Studies*, 13:1, 13–23.
Barish, Jonas (1981) *The Antitheatrical Prejudice*. Berkeley and Los Angeles, CA: University of California Press.
Barthes, Roland (2000) *Camera Lucida* tr. Richard Howard. London: Vintage Books.
Beckett, Samuel (1987) *Proust, and Three Dialogues with Georges Duthuit*. London: Calder.
Beckett, Samuel (1990) *The Complete Dramatic Works*. London: Faber and Faber.
Belsey, Catherine (1979) 'The Case of Hamlet's Conscience', *Studies in Philology*, 2, 127–48.
Bennett, Jane (2001) *The Enchantment of Modern Life: Attachments, Crossings and Ethics*. Princeton, NJ: Princeton University Press.
Bentley, Eric (1965) *The Life of the Drama*. London: Methuen.
Benzi, Nicoló (2021) 'Parmenides and the Tradition of Katabasis Narratives' in George Alexander Gazis and Anthony Hooper (eds), *Aspects of Death and the Afterlife in Greek Literature*. Liverpool: Liverpool University Press, 89–104.
Billington, Michael (1998) 'Art Reviews: The Wide Blue Yonder', *Guardian*, 13 October.
Billington, Michael (2006) 'The Seagull', *Guardian*, 28 June.
Billington, Michael (2014) 'Enda Walsh: "Pure Theatre Animal" Explores Solitude and the Void Below', *Guardian*, 18 September.
Blanchot, Maurice (1982) *The Space of Literature*, tr. with an introduction by Ann Smock. London: University of Nebraska Press.
Bonnechere, Pierre and Gabriella Cursaru (2016) 'Katábasis', *Cahiers des études anciennes*, 53, 7–14.

Booth, Michael R. (1988) 'Feydeau and the Farcical Imperative' in James Redmond (ed.), *Farce*. Cambridge: Cambridge University Press, 145–52.
Borney, Geoffrey (2006) *Interpreting Chekhov*. Canberra: Australian National University Press.
Brinkema, Eugenie (2014) *The Forms of the Affects*. Durham, NC: Duke University Press.
Briscoe, Joanna (2020) '*Hamnet* by Maggie O'Farrell Review – Immersive Shakespearean Drama', *Guardian*, 26 March.
Bronfen, Elisabeth (1992) *Over Her Dead Body: Death, Femininity and the Aesthetic*. Manchester: Manchester University Press.
Bulson, Eric (2012) *The Cambridge Introduction to James Joyce*. Cambridge: Cambridge University Press.
Campos, Liliane (2014) 'This is Not a Chair: Complicite's Master and Margarita', *New Theatre Quarterly*, 30:2, 175–82.
Carlson, Marvin (2003) *The Haunted Stage: The Theatre as Memory Machine*. Ann Arbor, MI: University of Michigan Press.
Chekhov, Anton (1993a) *The Seagull* tr. Michael Frayn in *Chekhov: Plays*. London: Methuen, 55–125.
Chekhov, Anton (1993b) *Three Sisters* tr. Michael Frayn in *Chekhov: Plays*. London: Methuen, 189–282.
Chekhov, Anton (2006) *The Seagull* tr. Martin Crimp. London: Faber.
Cheng, Vincent J. (2006) 'Empire and Patriarchy in "The Dead" in James Joyce, *Dubliners*, ed. Margot Norris. London and New York: W. W. Norton, 341–64.
Cixous, Hélène (1972) *The Exile of James Joyce* tr. S. A. J. Purcell. London: David Lewis.
The Clancy Brothers & Robert O'Connell (1988) 'Finnegan's Wake' with introductory material, www.youtube.com/watch?v=DU97TGbp6po
The Clancy Brothers with Tommy Makem (1961) 'Finnegan's Wake', www.youtube.com/watch?v=vnmg3ihDsAc
The Clancy Brothers with Tommy Makem (1986) 'The Ballad of William Bloat', www.youtube.com/watch?v=Im2ihKqvZwQ
Clapp, Susannah (2006) '*The Seagull* Has Landed – On Its Feet', *Observer*, 2 July.
Complicite (1997) *The Caucasian Chalk Circle* by Bertolt Brecht, dir. Simon McBurney.
Complicite (1999a) *Mnemonic* by Complicite, dir. Simon McBurney.
Complicite (1999b) *Mnemonic* by Theatre de Complicite. London: Methuen.
Costa, Maddy (2008) 'One Man and his Monsters', *Guardian*, 18 September.
Craig, George, Martha Dow Fehsenfeld, Dan Gunn and Lois More Overbeck (eds) (2014) *The Letters of Samuel Beckett, Volume III: 1957–1965*. Cambridge: Cambridge University Press.
de Grazia, Margreta (2007) *Hamlet without Hamlet*. Cambridge: Cambridge University Press.
Dean, Tanya (2015) 'Real Versus Illusory in Enda Walsh's *The Walworth Farce* and *The New Electric Ballroom*' in Mary P. Caulfield and

Ian R. Walsh (eds), *The Theatre of Enda Walsh*. Dublin: Carysfort Press, 119–30.
Derrida, Jacques (1998) *Monolingualism of the Other; or, the Prosthesis of Origin*. Stanford, CA: Stanford University Press.
Diderot, Denis (1875) *Entretiens sur le Fils naturel* in *Oeuvres completes*. Paris: J. Claye.
Didion, Joan (2012) *The Year of Magical Thinking*. London: Fourth Estate.
Doran, Gregory (dir.) (2008) *Hamlet* by William Shakespeare.
Dubliners (1966) 'Finnegan's Wake' (traditional), www.youtube.com/watch?v=nl7axmO4A24
Dubliners (1969), 'Navvy Boots On' (traditional), www.youtube.com/watch?v=T812Xlha3UU
Dubliners (1977) 'McAlpine's Fusiliers' by Dominic Behan, www.youtube.com/watch?v=xEk37t4LWp0
Dyce, Alexander (1904) *A General Glossary to Shakespeare's Works*. Boston, MA: Dana Estes.
Ellmann, Maud (2004) 'The Ghosts of Ulysses' in Derek Attridge (ed.), *James Joyce's Ulysses: A Casebook*. Oxford: Oxford University Press, 83–102.
Ellmann, Richard (1959) *James Joyce*. Oxford: Oxford University Press.
Enright, Anne (2021) 'Beautiful World, Where Are You by Sally Rooney Review – the Problem of Success', *Guardian*, 2 September.
Fehsenfeld, Martha Down and Lois More Overbeek (eds) (2009) *The Letters of Samuel Beckett, Volume I: 1929–1940*. Cambridge: Cambridge University Press.
Felski, Rita (2008) *The Uses of Literature*. Oxford: Blackwell.
Felski, Rita (2011) '"Context Stinks!"' *New Literary History*, 42:4, 573–91.
Fischer-Lichte, Erika (2002) *History of European Drama and Theatre*. London: Routledge.
Formalny Theatre (2001) *School for Fools*, dir. Andrey Moguchiy.
Frankcom, Sarah (dir.) (2014) *Hamlet* by William Shakespeare.
French, Percy, 'The Mountains of Mourne' (c. 1890s), version performed by Paddy Reilly www.youtube.com/watch?v=zkhE9qjbTLo
Freud, Sigmund (2003 [1919]) *The Uncanny* tr. David McLintock with an introduction by Hugh Haughton. London: Penguin.
Freud, Sigmund (1953) 'Mourning and Melancholia' in *The Standard Edition of the Complete Psychological Works of Sigmund Freud*, Vol. 14, tr. James Strachey. London: Hogarth Press, 243–58.
Fried, Michael (1980) *Absorption and Theatricality: Painting and Beholder in the Age of Diderot*. Chicago, IL: University of Chicago Press.
Gardner, Lyn (2002) 'School for Fools, Barbican', *Guardian*, 15 November.
Gardner, Lyn (2007) 'The Walworth Farce', review, *Guardian*, 6 August.
Gibbon, Edward (1762) *Essai sur l'étude de la littérature*. Geneva: T. Becket and P.A De Hondt.
Gielgud, John (dir.) (1964) *Hamlet* by William Shakespeare.

Golomb, Harai (2000) 'Referential Reflections around a Medallion: Reciprocal Art/Life Embeddings in Chekhov's The Seagull', *Poetics Today*, 21:4, 681–709.
Greenblatt, Stephen (2016) 'Introduction to Hamlet' in Stephen Greenblatt, Walter Cohen, Jean E. Howard and Katharine Eisaman Maus (eds), *The Norton Shakespeare*. 3rd ed. London and New York: W. W. Norton & Company.
Hackney Local Association (Boy Scouts) and Stanley E. Ince (1921) *The Hackney Scout Song Book*. London: Stacy & Son.
Hall, Joseph (1626) *Contemplations vpon the Historicall Part of the Old Testament*. London: M. Flesher for Nath. Butter.
Halliwell, Stephen (1987) *The Poetics of Aristotle*. Translation and commentary. Chapel Hill, NC: University of North Carolina Press.
Heaney, Seamus (2016) *Aeneid, Book VI*. London: Faber.
Henigan, Julie (2007) ' "The Old Irish Tonality": Folksong as Emotional Catalyst in "The Dead" ', *New Hibernia Review*, 11:4, 136–48.
Higgins, Kathleen Marie (2020) 'Aesthetics and the Containment of Grief', *The Journal of Aesthetics and Arts Criticism*, 78:1, 9–20.
Holinger, Dorothy. P. (2020) *The Anatomy of Grief*. New Haven, CT: Yale University Press.
Holmes, Jonathan (2004) *Merely Players? Actors' Accounts of Performing Shakespeare*. London: Routledge.
Homer (1919) *Odyssey* tr. A. T. Murray, revised by George E. Dimock. Cambridge, MA: Harvard University Press.
Hourihane, Ann Marie (2021) *Sorry for Your Trouble: The Irish Way of Death*. Dublin: Sandycove.
Howard, Tony (2007) *Women as Hamlet: Performance and Interpretation in Theatre, Film and Fiction*. Cambridge: Cambridge University Press.
Huffer, Lynn (1998) 'Blanchot's Mother', *Yale French Studies*, 93, 175–95.
Hughes, Ted (1997) *Tales from Ovid*. London: Faber.
Icke, Robert (dir.) (2017) *Hamlet* by William Shakespeare.
Johnson, Dominic (2012) *Theatre and the Visual*. Basingstoke: Palgrave.
Joyce, James (1992) *Finnegans Wake*. London: Penguin.
Joyce, James (2000) *Ulysses*. London: Penguin.
Joyce, James (2006) 'The Dead', in *Dubliners* ed. Margot Norris. London and New York: W. W. Norton & Company, 151–94.
Kellaway, Kate (2016) 'Aeneid Book VI Review by Seamus Heaney – a Pitch-Perfect Translation', *Observer*, 8 March.
Kennicott, Philip (2020) *Counterpoint: A Memoir of Bach and Mourning*. New York: W. W. Norton and Company.
Kerrigan, William (1994) *Hamlet's Perfection*. Baltimore, MD and London: Johns Hopkins University Press.
Kessler, David (2019) *Finding Meaning: The Sixth Stage of Grief*. London: Ebury.
Kirsch, Arthur (1981) 'Hamlet's Grief', *ELH*, 48:1, 17–36.

Knowlson, James (1997) *Damned to Fame: The Life of Samuel Beckett*. London: Bloomsbury.
Krasner, David (2012) *A History of Modern Drama, Volume I*. Oxford: Blackwell.
Kristeva, Julia (1991) *Strangers to Ourselves* tr. Leon S. Roudiez. London: Harvester Wheatsheaf; Columbia University Press.
Lacan, Jacques (1977) 'Desire and the Interpretation of Desire in *Hamlet*' tr. Jacques-Alain Miller and James Hulbert, *Yale French Studies*, 55/56, 11–52.
Laplanche, Jean (1998) 'Time and the Other' in John Fletcher (ed.), *Essays on Otherness*. London: Routledge, 234–59.
Larkin, Philip (1988) *Collected Poems*, ed. Anthony Thwaite. London: Faber and Faber.
Liapis, Vayos (2021) 'The Somatics of the Greek Dead' in George Alexander Gazis and Anthony Hooper (eds), *Aspects of Death and the Afterlife in Greek Literature*. Liverpool: Liverpool University Press, 33–48.
Linehan, Graham and Arthur Mathews (1995) *Father Ted*, 'Grant Unto Him Eternal Rest', S.1, E.6.
Loehlin, James N. (2012) *Cambridge Introduction to Chekhov*. Cambridge: Cambridge University Press.
Maguire, Laurie (2002) '"Actions That a Man Might Play": Mourning, Memory, Editing', *Performance Research*, 7:1, 66–76.
Marcoux, J. Paul (1988) 'Georges Feydeau and the "Serious" Farce', in James Redmond (ed.), *Farce*. Cambridge: Cambridge University Press, 131–43.
Marsh, Cynthia (2006) 'The Implications of Quotation in Performance: Masha's Lines from Pushkin in Chekhov's *Three Sisters*', *The Slavonic and East European Review*, 84, 446–59.
Marx, Karl (1907) *The Eighteenth Brumaire of Louis Bonaparte*. Chicago, IL: Charles H. Kerr.
McBride, Séan (1955) 'Homes of Donegal', version performed by Diedre: www.youtube.com/watch?v=Z74ykVDtVGs
McBurney, Simon, with Michael Morris (1999) 'Theater; Willing to Risk a Culture without Labels', *New York Times*, 17 October, www.nytimes.com/1999/10/17/arts/theater-willing-to-risk-a-culture-without-labels.html
McCoy, Narelle (2012) 'The Quick and the Dead: Sexuality and the Irish Merry Wake', *Journal of Media and Cultural Studies*, 26:4, 615–24.
McGee, Lisa (2019), *Derry Girls*, 'The Curse', S.2, E.4.
McIvor, Charlotte (2010) 'The Walworth Farce', *Theatre Journal*, 62:3, 462–4.
McMillan, Joyce (2007) 'Animal Attraction', *Scotsman*, 6 August.
McMullan, Anna (2010) *Performing Embodiment in Samuel Beckett's Drama*. London: Routledge.

McNally, Frank (2019) 'Manhattan Transfer', *Irish Times*, 6 November, www.irishtimes.com/opinion/manhattan-transfer-frank-mcnally-on-the-surprise-origins-of-a-classic-irish-drinking-ballad-finnegan-s-wake-1.4073488

Merritt, Stephanie (2020) '*Hamnet* by Maggie O'Farrell Review – Tragic Tale of the Latin Tutor's Son', *Observer*, 29 March.

Mesguich, Daniel (2006) *L'Éternel éphémère*. Paris: Verdier.

Mitchell, Katie (2009) *The Director's Craft: A Handbook for Theatre*. London: Routledge.

Nancy, Jean-Luc (2008) *Noli me tangere*, tr. Sarah Clift, Pascale-Anne Brault and Michael Naas. New York: Fordham University Press.

Nightingale, Benedict (2007) 'The Walworth Farce', *Times*, 8 August.

'Northern Lights of Old Aberdeen' (1952) Mel and Mary Webb, version performed by Robert Wilson: www.youtube.com/watch?v=QZh4 GMr4rEU

O'Brien, Karen (2011) 'New Ireland: The Enda Walsh Festival', *Theatre Journal*, 63, 4, 646–9.

O'Farrell, Maggie (2017) *I Am, I Am, I Am*. London: Tinder Press.

O'Farrell, Maggie (2020) *Hamnet*. London: Tinder Press.

O'Farrell, Maggie (2021) 'Maggie O'Farrell: In Conversation' with Afshan D'Souza-Lodhi (British Library), www.youtube.com/watch?v=VvTm xeOrZhk

O'Rourke, Fran, 'The Lass of Aughrim', (c. 1819–44), www.youtube.com/watch?v=5AN9YRPPIWY

Ovid (1916) *Metamorphoses*, Vol. 2, tr. Fran Justus Miller. Revised by G. P. Goold. Cambridge, MA: Harvard University Press.

Paull, Michelle C. (2015) '*Ballyturk*: Theatre and Event' in Mary P. Caulfield and Ian R. Walsh (eds), *The Theatre of Enda Walsh*. Dublin: Carysfort Press, 177–93.

Pavis, Patrice (1998) *Dictionary of the Theatre: Terms, Concepts, and Analysis*, tr. Christine Shantz. Toronto: University of Toronto Press.

Pavis, Patrice (1999) *La Mouette* by Anton Chekhov. Paris: Actes Sud.

Phelan, Peggy (1993) *Unmarked: The Politics of Performance*. London: Routledge.

Phelan, Peggy (1997) *Mourning Sex: Performing Public Memories*. London: Routledge.

Pilkington, Lionel (2010) *Theatre and Ireland*. Basingstoke: Palgrave Macmillan.

Pollard, Tanya (2012) 'What's Hecuba to Shakespeare?' *Renaissance Quarterly*, 65, 4, 1060–93.

Rayner, Alice (2006a) *Ghosts: Death's Double and the Phenomena of Theatre*. Minneapolis, MN: University of Minnesota Press.

Rayner, Alice (2006b) 'Presenting Objects, Presenting Things' in David Krasner and David Z. Saltz (eds), *Staging Philosophy: Intersections of Theater, Performance, and Philosophy*. Ann Arbor, MI: University of Michigan Press, 180–99.

Rebellato, Dan (2006) 'Anton Chekhov: Death of the Author', programme of *The Seagull*. London: National Theatre.
Redmond, James (ed.) (1988) *Farce*. Cambridge: Cambridge University Press.
Reynolds, Oliver (1999) 'Cold Collation' review of *Mnemonic* by Complicite], *Times Literary Supplement*, 17 December.
Ricoeur, Paul (1970) *Freud and Philosophy: An Essay on Interpretation*. New Haven, CT: Yale University Press.
Ridout, Nicholas (2006) *Stage Fright, Animals, and Other Theatrical Problems*. Cambridge: Cambridge University Press.
Ringer, Mark (1998) *Electra and the Empty Urn: Metatheater and Roleplaying in Sophocles*. Chapel Hill, NC: University of North Carolina Press.
Roach, Joseph (2010) 'Performance: The Blunders of Orpheus', *PMLA*, 125, 4, 1078–86.
Rooney, Sally (2021) *Beautiful World, Where Are You*. London: Faber.
Rose, Gillian (1995) *Love's Work*. London: Chatto and Windus.
Royal Court Theatre (2008) Podcast, 'Writer Martin Crimp, Director Katie Mitchell and Actors Benedict Cumberbatch and Hattie Morahan in Discussion with the Royal Court's Diversity Associate Ola Animashawun about Martin Crimp's Play', *The City*, 20 May, https://web.archive.org/web/20160201093351/http://www.royalcourttheatre.com/news/podcasts/the-city/
Saler, Michael T. (2016) *As If: Modern Enchantment and the Literary Prehistory of Virtual Reality*. Oxford: Oxford University Press.
Senelick, Laurence (1985) *Anton Chekhov*. Basingstoke: Macmillan.
Shakespeare, William (1987) *Hamlet*, ed. Richard Hibbard. Oxford: Oxford University Press.
Shakespeare, William (2016a) *The Tempest* in *The Norton Shakespeare*, 3rd ed., ed. Stephen Greenblatt, Walter Cohen, Jean E. Howard and Katharine Eisaman Maus. London and New York: W. W. Norton & Company.
Shakespeare, William (2016b) *Hamlet* in *The Norton Shakespeare*, 3rd ed., ed. Stephen Greenblatt, Walter Cohen, Jean E. Howard and Katharine Eisaman Maus. London and New York: W. W. Norton & Company.
Shakespeare, William (2016c) *Cymbeline* in *The Norton Shakespeare*, 3rd ed., ed. Stephen Greenblatt, Walter Cohen, Jean E. Howard and Katharine Eisaman Maus. London and New York: W. W. Norton & Company.
Silk, Sally M. (1994) 'The Orphic Moment and the Problematic of the Signified in Blanchot', *Neophilologus*, 78, 4, 537–47.
Smollett, Tobias (ed.) (1769) *The Critical Review; Or, Annals of Literature*, 27. London: S. Hamilton.
Smyth, Gerry (2009) *Music in Irish Cultural History*. Dublin: Irish Academic Press.
Societas Raffaello Sanzio (1997) *Giulio Cesare*, dir. Romeo Castellucci.

Sokolov, Sasha (2015) *A School for Fools* tr. Alexander Boguslawski. New York: New York Review of Books.
Solga, Kim (2011) 'Realism/Terrorism: The Walworth Farce', *Canadian Theatre Review*, 145, 89–91.
Sophocles (1995) *Electra* tr. Hugh Lloyd-Jones in *Ajax, Electra, Oedipus Tyrannus* Cambridge, MA: University of Harvard Press.
Stephens, Simon (2014) 'Why My Cherry Orchard is a Failure', *Guardian*, 16 October.
Styan, J. L. (2008) *Chekhov in Performance: A Commentary on the Major Plays*. Cambridge: Cambridge University Press.
Sword, Helen (1989) 'Orpheus and Eurydice in the Twentieth Century: Lawrence, H.D., and the Poetics of the Turn', *Twentieth Century Literature*, 35, 4, 407–28.
Szondi, Peter (1980) 'Tableau and Coup de Théâtre: On the Social Psychology of Diderot's Bourgeois Tragedy', *New Literary History*, 11, 2, 323–43.
Tarlow, Sarah (2023) *The Archaeology of Loss: Life, Love and the Art of Dying*. London: Picador.
Taylor, Edward (1774) *Cursory remarks on tragedy, on Shakespear, and on certain French and Italian poets, principally tragedians*. London: W. Owen.
Taylor, Paul (1997) 'Caucasian Chalk Circle, RNT London', *Independent*, 23 April.
Toolis, Kevin (2017) 'Why the Irish Get Death Right', *Guardian*, 9 September.
Turner, C. J. G. (1986) 'Time in Chekhov's *Tri Sestry* [*Three Sisters*]', *Canadian Slavonic Papers*, 28, 1, 64–79.
Turner, Susanne (2016) 'Sight and Death: Seeing the Dead through Ancient Eyes' in Michael Squire (ed.), *Sight and the Ancient Senses*. London: Routledge, 143–60.
Ubersfeld, Anne (1981) *L'école du spectateur*. Paris: Les éditions sociales.
Van Hulle, Dirk and Vincent Neyt (n.d.) Beckett manuscripts, www.beckettarchive.org/krapp/comparesentences/0234
Virgil (1999) *Aeneid*, tr. H. R. Fairclough. Revised by G. P. Goold in *Eclogues, Georgics, Aeneid, Books 1–6*. Cambridge, MA: University of Harvard Press.
Virgil (1999) *Georgics*, tr. H. R. Fairclough. Revised by G. P. Goold in *Eclogues, Georgics, Aeneid, Books 1–6*. Cambridge, MA: University of Harvard Press.
Walsh, Enda (2006) *The Walworth Farce*. London: Nick Hern Books.
Walsh, Enda (2004) *The New Electric Ballroom*. London: Nick Hern Books.
Walsh, Enda (2009) 'In Conversation: Joe Dowling and Enda Walsh', Walkerart.org, 25 October, www.walkerart.org/channel/2009/in-conversation-joe-dowling-and-enda-walsh
Ward, Brendan (2018) 'Finnegan's Wake – Origins', https://steemit.com/finneganswake/@harlotscurse/finnegan-s-wake-origins.

Ward, Brendan (2018) 'Finnegan's Wake – The Origin of the Species', https://steemit.com/finneganswake/@harlotscurse/finnegan-s-wake-the-origin-of-the-species

Whelan, Kevin (2002) 'The Memories of "The Dead"', *The Yale Journal of Criticism*, 15, 1, 59–97.

White, Harry (2005) *The Progress of Music in Ireland*. Dublin: Four Courts Press.

Williams, Sean (2009) *Focus: Irish Traditional Music*. London: Routledge.

Wilson, Harry Robert (2019) 'The Theatricality of Grief: Suspending Movement, Mourning and Meaning with Roland Barthes', *Performance Research*, 24, 4, 103–9.

Wisniewski, Tomasz (2016) *Complicite, Theatre and Aesthetics: From Scraps of Leather*. London: Palgrave.

Wolfe Tones (1972) 'Men Behind the Wire', www.youtube.com/watch?v=DXzhEokVn0s

Woods, Gillian (2016) '*Hamlet*: The Play within the Play', https://eprints.bbk.ac.uk/id/eprint/16275/

Woodward, Kathleen (1990) 'Freud and Barthes: Theorizing Mourning, Sustaining Grief', *Discourse*, 13, 1, 93–110.

Wyman, Sarah (2017) 'Chekhov's *Three Sisters*: A Proto-Poststructuralist Experiment', *Theatre History Studies*, 36, 183–210.

Young, Lin (2017) '"To Talk of Many Things": Chaotic Empathy and Anxieties of Victorian Taxidermy in *Alice's Adventures in Wonderland*', *Victorian Review*, 43, 1, 47–65.

Index

'A Nation Once Again' (song) 127, 132, 152
Adams, Gerry 149, 167
Aeneas 22–4, 67, 68
Aeneid 9, 18, 19, 22, 32, 46, 67, 87
Alexander, Rachel K. 20, 21
An Irish Lullaby (song) 127, 152
Anchises (Aeneas's father) 22
animacy 4, 7, 10, 16, 37, 38, 41, 43, 50, 52, 56, 57, 60, 91, 92, 178, 179
animals 15, 26, 47, 91, 92, 124
Anticlea (Odysseus's mother) 19–22
Aristotle 46
Ashmolean Museum, Oxford 32
Aurora Nova 52
autobiographical 14, 149
avant-garde 16, 91, 92, 102, 108, 110, 113, 120, 122, 125, 126, 131

Babula, William 102
Bailegangaire (play by Tom Murphy) 128
Bal, Mieke 3, 4
ballad 16, 34, 132–4, 139, 141, 143, 150–8, 162, 168–72, 175, 176, 179
Ballyturk 122
Barish, Jonas 69, 87

Barthes, Roland 12, 13, 108, 149, 180
bathos 54, 57, 59, 60, 170
Bausch, Pina 58
Beautiful World, Where Are You 16, 134, 135, 142, 144, 146
Beckett, Samuel 13, 16, 112–27, 130, 131
Belfast 167–9, 171
Belsey, Catherine 74
Bennett, Jane 43, 44
Bentley, Eric 127, 129
Benzi, Nicoló 19
bereavement 1, 2, 4, 9, 10, 32, 42, 78, 82, 85, 132, 133, 177, 178
Bible 18
Billington, Michael 47, 98, 99, 100, 121, 130
Blanchot, Maurice 26, 27
Booth, Michael R. 127, 128
Breath (piece by Beckett) 113
Brecht, Bertolt 55
Bright Colours Only 162
Brinkema, Eugenie 5, 11–13
Briscoe, Joanna 82, 83
Bronfen, Elisabeth 157, 176
burial 1, 12, 14, 31, 35, 53, 61, 62, 77, 84, 113, 117, 119, 123, 139, 155, 165
Burton, Richard 80

Camera Lucida 12, 13, 149, 180
Campos, Liliane 50, 51
Carlson, Marvin 80
Castellucci, Romeo 15, 41, 42,
 47–9, 54, 56, 57
cemetery 42, 53, 76
chair (in performance) 41, 42, 50,
 51, 52, 84, 106
Chairs (Ionesco) 51
Chekhov, Anton 13–15, 88–108,
 111, 113, 123
Cheng, Vincent J. 136, 139
childhood 3, 14, 17, 20, 21, 40,
 56, 63, 65, 76, 86, 88, 104,
 105, 109, 113, 118, 149,
 150, 168
Cixous, Hélène 138
Clancy Brothers 152, 157, 159,
 160, 176
Clancy, Paddy 157
coffin 113, 120, 123–6, 138, 156,
 158, 162, 163, 177
Complicite 15, 41, 42, 50–2, 54–8
conscience 73–5, 80
corpse 5, 32, 36, 39, 52, 78, 90,
 125, 150, 151, 153, 156–8,
 162–4, 175
coup de théâtre 10, 13, 40–60, 180
Crespi, Giuseppe Maria 32, 33
crime 62, 64, 66, 68, 69, 71–4, 112,
 124, 126, 128, 166, 175, 179
Crimp, Martin 94–100
critical and creative writing 14
Cymbeline 19, 34, 37, 38

Dean, Tanya 125
decay 21, 22, 36, 42, 53, 54,
 63, 78, 80
denegation 48
Derrida, Jacques 161, 162
Derry Girls 163
Diderot, Denis 46
Didion, Joan 4, 8, 9, 12
Dido (Queen of Carthage)
 67, 68, 87

Dido's Lament 67, 87
Doran, Gregory 74
doubleness 30, 32, 34, 38,
 52, 56, 76
dream 20, 21, 23, 24, 61, 68, 70,
 71, 80, 82, 85, 106, 128
Drew, Ronnie 149, 150, 152, 159,
 160, 171, 173
Dubliners (band) 132, 148, 150,
 152, 154, 159, 160, 171,
 172, 173
Dubliners (Joyce) 134, 135, 150

Edinburgh Festival 52, 121,
 129, 162
Electra 10, 18, 29–32, 34,
 38, 179
Ellmann, Maud 1, 64
Ellmann, Richard 138, 150, 159
enchantment 1, 4, 9, 11, 38,
 43–5, 50, 51, 53, 56, 57, 58,
 59, 138
Endgame 117, 123
Enright, Anne 142
ephemerality 13, 22, 35, 41, 58,
 60, 71, 95, 109, 111
epiphany 134, 137, 140
Eurydice (Orpheus myth)
 19, 24–9

farce (as genre) 126, 127
father 4, 22–4, 29, 35, 36, 51,
 61–6, 71, 72, 75, 77, 79, 82,
 85, 89, 102, 103, 112, 124,
 129, 131, 133, 140, 161,
 174, 176, 177, 179
Father Ted 162
'Fear no more the heat o' th' sun'
 (Shakespeare) 34
Felski, Rita 4, 43–5
fiction (as concept) 2, 4, 9, 10, 11,
 14, 30, 35, 38, 61, 68, 70, 71,
 80, 82–4, 87, 89, 90, 96, 97,
 130, 134, 146, 160, 178, 180
fictionality 48, 49, 69

Finnegan's Wake (song) 3, 16,
    19, 34, 132, 133, 149–52,
    154, 156, 157, 158, 160,
    161, 162, 165, 171, 172,
    175, 179
Finnegans Wake 3, 155
Fischer-Lichte, Erika 105
folk music 149
Footfalls 117
Formalny Theatre 41, 42, 52, 53
Freud, Sigmund 7, 12, 13, 41,
    55–7, 59, 60, 62, 63
Fried, Michael 46, 47
'Full fathom five thy father lies'
    (Shakespeare) 35
funeral 3, 31, 34, 61, 77, 155, 156,
    162, 165, 175

Gardner, Lyn 52, 129, 176
gaze 27, 64, 136, 137, 143
Georgics 25
gesture 33, 42, 52, 53–5, 57, 58,
    60, 70, 98, 130, 131, 174
ghosts 2, 4, 5, 8, 9, 10, 13, 14, 17,
    18–22, 24, 29, 30, 32, 35,
    37, 38, 40, 59, 61–7, 80, 82,
    84, 86, 89, 174, 178
Gielgud, John 80
Giulio Cesare 42, 47, 48
Globe Theatre 82, 85
Golomb, Harai 97
grave 34, 42, 53, 54, 61, 76, 77,
    80, 117, 120, 177
Greenblatt, Stephen 62, 64, 72
grief
    and contradiction 5, 9, 14,
        21, 66, 68
    in contrast to mourning
        11, 12
    as effeminate 28, 179
    and gender 83, 179
    maternal 83
    and negation/negativity 5,
        38, 116
    as perceptual chaos 29

guilt 2, 3, 8, 64, 67, 69, 71–3, 112,
    121, 128–31, 133, 168, 178

Hall, Joseph 5
Halliwell, Stephen 46
Hamlet 5, 10, 12, 13, 15, 30,
    104, 179
    Chapter 3 (passim) 61
Hamnet 15, 82, 83, 84, 86,
    179, 180
Happy Days 113, 117–21, 172
haunting 7, 9, 10, 14, 68, 80,
    104, 144
Heaney, Seamus 22, 23
Hecuba 70, 71, 80, 81
Henigan, Julie 136, 141
hermeneutics of suspicion
    43, 44
Holinger, Dorothy P. 7
Homes of Donegal 175
horse 41, 42, 47–50, 52, 54, 57
Hourihane, Ann Marie 156
Howard, Tony 80
Huffer, Lynne 27
Hughes, Ted 28

I Am, I Am, I Am 83
Icke, Robert 81
inanimacy 4, 7, 10, 16, 37, 38, 41,
    43, 50, 60, 178
intertextuality 9, 51, 86, 97, 98,
    104, 134, 143, 145, 178
Irishness 141, 151, 152, 169

Jesus Christ 32–4, 39, 163
Johnson, Dominic 95
Joyce, James 3, 16, 133–47, 150,
    151, 155, 157, 159, 175, 176

katabasis 19, 22, 24
Kellaway, Kate 22, 23
Kennicott, Philip 8, 9, 38, 178
Kerrigan, William 78, 79
Kessler, David 11
Kirsch, Arthur 79

Krapp's Last Tape 112–14, 117, 121, 127
Krasner, David 101, 107, 108, 110
Kristeva, Julia 161

Lacan, Jacques 62, 63
Laplanche, Jean 8, 9
Larkin, Philip 177
Liapis, Vayos 19, 20
Loehlin, James N. 101, 102

magic 1, 4, 9, 26, 28, 37, 42, 45, 55, 62, 71, 179
Maguire, Laurie 12, 62, 63, 66
Makem, Tommy 152, 159, 166, 167, 170
Mantel, Hilary 84
Marsh, Cynthia 104
Marx, Karl 126
McAlpine's Fusiliers 171, 172, 175
McBurney, Simon 41, 42, 50, 113, 114
McCoy, Narelle 156
McGee, Lisa 163
McIvor, Charlotte 128
McMillan, Joyce 124, 126
McMullan, Anna 118, 119
McNally, Frank 151, 176
melancholia 5, 63
memory
 acoustic or auditory 2, 16
 of artwork 180
 of the dead 11, 22, 26, 59, 67
 as fragmentary 119
 of grief 106, 136, 137
 of performance 40, 54
 of voices 22
Mesguich, Daniel 48
metatheatre/metatheatricality 5, 15, 30, 31, 40, 62, 65, 83, 94, 103, 113, 124–6
metonymy 32, 110
migration 122, 125, 126–9, 151
mishearings 11, 149, 159

Mitchell, Katie 95–100
Mnemonic 15, 42, 50, 51
monstrous/monstrosity 73
mortality 8, 11, 20, 22, 30, 38, 62–4, 76, 79, 138, 142, 151
mother/the maternal 20–2, 83, 86, 114, 116, 125, 161
mourning
 in contrast to melancholia 63
 definition 11
 as performative 12
 as public 12
music 11

Nancy, Jean-Luc 1, 19, 33, 34, 38
naturalism 52, 89, 90
Navvy Boots On 150, 171, 172, 174, 177
Nightingale, Benedict 124, 128
'Noli me tangere' 32
nostalgia 6, 88, 122, 161, 172, 174
Not I 117

'O, what a rogue and peasant slave am I' (Shakespeare) 68, 70, 81
O'Brien, Karen 126
O'Farrell, Maggie 15, 82–6, 94, 179, 180
objects 3, 4, 7, 15, 18, 26, 29, 37, 38, 40, 41, 43, 49, 50, 52–4, 56, 58–60, 88, 94, 99, 119, 125, 131, 139, 179
Odysseus 19–22
Odyssey 9, 18, 19, 22, 32
Orpheus 18, 19, 24, 25–9, 37
Orton, Joe 123
Ovid 18, 19, 24, 28, 29, 38

Paull, Michelle C. 122
Pavis, Patrice 43, 48, 90, 91
Peake, Maxine 80, 81
performability 94, 96, 99

Phelan, Peggy 10, 39
photograph 13, 107–9, 179
photographic 12, 91, 94, 103, 107, 109, 110
Pilkington, Lionel 123
Play (piece by Beckett) 117
play-within-a-play 90, 91, 121
Pollard, Tanya 71
puppet/puppetry 42, 49–52, 55–8
Purcell, Henry 67, 68
Pushkin, Alexander 104

Quad 118
queer/queerness 28, 133, 144, 145
quotations (their use in plays) 104, 106, 110, 118, 119, 171, 172

Rayner, Alice 2, 10, 43, 49, 58, 59, 66
reading 2, 16, 18, 81, 97, 179
realism 13, 16, 52, 55, 56, 58, 77, 88–94, 98–104, 107, 109, 110, 111, 130, 134, 137, 139, 142, 146
reanimation
  conceptualising death 7
  as contradiction 5, 7
  definition 2
  and enchantment/magic 9
  etymology and early uses 5, 6, 7
  and fictionality 14
  and guilt 8, 71, 73
  and justice 71
  and transformation 9
  as utopian 71
Rebellato, Dan 97
rehearsal 6, 10, 11, 129, 130, 152
remember me (phrase) 64, 66, 67, 87, 179
repetition 6, 7, 10, 11, 66, 69, 80, 106, 110, 114, 116, 121, 122, 139

resurrection 19, 32–4, 38, 39, 133, 151, 154, 158, 160, 165, 178
revival 7, 16, 33, 57, 79, 133, 159, 160, 162
Ricoeur, Paul 45
Ridout, Nicholas 47, 48, 56, 162
Ringer, Mark 30, 32
Roach, Joseph 26
Rockaby 117
Rooney, Sally 16, 134, 135, 142–7
Rose, Gillian 14, 15

Saler, Michael 4
School for Fools 52
science 35, 73, 92
Scott, Andrew 81
Shakespeare, William 5, 15, 17, 18, 34–7, 42, 47, 64–78, 82, 83, 85, 86
Silk, Sally M. 27
skull 61, 63–5, 76, 78, 79, 86, 153
Smyth, Gerry 141, 144
Societas Raffaello Sanzio 15, 42
Sokolov, Sasha 42
Solga, Kim 129
songs 3, 6, 11, 14, 16, 27, 28, 32, 35, 76, 77, 127, 132–4, 143, 144, 148–52, 167, 171–6, 180
Stephens, Simon 99
Styan, J. L. 101, 104
Sword, Helen 24, 26
Synge, J. M. 128
Szondi, Peter 46

Tarlow, Sarah 4, 5
Tate, Nahum 67
taxidermy 91, 92
Taylor, Paul 55
temporality 6, 16, 41, 54, 165, 180
Tennant, David 74, 80

The Ballad of William Bloat 150,
    166–8, 172
The Caucasian Chalk Circle 42, 55
The Cherry Orchard 99, 106
The Dead (Joyce) 9, 16, 133–8,
    140–6, 175
The Director's Craft 99
The Lass of Aughrim 16, 134–6,
    139, 141–6, 175
The Mountains of Mourne 149,
    172, 176
The New Electric Ballroom 121–4,
    127, 128
The Seagull 15, 88–92, 94, 98–104,
    107, 108, 110, 111, 113, 172
The Sisters (Joyce) 150
The Tempest 15, 19, 34–8
The Troubles 159, 167, 170
The Walworth Farce 5, 16,
    112–32, 152, 162
Three Sisters 15, 88–90, 100–11
Toolis, Kevin 155
touch
    and the dead body 163
    and ghosts 20, 21, 24
    and reconciliation 145
    and the resurrected
        Christ 32, 33
    and Yorick 76
tragedy 18, 30, 32, 46, 64, 71, 94,
    125–7, 129, 130, 131, 170
translation 22, 23, 29, 48, 59, 91,
    94–8, 112, 115, 156

Turner, C.J.G. 101
Turner, Susanne 20, 22

Ubersfeld, Anne 48
Ulysses 138, 147
uncanny 7, 24, 30, 33, 38, 41, 52,
    54–9, 61, 151
underworld 19, 20, 24–9
urn 31, 32, 117

Virgil 18, 19, 22–6, 37, 46, 87
voice 2, 10, 17, 18, 21, 22, 24,
    26, 37, 67, 68, 70, 72, 77,
    80, 85, 86, 91, 104, 114,
    116, 117, 134, 136, 143, 145,
    149, 150, 160, 161, 167,
    175, 177

Waiting for Godot 117–20
wake
    and comedy 162
    as cultural practice 155
    etymology 155
Walsh, Enda 5, 16, 112, 113, 152
Whelan, Kevin 135, 139, 146
Whitelaw, Billie 121
Williams, Sean 139, 143, 159
Wilson, Harry Robert 11, 12
Woods, Gillian 72
Woodward, Kathleen 13, 14
Wyman, Sarah 102, 103

Yorick (Shakespeare) 64, 65, 76–9

EU authorised representative for GPSR:
Easy Access System Europe, Mustamäe tee 50,
10621 Tallinn, Estonia
gpsr.requests@easproject.com

www.ingramcontent.com/pod-product-compliance
Lightning Source LLC
Chambersburg PA
CBHW071204240426
43668CB00032B/2086